Casemates and Cannonballs

Casemates and Cannonballs

Archeological Investigations at Fort Stanwix, Rome, New York

by
Lee Hanson and Dick Ping Hsu

Publications in Archeology 14

U.S. Department of the Interior
National Park Service

Washington 1975

As the Nation's principal conservation agency, the Department of the Interior has responsibility for most of our nationally owned public lands and natural resources. This includes fostering the wisest use of our land and water resources, protecting our fish and wildlife, preserving the environmental and cultural values of our national parks and historical places, and providing for the enjoyment of life through outdoor recreation. The Department assesses our energy and mineral resources and works to assure that their development is in the best interests of all our people. The Department also has a major responsibility for American Indian reservation communities and for people who live in Island Territories under U.S. administration.

Library of Congress Cataloging in Publication Data

Hanson, Lee H
    Casemates and cannonballs.

    (Publications in archeology; 14)
    Bibliography: p.
    Includes index.
    Supt. of Docs. no.: I 29.59:14
    1. Stanwix, Fort, N. Y.   I. Hsu, Dick Ping, joint author. II. Title. III. Series.
E51.U75 no. 14 [F129.R82] 623'.1'097462 75-619143

For sale by the Superintendent of Documents, U.S. Government Printing Office
Washington, D.C. 20402 - Price $3.60
Stock Number 024-005-00604-4

Foreword

One of the major efforts of National Park Service researchers during the years immediately preceding the bicentennial celebration of the United States has been the study of Fort Stanwix National Monument, an archeological site of extraordinary importance. This book reports on the excavations of the fort, an essential prerequisite to its reconstruction and interpretation.

Fort Stanwix was built by the British in 1758 to protect the Oneida Carrying Place between the Mohawk River and Wood Creek, the principal route between the Hudson River and the Great Lakes. It was the site of the Treaty of Fort Stanwix in 1768. Abandoned prior to the Revolution, it was occupied by American forces in 1776 and was unsuccessfully besieged, at great costs to both sides, by the British under Colonel Barry St. Leger in August 1777 during the Burgoyne campaign.

An understanding of the role Fort Stanwix played in the American Revolution will provide the reader with a better understanding of the military activity of the Revolution itself. In addition, an archeological report of this nature provides us with a fascinating insight into the day-to-day activities of the soldiers who were garrisoned at the fort. Inclusion in this book of reconstruction drawings based upon the archeological evidence leaves us with a clearer picture of the fort's appearance.

While it will be the subject of continuing research by historians in future years, the importance of Fort Stanwix as it relates to Burgoyne's defeat at Saratoga, "the Turning Point of the Revolution," is well known and recognized. As National Park Service historian John Luzader has so aptly put it, "St. Leger's failure to secure the Mohawk and reach Albany to form a junction with Burgoyne contributed to American victory at a critical time when British victory *might* have been a death-blow to the fight for independence."

Gary Everhardt
Director, National Park Service

Acknowledgments

Although we run the risk of forgetting the contributions of some individuals involved in an archeological project of this magnitude, certain persons and institutions are particularly deserving of our gratitude, and must be mentioned here. Many individuals and representatives of local, State, and Federal organizations cooperated with us. The assistance of the private citizens of Rome, New York, was matched by their justified pride in Fort Stanwix, a historic site of national significance.

We are particularly indebted to Edwin Ball, President of the Rome Historical Society, E. Stevens Wright and Frederick Rahmer, Directors of the Society's Fort Stanwix Museum, for the use of their historical files and library. And we are especially grateful to Curry M. Bartlett Jr., and Edward Ratazzi of the Rome Chamber of Commerce for providing interpretive assistance in the form of pamphlets and signs during the time of excavation.

Representatives of State and local organizations who assisted include Gordon A. DeAngelo of the New York State Department of Transportation, who helped us in the excavation and allowed us access to his personal library; William Flinchbaugh, Executive Director of the Rome Urban Renewal Agency, for facilitating the demolition and clearing of the site; the Honorable William Valentine, Mayor of the City of Rome, for extending the hospitality and services of the community; Stephen Zingerline and Frank Clark of the Rome City Engineer's Office, and staff members of the Rome Water Department for information on elevations and underground lines; and the Rome Fire Department for cutting pipes and trees in the excavation, and the loan of equipment.

Certain members of the National Park Service deserve recognition for their work on the Fort Stanwix project. They include John Luzader, historian, whose report on the construction and military history of Fort Stanwix provided a most valuable resource; Orville W. Carroll, historical architect, for his interpretation of structural remains and conjectural elevation and projection drawings included in this book; John L. Cotter, archeologist, for advice and assistance in this project; and Harold Peterson, Chief of Curatorial Services, for identification of artifacts.

The contributions of several staff members of the *Rome Daily Sentinel* are most appreciated. They include Fritz S. Updike, Editor, who served as a liaison for us with the entire community; and Edwin Miller, who assisted us during excavation and offered the use of his photographic darkroom after ours was closed.

The individual members and staffs of several learned institutions and libraries were of particular help. They include Howard Miller, Professor of Entomology and Pathology, State University of New York (Syracuse), for identifying faunal and floral remains; the staff of the Jervis Public Library who spent countless hours searching for obscure facts and locating rare books; and the Oneida Historical Society for the use of their extensive collection of documents.

Among those corporate and private businesses that assisted us are the Niagara Mohawk Power Corporation for work at the site; the Pettibone Corporation for the use of their cranes; Revere Copper and Brass, Inc., for examining metal specimens to determine origin; the Rome Sentinel Corporation for the loan of tools; and United Contractors for the special care they exercised in demolishing buildings in such a way as not to destroy archeological evidence.

We are grateful to many private citizens of Rome. Foremost among them is William Scripture for his tireless efforts in locating and transcribing original documents pertaining to Fort Stanwix. Others include David Wright, who gave up a part of his vacation to search the British Museum for early plans of Fort Stanwix; Chester Williams who made his collection available for our study, the McGraw powder horn in particular; and David Wertheimer, whose photography aided us materially.

Our special thanks go to Roselyn I. Gillard, Marguerite Burek and Vivian Crawford for typing the manuscript.

L.H.H. and D.P.H.
August 1974
Rome, N.Y.

Contents

Illustrations

Tables

Chapter 1

Introduction

In 1965, the second phase of the Rome, New York, urban renewal project was begun, encompassing 12 city blocks in downtown Rome (figs. 1, 2). One of these blocks was traditionally held to be the site of Fort Stanwix, 1758-1781. The land was purchased and cleared by the city of Rome and donated to the Federal Government. The National Park Service prepared a master plan for the development of the site as a national monument.

Buildings were scattered over the 12-block area, and it was feared that most of the fort had been destroyed by foundations and utility lines. However, excavations by Col. J. Duncan Campbell for the Rome Urban Renewal Agency in 1965 indicated that substantial parts of the fort's foundations were intact, although buried under 2 feet of topsoil (Campbell, 1965).

This report describes the archeological remains of Fort Stanwix and presents only a synopsis of the post-1781 components of the site. It is hoped that further information on these later components will be made available in future reports.

Fort Stanwix played a key role in the American Revolution, serving as a plug to one of the two main invasion routes between Canada and the American Colonies. For this reason, it was determined that the fort should be a focal point of interest during the bicentennial observance of the American Revolution. A historical report for the National Park Service by John Luzader (1969) draws together references to Fort Stanwix, its role in the French and Indian War, the American Revolution and details of construction to be used in rebuilding the fort as much like the original as possible. The records were scanty and many details remained conjectural. Archeological investigations were required to establish the location of the fort, its configuration, the interior arrangement of buildings, and to describe the artifacts left by the occupants in an attempt to supplement historical data on garrison life.

The National Park Service began archeological investigations in July, 1970, under Dick Ping Hsu. The senior author joined the staff in September of that year. Because of a lack of time and a limit to the area available for excavation (the site was still inhabited) work during the first season was concentrated on locating the fort, and identifying key features to which 18th-century plans could be related. It was discovered that the fort was not quite in the traditional location but conformed very well, internally, to the 18th-century plans. In 1896, an engineer attempted to locate the fort and, while determining its approximate position, decided that it was trapezoidal in shape rather than square as shown on 18th-century plans (figs. 4, 5, 7). Our investigations demonstrate that the fort was square. The next two summers were spent excavating the structures inside the main fort and sampling other parts of the fortifications to determine their location and dimensions. It is estimated that 33 percent of the main fort was excavated, 15 percent of which had been disturbed in the 19th and 20th centuries. An estimated 13 percent more was disturbed in unexcavated areas.

Five reference points were established in the fort area in lieu of a grid system, and all excavated features and many artifacts were mapped in relation to these stakes (fig. 10). Map tables were set up for each unit and all finds were recorded as they were uncovered. Units and sub-units were established as needed and were related to the structures found on the site. Small features, such as cellar holes or 19th-century privies were separately identified. A maximum of horizontal control was maintained, and material could be instantly identified in the la-

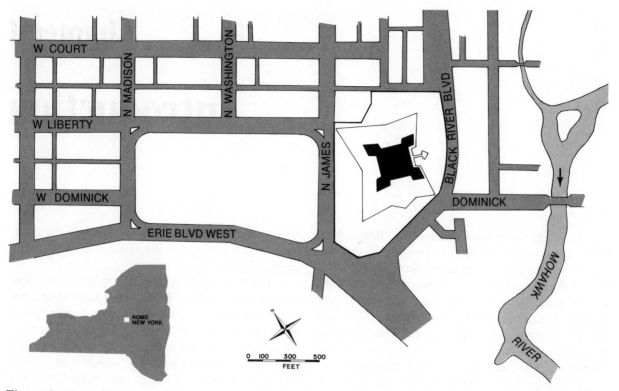

Figure 1. Plan of downtown Rome, New York, showing the location of Fort Stanwix National Monument.

boratory as to the fort feature from which it came by the field catalog number. In the one instance where we imposed an arbitrary grid system over a structure we gained nothing in terms of increased horizontal control. It should be noted that this method can be used only in a situation where the site is highly structured and contemporary plans can be tied to the archeological work from the beginning of the excavation.

The natural stratigraphy of the site was used to maintain vertical control of the artifacts. With the exception of the ditch around the fort and pits dug into it, the stratigraphy consisted of three layers. The bottommost was a sterile, yellow-brown sandy gravel. Above this lay a thin sandy brown loam layer (Level II) containing fort debris. On top was a thick gray loam that contained 18th- to 20th-century artifacts (Level I). The entire deposit averaged about 2 feet in thickness.

The stratigraphy of the ditch surrounding the fort on three sides was more complex; essentially the same three layers were found, but instead of the brown sandy loam layer with fort debris, we en-

countered a dark gray loam lining the scarp, counterscarp and bottom of the ditch (Level XI). There were a series of 19th- and 20th-century strata (Levels I-X) as the ditch was filled to level the ground surface (fig. 32). The dark gray loam lining was thicker at the base of the scarp and counterscarp and was interpreted as the remains of a sod lining. In the bridge area the stratigraphy was more complex and Level XI was divisible into Levels XI-XV.

Most of the fort-related artifacts were found in cellar holes in the east and west barracks, pits in the casemates and garbage dumps on the east scarp and in the sally port communication. A few artifacts, such as gunflints, could be identified on morphological grounds as being fort-related regardless of the levels in which they were found.

Intrusions

Most sites of any size have sections that have been disturbed by later components and Fort Stanwix, in an urban setting, was no exception. The

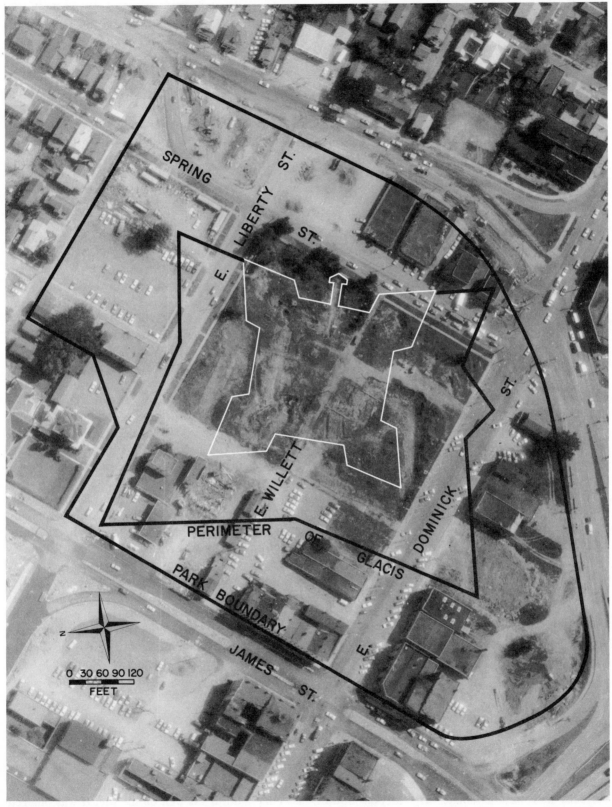

Figure 2. Aerial view of the site of Fort Stanwix during excavation. The fine white line defines the periphery of the fort.

disturbance at the fort date back to the late 18th century. In 1807, Christian Schultz observed:

Rome, formerly known as Fort Stanwix, is delightfully situated in an elevated and level country commanding an extensive view for miles around. This Village . . . seems quite destitute of every kind of trade, and rather upon the decline. The only spirit which I perceived stirring among them was that of money digging, and the old Fort betrayed evident signs of the prevalence of this mania, as it had literally been turned inside out for the purpose of discovering concealed treasures (Green, 1915, p. 183).

The newspapers of the day did not record the finding of any great treasures, although from time to time there appeared entries such as the following: "Mr. Alva Mudge, who resides on the site of old Fort Stanwix, recently found a British copper in his garden bearing the date of 1738." (Anon., Aug. 15, 1879).

For the purposes of this report, an intrusion shall be defined as any post-1781 disturbance of the earth which usually, but not always, was characterized by the inclusion of post-1781 artifacts in the fill and/or an orientation aligned to the present street system. Figure 2 depicts the position of the fort relative to surrounding buildings. The buildings which were once over the fort are described below by category of intrusion. Unless otherwise noted, they were torn down in 1970 and 1971. The names of the various houses are merely convenient labels that have been traditionally applied, and are not necessarily those of the last owners of the property.

Streets

Three major streets and two alleys traversed the site, all of which covered water, sewer and gas lines at depths to 9 feet. Only the utilities under Willett Street (an alley) damaged the site since these lines ran through the center of the fort. Spring Street cut off the tip of the southeast bastion.

Cellars

Eleven major structures with cellars were located on the central portion of the fort with several more situated on the glacis. Included in this total was one indoor swimming pool built *ca.* 1920 on Willett Street which destroyed parts of the west barracks and west casemate. The Stryker house, built in 1839 (Waite, 1972, p. 60) had a full cellar, the digging of which destroyed the east face of the northeast bastion. The Brockett house built *ca.* 1842 (Waite, 1972, p. 40) had a full cellar which destroyed the east flank of the southeast bastion, a portion of the bakehouse and a large part of the 1758 powder magazine. This house was torn down in 1927. The Draper house, built *ca.* 1825 (Waite, 1972, p. 39) replaced an earlier structure dating from *ca.* 1800 (Cookinham, 1912, p. 224). It had a full basement which destroyed part of the south face of the southeast bastion and the counterscarp. The Martin house, built *ca.* 1878 (city directory), and torn down in 1964, had a full basement which destroyed part of the ravelin and counterscarp. The Fort Stanwix Museum, built in 1910 (city directory), had a partial basement which cut out part of the southwest casemate. The Barnes-Mudge house, built in 1828 (Waite, 1972, p. 13), had a full cellar. It destroyed most of the southwest bastion and part of the southwest bombproof. The Henderson house, constructed *ca.* 1870 (city directory) with a full cellar destroyed part of the west flank of the northwest bastion. The Ward house, built *ca.* 1841 (Wager, 1896, p. 115), was replaced *ca.* 1895 (city directory) by the Carpenters' Temple. Both had full cellars and destroyed part of the counterscarp opposite the northwest bastion. The Cole-Kingsley house, erected in 1846 (Waite, 1972, p. 25) with a full basement, damaged part of the north casemate and the counterscarp. Another structure, the Prince house, was erected in 1839 (Waite, 1972, p. 61) and was moved from the site in 1871 (Wager, 1871). No trace of it was found and presumably it had no cellar. The same was true of the Huntington office which was built *ca.* 1877 (city directory) and moved *ca.* 1910 to another part of the site. It was torn down in 1960. One cellar hole was found which could not be related to any known buildings. A total of 14 wood or stone lined privies were found on the site (Hanson, 1974). Most of these resulted in a minimum of damage, although one did intrude into the northwest bombproof and three others went through the gateway and bridge.

Utilities

Nine cisterns and three wells were found, but the damage from these was negligible except for one cistern in the northeast bombproof. There was also one natural gas well on the site. It was plugged as a safety measure, but did not destroy anything. A number of drain pipes and water and gas feeder lines crossed the site to service the various buildings on it. These were more of a nuisance than an intrusion, although the southwest and northeast bombproofs suffered some destruction.

Other Intrusions

A flower garden on the Stryker property left some plow scars on the east barracks. There were a number of trees on the site, particularly 13 large elms. One of these was reportedly growing from the wall of the southwest bastion in 1804 (Durant, 1878, p. 385), an observation confirmed by counting the rings when it was removed. The Dutch elm disease destroyed it before we did.

In 1965, Col. J. Duncan Campbell conducted exploratory excavations at Fort Stanwix (Campbell, 1965). He excavated the bakehouse and part of the southeast casemate. He also dug a backhoe trench through the gateway area obliterating part of it.

Organization

This report is divided into four parts dealing with the history, structural details, artifacts, and a reconstruction of life at the fort. We relied mainly on the research of John Luzader and Orville Carroll for the section on history. Inasmuch as the main purpose of excavating Fort Stanwix was to get structural information for a reconstruction, we have devoted considerable space to the layout of the fort and building design. Principal elements of the fort are presented in chapter 3 in glossary form as an aid to those readers who are unfamiliar with fort terminology. In the course of our excavations we unearthed a quantity of 18th-century artifacts left by the fort's garrisons. These offer some evidence of the activities which took place in the fort, and the technloogy of the period. To elaborate on the topic of life in the fort, we gathered details from orderly books, diaries and letters for the final chapter.

Chapter 2

From Portage to Park

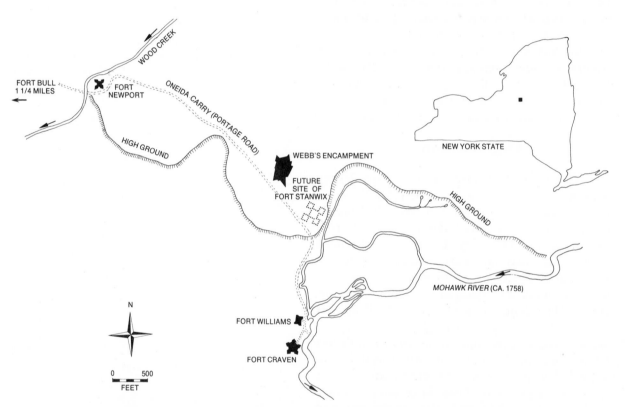

Figure 3. The Oneida Carrying Place and the location of pre-1758 forts.

Known as the Oneida Carrying Place (fig. 3), the portage was only a narrow trail across a low ridge in what is now central New York. In the 250 years after white men first used the portage, it became a funnel for fur trade, military activity and, eventually, settlement. Its strategic importance led finally to the construction of Fort Stanwix. The ridge lay between two major watersheds—the Mohawk River flowing eastward to the Hudson River and the Atlantic, and Wood Creek flowing westward to the Great Lakes by way of Oneida Lake and the Oswego River. During the spring thaws, when both watersheds were full, the distance across the portage was only 1 mile, while in the fall, after a drought, a man might have to walk 5 miles to find water deep enough to launch a bateau (O'Callaghan, 1854, p. 726). The importance of this portage can only be realized when one understands how poor the roads and trails were in colonial days. Most were mere ruts worn in the soil by travelers and were extremely difficult to negotiate on horseback, let alone by wagon. Rivers were the principal arteries of transportation and bateaus were developed to hold several tons of cargo. They could be propelled by three men paddling or, if the wind was right, with a sail. The Oneida Carry offered the second shortest route from the Atlantic to the Great Lakes. The St. Lawrence River, under French control until 1760, was the shortest.

Indians and Trade

The Iroquois Confederation consisted of the Mohawk, Onondaga, Cayuga, Oneida, Seneca and Tuscarora tribes that dominated the central New York area. French traders and missionaries from the north reached the Great Lakes by way of Canada as early as the 1640's, trading with the Indians for valuable pelts, particularly beaver. To maintain their trade, the Iroquois pushed westward after their own supply of furs was exhausted (Graymont, 1972, p. 24). Thus, the Iroquois, economic competitors of the French, allied themselves first with the Dutch and, after 1664, with the English.

The Dutch attempted to control trade by establishing state sanctioned posts such as Fort Orange at Albany, New York, and waiting for the Indians to come to them rather than sending independent traders among the Indians, as the French did. Although this led to fewer abuses to the Indians, the profit margin was much less. Finally, the Dutch were forced to modify their system to remain in competition, but by the time they became organized the English had taken control of the Dutch colony.

From the Indian point of view, English trade was a definite improvement. The French traders constantly complained that the English were paying higher prices for furs, thus drawing more Indians to them because they could produce and distribute trade goods at less cost than the French (Graymont, 1972, p. 26). For a considerable time, the Iroquois were divided over whether to remain neutral or to support the English or French in their recurring wars. The appointment of Sir William Johnson as New York's commissioner to the Indians in 1746 did much to strengthen Iroquois-English ties (Buffington, 1933, p. 228) particularly among the Mohawks. Johnson counteracted the hostility among the Iroquois caused by English encroach-

ments on their land. In 1756 he was made Superintendent of Indian Affairs by the Crown.

During this time the Carrying Place was a sort of "no man's land," or frontier between the English and French.

French and Indian War

In 1755, during the French and Indian War, Major General William Shirley, Governor of Massachusetts, led an expedition to the Great Lakes, pausing at the Oneida Carry. Here he took command of the English forces in North America after learning of the death of General Braddock (Luzader, 1969, pp. 4-5). He established a permanent post at Oswego, on Lake Ontario, and fortified the Carry with Fort Williams at the eastern end, built to hold 150 men and a stockade on Wood Creek to house 30 men and a storehouse.

This weaker post was named Fort Bull and became the target of a French and Indian raid in March, 1756. The garrison was overwhelmed when the stockade was broken through. In the midst of the battle, the explosion of the powder magazine hurled bodies, supplies and palisade logs over the countryside (Hagerty, 1971, pp. 57-60). The French completed the destruction of supplies waiting to be loaded into bateaus on the bank of Wood Creek and retired to Canada before the garrison at Fort Williams could pursue them.

Almost immediately the English began refortifying the Carry. Fort Bull was replaced by Fort Wood Creek, Fort Newport was added to store supplies and to protect a dam, and the pentagonal Fort Cravens was begun to replace Fort Williams (Luzader, 1969, p. 10). In the midst of this effort the English made a rapid succession of changes in the military leadership, all but paralyzing the war effort. General Daniel Webb took command at the Carry in August where he learned the garrison at Oswego had surrendered to the French. He ordered all the forts on the Oneida Carry destroyed and withdrew his troops back down the Mohawk Valley (Luzader, 1969, p. 14).

Except for a raid in the upper Mohawk Valley, the French failed to follow up their advantage and establish a permanent post at the Carry. In 1758, the British decided to reoccupy the Carry and build a larger fort which would be capable of withstanding the type of raid made on Fort Bull. Permission to rebuild was given by the Oneida Indians on the

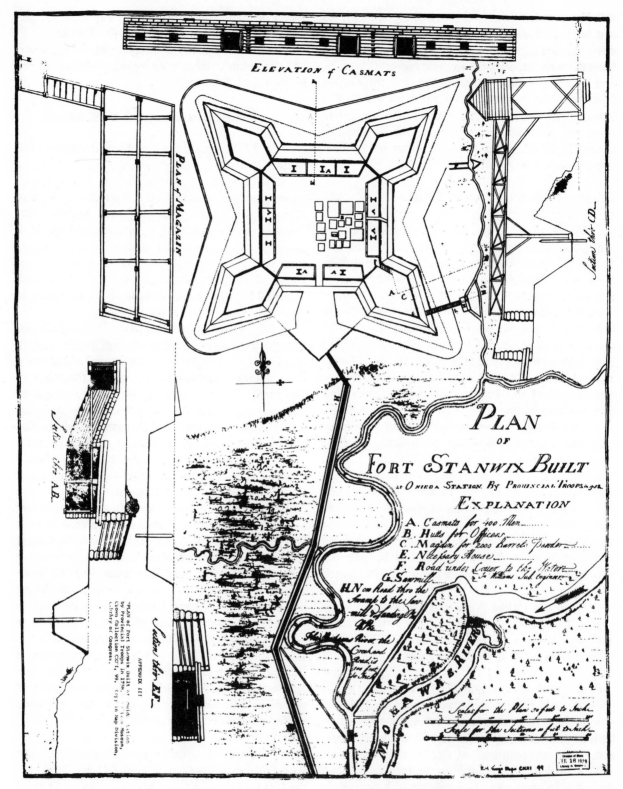

Figure 4. Plan of Fort Stanwix in 1758, from the Crown Collection (No. CXXI, 99).

condition that the fort be razed at the end of the war and that trade would be plentiful (Luzader, 1969, p. 19).

An adjunct to the building of the fort was Lt. Col. John Bradstreet's expedition against Fort Frontenac that destroyed that post and cut the French supply lines to the western Great Lakes. Work on Fort Stanwix began in the fall of that year (fig. 4). It was named for Brigadier General John Stanwix, who commanded the troops on the Carry. Up to 2,750 troops worked on the fort, digging the ditch and hewing the logs for the walls, but scurvy and exposure took a heavy toll of the work force and the number of available troops was often far less. While Bradstreet was gone, Stanwix had approximately 400 men fit for duty (Luzader, 1969, p. 30). By winter, the fort was sufficiently complete to house 400 men of Fraser's Highlanders (the 71st Regt. of Foot). A company of rangers, men hardened to frontier warfare and capable of fighting Indian-fashion, occupied huts outside the fort (Luzader, 1969, p. 42). The fort contained five casemates, a cluster of officers' huts on the parade ground and a powder magazine in the southeast bastion. Entrance to the fort was over a causeway. A row of pickets was placed in the ditch. The fort was essentially completed the following summer, but taking into account the haste with which it was constructed, the green wood used, and the skill (or lack thereof) of the colonial troops who erected it, it was in constant need of repairs. This was accelerated by the diminishing size of the garrison as the war zone moved further west. By 1761, there were only 50 men stationed at the fort (Luzader, 1969, p. 47).

Pontiac Conspiracy

In 1763, the Pontiac conspiracy inflamed the frontier, resulting in the destruction of settlements and forts (Peckham, 1961). Pontiac, an Ottawa Indian, persuaded the tribes in the area of the Great Lakes to the Ohio River to revolt and drive the British from their forts. Although several forts fell, Indian losses were heavy and expected French aid never materialized. Fort Stanwix was hastily rebuilt as a defensive measure when it was feared that the Iroquois confederacy would join Pontiac (fig. 5). The cluster of officers' huts was replaced by three barracks around the parade ground and a bridge replaced the causeway. A redout was raised before the sally port and connected with a covered communication. The movement collapsed in September of 1763 and within two years Fort Stanwix had again become inactive and fallen into disrepair.

Missionaries and Settlers

Next to traders and military men, missionaries probably had the greatest influence on the Indians. Their first contacts were with French Jesuits and later with English and Colonial protestants. In 1764, Samuel Kirkland, a Presbyterian missionary from Connecticut, settled among the Senecas and two years later moved to the Oneidas (Graymont, 1972, p. 34). He exerted a strong influence on the Indians and may be credited with causing the Oneidas and Tuscaroras to side with the Americans in the American Revolution. By contrast, the Anglican missionary, John Stuart, exerted his energies to keep the Mohawks loyal to the Crown.

In 1763, King George III had proclaimed the ridgeline of the Alleghenies as a boundary between Indians and Europeans to permit the development of an imperial policy to deal with frontier problems, i.e., land speculation, Indian relations, and the fur trade. But the colonists continued to push westward despite English efforts to enforce the proclamation. In October 1768, Sir William Johnson called all the leaders of the Iroquois to a grand council at Fort Stanwix to establish the line between the colonies and the Indians. The Treaty of 1768, or the Boundary Line Treaty, was an effort to stem the tide. The boundary set at the treaty ran from Fort Stanwix in a southwesterly direction to the mouth of the Tennessee River in what is now western Kentucky (fig. 6).

A garrison was stationed at Fort Stanwix at least until 1767. After that date a few men remained to forward mail and supplies to the western forts, but the fort ceased its military function. In 1774, the barracks burned to the ground and nothing remained but a room occupied by a trader (Duncan, 1969).

At the outbreak of the American Revolution, five families resided in the vicinity of Fort Stanwix (Duncan, 1969). John Roof had settled ca. 1760 under the protection of the fort. His home served as a stopping place for travelers. The beginning of hostilities forced these settlers to move

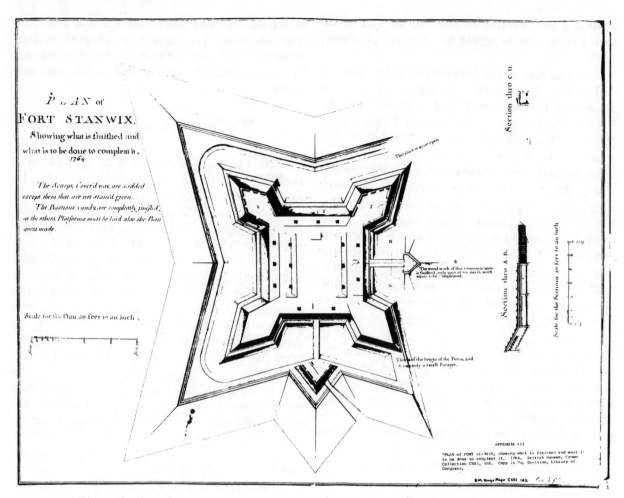

Figure 5. Plan of Fort Stanwix in 1764, from the Crown Collection (No. CXXI, 102).

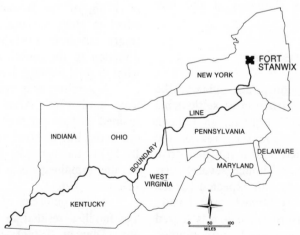

Figure 6. Boundary line esablished by the 1768 Treaty of Fort Stanwix.

down the Mohawk Valley to the relative security of the permanent settlements.

American Revolution

In the summer of 1776, the Americans occupied the Carry and began rebuilding Fort Stanwix with troops from New Jersey and New York. These were relieved by Connecticut troops over the winter. The Third New York Regiment arrived in the spring and continued the rebuilding. Hampering their efforts were a lack of skilled craftsmen and an incompetent French engineer. (W. Willett, 1831, p. 45).

The residents of the Mohawk Valley reflected the general attitude of the colonies in the break with Great Britain: some favored a break, others maintained loyalty to the Crown, but most just wanted to be left alone. Pressures from the rebels, who were not above using the present hostilities to settle old scores, drove many of the loyalists (Tories) to Canada. A few professed support for the rebellion and kept their sympathies secret. These secret Tories were one of the great British illusions until the end of the Revolution. Several campaigns were begun under the misapprehension that Tories would flock to the Crown's colors. The Burgoyne Campaign of 1777 was no exception. How this illusion was maintained remains a mystery; the British constantly suffered reverses from too much reliance on this support. It must be noted that those Tories who did unite with the British troops generally gave a good account of themselves in battle when they had good leadership. Furthermore, their leaders were constantly promoting the idea that the hinterlands were filled with men waiting to join the Crown. Perhaps the British generals, in an unfamiliar land, were too willing to believe their allies.

The Burgoyne plan (Luzader, 1969, Appendix XI), while bold in concept, was not really new. General Carleton had attempted a similar move the previous year but it was aborted by lateness of the season and Benedict Arnold's naval actions on Lake Champlain. The French had used the same route in the French and Indian War.

Burgoyne's plan for 1777 provided for the bringing of an army from Canada to Albany, where it would come upon Gen. Sir William Howe's command, open communications between New York City and Montreal, and permit Howe to "act to the southward." Howe was expected to cooperate by taking unspecified action on the Hudson, but he was not expected to effect a personal junction with Burgoyne at Albany. Howe was authorized to proceed against Philadelphia in such a manner as to permit "cooperation." He fulfilled the letter of that requirement by ordering the commander at New York, Sir Henry Clinton, to act on the lower Hudson. Clinton sent Vaughan and Wallace upstream, whereupon they burned Esopus (Kingston) and got as far as Livingston Manor, but were too late to help take the pressure off Burgoyne in time to save him (Luzader, personal communication). A third army would come from Canada by way of the Mohawk Valley to create a diversion, and thereby weaken the American forces opposing the main army and gather Tory sympathizers for the King's forces.

The western army, under the command of Lt. Colonel Barry St. Leger (a brevet general for the campaign), consisted of 100 men each from the 8th and 34th Regiments of Foot, a company of Hanau Chasseurs (German light infantry), Sir John Johnson's Regiment (Royal Yorkers, or Johnson's Greens), a company of Butler's Rangers, 40 artillerymen, Canadian militia and Indians (Luzader, 1969, p. 96). St. Leger had an effective force of about 700-800 whites and 800-1,000 Indians. By the end of July, Fort Stanwix was garrisoned with 450 men from the 3rd New York Regiment and 150 men of the 9th Massachusetts Regiment (Luzader, 1969, p. 106).

On July 3, a work detail cutting sod for the fort walls was ambushed by a raiding party that killed four men and took five prisoners (Graymont, 1972, p. 118. From these prisoners St. Leger learned that Fort Stanwix was stronger than he anticipated but he decided to continue forward.

The siege of Fort Stanwix officially began on Sunday, August 3, when Lt. Bird invested the fort with a small party of English troops and Indians (Luzader, 1969, p. 110). He was too late to prevent 100 more men from the 9th Massachusetts Regiment and four bateaus of supplies from entering the fort at the last minute, but did cut off the guard left behind at the river with the boats. This stroke of good fortune greatly aided the American defense of the fort and brought the numbers of the defenders nearly to a par with the British troops, excluding their Indian allies.

At 3 o'clock in the afternoon, St. Leger sent a captain under a flag of truce to demand the fort's surrender (Luzader, 1969, p. 118). The Americans refused. On this date, the garrison first raised their flag before the enemy. The officers had made the flag themselves because Congress had never supplied one for the fort. Two written references to the flag call it a "Continental Flagg" (Reid, 1905, pp. 95–96), (W. Willett, 1831, p. 54) and note that it was made from red, white and blue material, the latter a blue cloak owned by Captain Swartwout (Gansevoort-Lansing Papers). The material was cut into stripes but there was no mention of stars. This fact is important because a local tradition, traceable back to 1851, states that this flag was "the first stars and stripes to fly in the face of the enemy." The evidence, unfortunately, is not conclusive. There are four purportedly contemporary sketches of the flag of Fort Stanwix engraved on powder horns. Three of these show a Grand Union flag, which was first introduced at Boston in 1775, and the other appears to have stars and stripes, although the pattern of the stars is not discernable. On June 14, 1777, Congress passed a resolution adopting the stars and stripes but did not specify how the stars were to be arranged. The news did not reach Albany, New York, until early August (Thatcher, 1862, p. 87) which would have been too late for the news to have reached Fort Stanwix. So far as is known, none of the garrison claimed to have flown a stars and stripes flag, although several later went into politics.

During the night of August 4th, the Americans sent out parties to bring in hay for cattle penned in the ditch and to burn a house and barn in their field of fire (Luzader, 1969, pp. 121–22).

It took St. Leger until August 7th to clear the obstructions from Wood Creek, build a road, and bring up his artillery and stores (Luzader, 1969, p. 132). During this time, events were shaping up for one of the major engagements of the Revolution. Even before the beginning of the siege, word of the British advance raced down the Mohawk Valley. By August 4th, General Nicholas Herkimer mustered about 800 militiamen at Fort Dayton, 50 miles to the east, and set out for Fort Stanwix (Luzader, 1969, p. 122). The night of August 5th he camped at the Indian Village of Oriska and sent scouts ahead to alert the fort that he was coming. The next morning his army set out for Fort Stanwix without waiting for word that the garrison had received the message. In a ravine 6 miles from the fort, the American column was ambushed by 400 British and Indian troops. The

American rear guard of 200 men managed to escape while the remainder took any available cover they could find, firing at point-blank range. After 45 minutes, a cloudburst enabled the wounded Herkimer to regroup his forces to more defensible positions. The battle was at times a hand-to-hand combat, and lasted for 8 hours. Finally, the British, having lost 72 of their men, left the field (Graymont, 1972, pp. 131–138). The Americans, with at least 150 casualties, were in no condition to follow and fell back to Fort Dayton (Luzader, 1969, p. 125).

Meanwhile, the three messengers from Herkimer reached Fort Stanwix. Guns were fired by the fort's garrison to let General Herkimer know that the messengers arrived safely. A detachment of 250 Massachusetts and New York troops, with a 3-pound cannon, were dispatched to meet him. They did not know of the battle raging only a few miles away when they came upon two deserted British camps. Instead of proceeding to Oriskany they began to loot the camps, carrying off approximately 50 brass kettles, 100 blankets, muskets, tomahawks, spears, ammunition, clothing, deer skins, other Indian goods and papers of St. Leger (M. Willett, 1777). They also recovered an intercepted bundle of letters for the garrison.

During their return to the fort, the party was ambushed by a British detachment, but were able to return to the fort without losing a man. While at the camps, Willett learned of the battle at Oriskany from prisoners and did not continue on to meet Herkimer (Luzader, 1969, p. 129). The prisoners may have led him to believe that Herkimer had been defeated and he was under orders to meet Herkimer, not to go hunting for him. In any event, the raiding party was organized too late to influence the outcome of the battle at Oriskany since it did not leave the fort until after the heavy rain (Luzader, 1969, p. 130).

About 5 p.m. on August 8th, Colonel Butler and two other officers came into the fort under a flag of truce (Luzader, 1969, p. 132). They were blindfolded and led into a closed room at headquarters so they could not see the fort's defenses. They threatened that their Indian allies would devastate the Mohawk Valley and its inhabitants if the garrison did not surrender Lt. Col. Willett noted that the British would be held responsible for the actions of their allies, and that the garrison had no intention of surrendering (W. Willett, 1831, pp. 57–58). If Willett's account was accurate, it indicated that the Indians were already discouraged with the way the campaign was going and their recent losses of men and equipment. That night, Marinus Willett and Lt. Levi Stockwell slipped out of the fort and made their way down the Mohawk Valley to organize another relief expedition.

The next day St. Leger repeated his demands in writing. Colonel Gansevoort's reply was a classic for clarity and brevity:

Fort Schuyler, Aug. 9, 1777

Sir:
Your letter of this day's Date I have Receiv'd, in answer to which I say, that it is my Determined resolution with the Forces under my Command, to defend this Fort to the last Extremity in behalf of the United American States who have placed me here to Defend it against all their Enemies.
I have the Honour to be
Sir Your most ob^t Hum^l serv^t
P Gansevoort Col^o
Commanding F^t Schuyler
Gen. Barry St. Leger   (W. Stone, 1838, facing p. 252)

During the next two weeks the combatants engaged in intermittent shelling and sniping. Finding cannon ineffective against the fort, the British began a siege trench toward the northwest bastion, either to bring their cannon closer, or to dig a mine under the bastion.

Unaware of Herkimer's actions, General Schuyler ordered Brig. General Ebenezer Learned's brigade of Massachusetts troops up the Mohawk Valley to relieve Fort Stanwix on August 6th. On August 13th, Major General Benedict Arnold was sent to take command of the brigade and any militia that could be raised for the relief expedition. By August 20th, the troops began assembling at Fort Dayton (Luzader, 1969, pp. 146–151).

By a stroke of fortune, a group of Tories was apprehended at German Flatts. Among those captured was a mentally retarded man, Hon Yoost Schuyler, his brother and mother (Luzader, 1969, p. 156). The Indians believed that Hon Yoost could commune with the spirits. Holding the brother and mother as hostages, Arnold sent him and a friendly Oneida Indian to St. Leger's camps to spread the rumor that Arnold was coming with an army larger than he actually had. The plan was to scare the Indians into deserting St. Leger thereby giving Arnold's army superiority. The plan

worked too well; before Arnold's army could reach Fort Stanwix, the Indians had deserted, forcing St. Leger to lift the siege and retreat to Canada. The retreat was nearly a rout. Much equipment, including artillery, was abandoned.

This ended the military actions against Fort Stanwix. Two months later, surrounded and cut off, General Burgoyne surrendered his forces at Saratoga. General Clinton had been left at New York City by General Howe. After being reinforced, he attempted to aid Burgoyne but was too late to extricate him. The surrender at Saratoga was the turning point of the Revolution inasmuch as it led to the formal French alliance.

During this period, Fort Stanwix was essentially rebuilt along the lines of the British occupation (fig. 7). There were five casemates, three barracks around the parade ground (one used as headquarters) and a guard house and storehouse flanking the gate on the parade ground. The major difference was the moving of the line of pickets from the ditch to the covered way (W. Willett, 1831, p. 44). The northwest and southwest bombproofs were also erected in 1777 (Reid, 1905, p. 99), (W. Willett, 1831, p. 49).

Arnold's troops and the 9th Massachusetts returned to take part in the battles at Saratoga while the 3rd New York remained at Fort Stanwix until 1779 when they were relieved by the 1st New York which, in turn, was replaced by the 4th New York (later the 2d New York after a reorganization of the New York line) in 1780.

Fort Stanwix played a minor role in the Sullivan expedition in 1779. This campaign destroyed Indian settlements in western New York, but failed to stop Indian raids which by this time originated primarily in Canada.

Although Fort Stanwix was garrisoned until 1781, the Revolution swirled about it without much effect. The Tories and Indians bypassed it, and attacked the settlements of the Mohawk Valley. The garrison was isolated and constantly short of supplies. On May 13, 1781, the barracks caught fire and Fort Stanwix burned to the ground. The circumstances of the fire were very unusual; arson was suspected but never proven. Within a few days, the garrison was ordered to evacuate the fort and take everything, even scrap iron, with them (Lauber, 1932, p. 581).

In the fall of 1783, a blockhouse was erected near the site of Fort Stanwix, but there is no evidence that it was ever garrisoned.

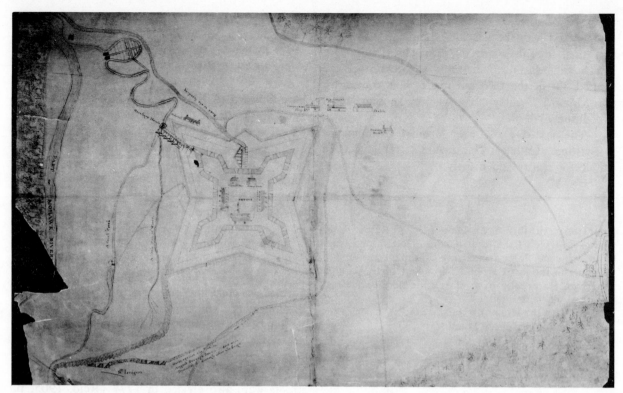

Figure 7. Fort Stanwix, *ca.* 1777, commonly known as the Gansevoort Plan (New York Public Library).

Peace

Although the Treaty of Paris (1783) ostensibly ended the American Revolution, the British abandoned their Indian allies and so a separate peace had to be made. Accordingly, commissioners of the Congress, with representatives from Pennsylvania, met with the Iroquois in October 1784, to set the terms for peace (Graymont, 1972, p. 273). The State of New York tried to negotiate a separate treaty to prevent the Congressional delegation from taking land in Congress' name. Important visitors to the meetings included the Marquis de LaFayette and James Madison.

Not only were the Iroquois divided among themselves as a result of the war, but they were shocked to learn that the British had made no provision for them in the Treaty of Paris. In the Treaty of Fort Stanwix of 1784, the Iroquois Confederacy (with the exception of the Oneidas and Tuscaroras who had generally supported the Americans) was forced to cede a large part of its territory to the Congress, and another parcel was bought by Pennsylvania for $5,000 (Graymont, 1972, p. 283). Much of the land obtained from the Indians was subdivided for sale to pay Revolutionary War debts or granted to soldiers in lieu of back pay. The site of Fort Stanwix, included in the Expense Grant to pay for the costs of this program, was purchased by Dominick Lynch, a wealthy land speculator from Long Island (Waite, 1972, p. 38).

Settlement

By 1796, there were already several settlers in the area, including soldiers who had served at Fort Stanwix. In that year, the Western Inland Lock and Navigation Company began a canal across Oneida Carry to replace the portage. In 1817 the Erie Canal was begun at Rome.

About 1800, Lynch built a house over the ditch just off the southeast bastion. His son occupied it until it burned in 1825. After a period of unsuccessful attempts to lease the land, Lynch began to sell off lots. Buildings were constructed over the site from 1828 to 1850. Remaining portions of the earthen walls were scraped into the ditch to level the area, and the remains of a 1794 blockhouse were razed. The houses were large and surrounded by big yards. The expense of maintaining these dwellings was great and by 1925 most had been sold to organizations such as the American Legion and Rome Club (Waite, 1972, p. 40).

Park

In 1927, a small plot of land was bought by the State of New York to commemorate the Fort, and in 1935 Congress declared the site a National Monument subject to the land becoming Federal property (49 Stat. 665). This was made possible by the inclusion of the site in the Urban Renewal District of the City of Rome which purchased the land and donated it in 1973 to the Federal Government for the reconstruction of the fort.

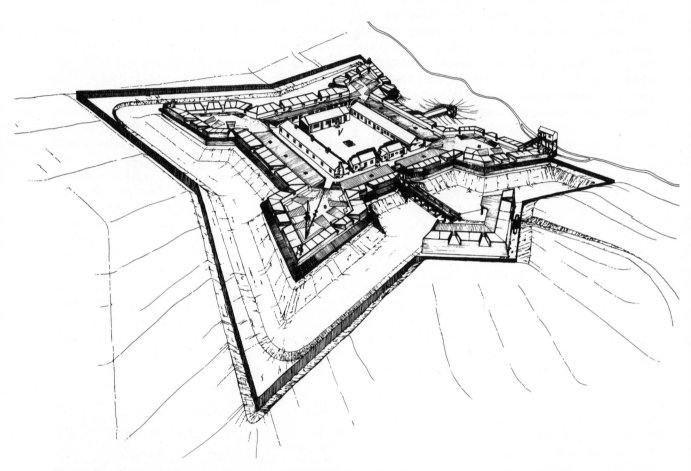

Figure 8. Architectural reconstruction (three-dimensional projection view) of Fort Stanwix, view to east (after a drawing by Orville W. Carroll).

Chapter 3

The Fort and Its Structure

In this section we will detail the 18th-century archeological features uncovered at Fort Stanwix (fig. 10). The major structural elements of the fort are presented in glossary form. Definitions of terms are taken from 18th-century sources, and the spelling of terms generally follows 18th-century usage. The principal elements of the fort are identified on the reconstruction drawings depicted as figures 8 and 9.

All structural measurements are in the English system as used in laying out the fort in 1758. All elevations are taken from Rome City Benchmark No. 128, 745 feet south-southwest of the fort. The parade ground averaged 451 feet above mean sea level with a variation of less than 6 inches between high and low readings. All depths are given in relation to a datum of 451 feet. All measurements of structures given are exterior dimensions unless otherwise noted. Approximate dimensions are those based on projections of existing walls and angles and, in some cases, on assumed building symmetry when the actual dimensions could not be measured. A measurement relative to the wall of a structure was taken from the exterior of the wall to the nearest point or side of the feature being described. See Appendix C for a list of features, their locations, and approximate dates of origin.

Wood samples were identified by the College of Environmental Science and Forestry, State University of New York, Syracuse.

Bakehouse

The Bakers who are Daily employ'd in Baking bread for this Garrison shall under no pretence Whatsover, take more than One Shilling, for a Loaf of Bread which shall weigh 6 lb. (M. Willett, 12/4/77)

The bakehouse for Fort Stanwix was located inside the southeast bastion (fig. 11). Although we are not certain when the bakehouse was built, one was certainly used during the Revolution (M. Willett, 1777; Lauber, 1932, pp. 541, 572, 577). We know also that it was constructed after the 1758 powder magazine was abandoned since the oven and one corner of the bakehouse were built over the hole created by the collapsed roof of the magazine after that hole had been filled with soil and leveled off. The 1758 magazine was still shown on a 1764 plan (Crown Collection CXXI, 103), the last known plan from the British occupation. Since the Americans built new magazines in 1777 (W. Willett, 1831, p. 49), it had presumably collapsed by that time.

The original excavation of the bakehouse was undertaken in 1965 by J. Duncan Campbell (1965). His report was available but we decided to reexcavate the structure to relate it to our plans, and to find its relationship to the 1758 powder

Figure 11. View of the bakehouse excavation, looking east-northeast. Note the oven to the right, and the 19th-century foundation intruding the north corner of the structure. The bakehouse measures 20.3 feet long along the near wall, and 18.4 feet across.

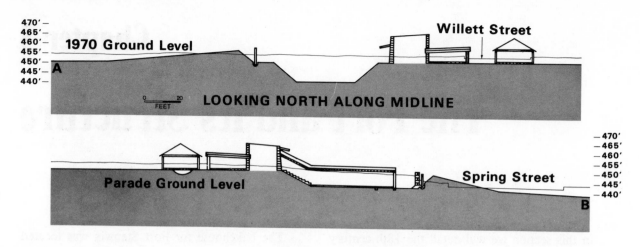

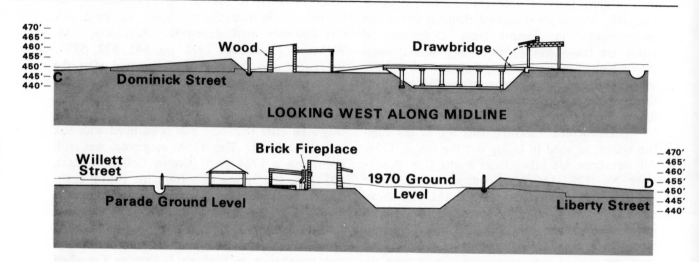

Figure 9. Architectural reconstruction (side elevation) of Fort Stanwix. These sections are based on archeological evidence, historic plans, contemporary descriptions and comparable forts (after drawings by Orville W. Carroll).

magazine. The foot-wide sill beams were charred and the corners of the bakehouse were sufficiently destroyed so that it was not possible to determine the method of joining, except that no nails were used. The east wall sill beam was made from eastern white pine (*Pinus strobus*).

The building was not quite square, being approximately 21 feet long on the east side, 20.3 feet long on the west, approximately 19.5 feet long on the north, and 18.4 feet long on the south side. The northeast corner was destroyed by a post-1840 stone-lined cellar. Campbell reported finding clapboards 1.1 feet wide and 1 inch thick along the east wall which he thought were an exterior facing of the building. These should have

required a heavy timber framing. We recovered no evidence of the roof, but it was probably sloped for drainage and made from heavy timbers like those found on the bombproofs under the other bastions.

Campbell reported the finding of window glass. However, a window would not have been in the walls since this structure was buried in the southeast bastion, and it is highly unlikely that there would have been a skylight. There may have been a window in the door.

The floor consisted of hard-packed earth. In several areas, especially the three remaining corners of the building, the earth was fire reddened and charcoal was abundant. This probably resulted

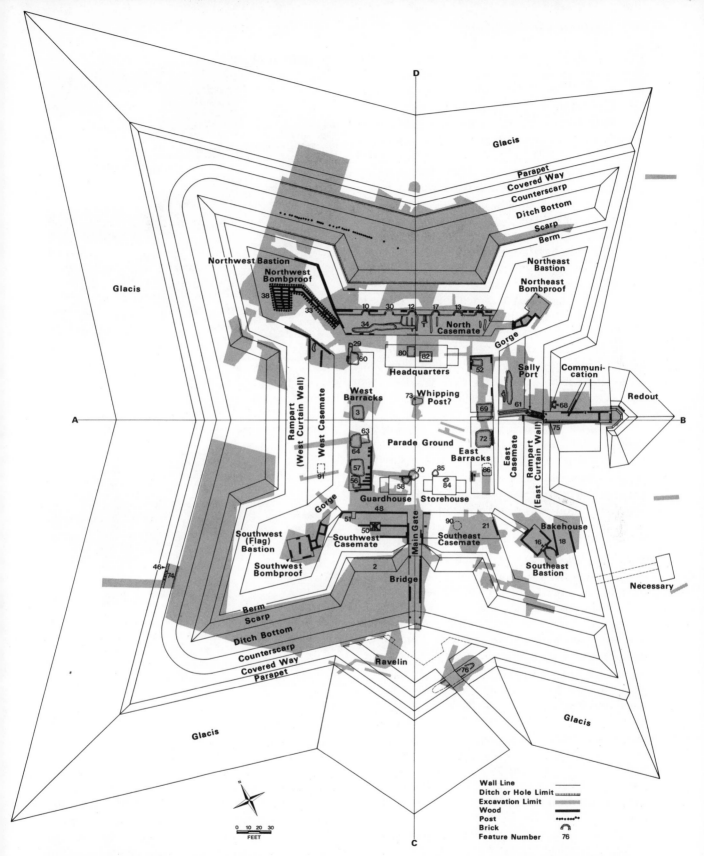

Figure 10. Plan of the 18th-century remains of Fort Stanwix located by excavation. See figure 9 for sections along the A-B and C-D lines.

from the fire that destroyed the structure rather than a deliberate burning of the floor to harden it. The floor was at an elevation of 450.05 feet or 1 foot below the parade ground level.

Entrance to the bakehouse was made down a flight of steps constructed of hewn logs resting on sterile soil (fig. 12). Except where burned, the wood had decomposed. The treads were approximately 1 foot deep, the risers were 5 inches, 10 inches and 3 inches high respectively from bottom to top, although the top step, or landing, was truncated by modern landscaping activities and may once have been higher. The steps were 5 feet wide while Campbell reported the doorway to be 3.75 feet wide flanked by vertical jambs on the bottom step which was actually the sill beam for the wall. One pintle for the door was located in the east jamb; another was lying on the floor. These had been removed prior to our excavation and are presently in the collection of the Rome Historical Society. The steps were 6.7 feet from the west wall and approximately 7.8 feet from the east wall.

A brick fireplace was situated opposite the doorway, fully recessed in the south wall 5.7 feet from the west wall and 6.3 feet wide (fig. 13). It was 2 feet deep with a back wall and jambs .6 foot thick. The back narrowed to 5.5 feet in width. The hearth floor was paved with bricks laid parallel to the back wall of the fireplace and extended 1.5 feet out in front of it. The fireplace stood 1.6 feet high but the top had been removed. There was a rodent burrow or intrusive pit (Feature 16) through the hearth and part of the back wall.

Behind the fireplace at an elevation of 451.80 feet stood an egg-shaped, arched oven approximately 12 feet long and 10 feet wide. Parts of this were destroyed by a tree and a gas line. Campbell reported a brick paving under the oven which we were not able to find, although we did observe a wood and mortar base under the walls of the oven that probably extended beneath such a floor. The gap in the oven walls to the hearth was 2.3 feet in width, but the actual opening into the hearth had been destroyed and may have been somewhat narrower. The oven was probably heated by wood embers, the coals scraped out into the fireplace and the bread inserted, after which the opening was sealed. The oven could have accommodated about 20 6-pound loaves at one time. Because the oven was underground and well insulated, several batches could have been baked before the oven

Figure 12. View of the charred steps of the bakehouse, looking west. The bottom step is five feet wide.

Figure 13. View of the fireplace and oven of the bakehouse, looking south-southeast. Slumping of the back wall was caused by a rodent burrow (Feature 16), roots or previous excavation. The rear wall of the fireplace measures 5.5 feet wide.

had to be reheated. At its peak, the garrison would have required only 200 loaves a day at full rations, which was probably rare. This was well within the capacity of this oven and most of the time they probably did not require over 60 loaves a day.

Campbell's excavations removed all *in situ* artifacts and building debris. Level I was his backfill and extended to the floor level. The few artifacts we recovered in this fill that compares to our documented, 18th-century specimens may have come from elsewhere in his excavations.

Banquette

. . . a kind of step made on the rampart of a work near the parapet, for the troops to stand upon, in order to fire over the parapet: it is generally 3 feet high when double, and 1½ when single and about 3 feet broad, and 4½ feet lower than the parapet. (G. Smith, 1779, p. 99)

The only evidence of a banquette at Fort Stanwix was found in the redout of the sally port. Here, we uncovered the base of an earthen banquette, probably revetted with sod, at an elevation of 443 feet. It was approximately 3.5 feet broad at the base. A 1764 plan of the fort (fig. 5) showed an overall width of 3.5 feet with a vertical height of 1.5 feet. The top of the banquette was shown as 2 feet wide with .5 foot taken up by a row of pickets. This produced a 45-degree slope to the face. The banquette on the rampart, which was probably wooden, was gone and no evidence of a banquette was found on the covered way.

Barracks

. . . are places erected for both officers and men to lodge in; they are built different ways, according to their different situations. When there is sufficient room to make a large square, surrounded with buildings, they are very convenient . . . (G. Smith, 1779, p. 20)

By November of 1764 two barracks were erected inside the fort (Crown Collection CXXI, 103). These, or their replacements, burned down in the fall of 1774 (Duncan, 1969). Americans occupied the fort from 1776 to 1777 and rebuilt the barracks. The west barracks were partly dismantled in 1780 when the guardhouse burned down (Van Dyck, 1780) and then rebuilt. All the barracks in the fort were destroyed in a general fire in May 1781 (Lauber, 1932, p. 581). Plans and contemporary powder horn engravings indicate that these were gabled roofed frame structures. (Carroll, 1973).

East Barracks

This structure measured 20 feet wide by at least 110 feet long, based upon the remaining timbers (figs. 14, 15). The southern end was disturbed, but assuming that it extended as far south as the west barracks, it was 120 feet in total length.

The remnants of the foundations consisted of 1-foot-wide beams that lay on sterile soil. Two samples were identified as eastern white pine (*Pinus strobus*). They had collapsed from decay and were charred on their upper surfaces. The beam at the north end was 18 feet long with the side beams flanking the ends at the corners. At the northwest corner was a .5 foot wide beam, 3 feet from the corner, tying together the end and side sleepers. A soil change at the northeast corner indicated a similar structural detail. The only trace of a cross sleeper beneath the floor was approximately 16.5 feet from the south wall. This structure was 2 degrees out of line with the axis of the fort, the only structure so situated. A number of burned or corroded wrought iron nails were found on the sleepers and within the perimeter of the barracks.

No fireplaces were found. This cannot be explained except by disturbance, since all 18th-century plans and sketches show chimneys on this building. Brick rubble found in cellar holes probably represents the remains of fireplaces. The floor was probably wooden planks running lengthwise to the building and nailed to sleepers resting on sterile soil. This inference was based on the presence of cellar holes, the absence of a packed dirt floor and sleepers in the west barracks.

Level I was 1 foot thick at the north end of the barracks and 2 feet thick over the middle and southern two-thirds. It contained post-1781 artifacts in a gray loam. Level II was the surface of the undisturbed sterile subsoil but also had post-1781 artifacts on it.

Four cellar holes were found under this barracks. The dates for these are discussed following a description of the west barracks. The artifacts listed for each cellar do not represent the total inventory for each, rather only those types which might give some indication of the age of the cellars. Feature 52 was a 6- by 9-foot hole, 2 feet from the west wall and 3 feet from the north wall. It was 5 feet deep and was probably wood-lined but no trace of the lining remained. This is inferred from the observation that the sand walls were nearly vertical. Intruding this was a 6- by 8-foot hole against the west wall and 5 feet from the north wall. This was 2.5 feet deep. The former hole was designated Level IV and the latter Level III. Intruding Level III was an oval pit, Feature 53, which contained, among other things, a modern soft drink bottle in a fill of gray loam and brickbats. The fill of Level III in Feature 52 consisted almost entirely of brick-

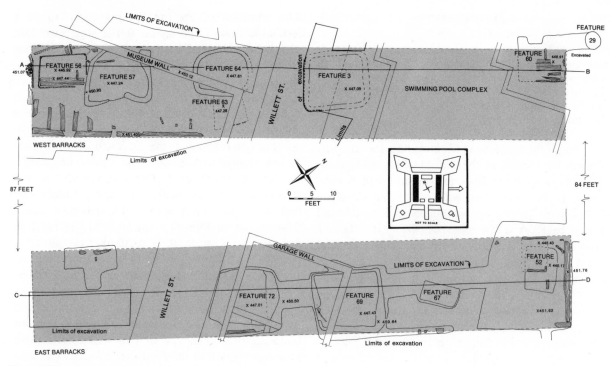

Figure 14. Ground plans of the east and west barracks. See figure 15 for sections along the A-B and C-D lines.

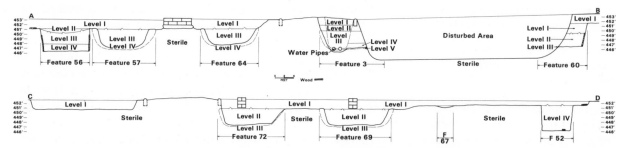

Figure 15. Sections through the east and west barracks.

Figure 16. View of a clay-lined cellar hole (Feature 69) in the east barracks, looking southeast. The concrete on the floor at left was broken from an intrusive garage foundation. Width of the cellar is 15.5 feet.

bats and mortar with some charcoal and almost no soil. The artifacts in this level included a 1734 British halfpenny, two Type 3A axe fragments, three Dutch gunflints, a mortar bomb fragment, two Type A-1a buttons, a Type B-1 button, a Type F-2 button, six Type 1a porcelain potsherds, 11 Type 1b porcelain potsherds, six Type 1a stoneware potsherds, two Type 1b stoneware potsherds, a Type 1a earthenware potsherd, three Type 1b earthenware potsherds, four Type 2a earthenware potsherds and a Type 4 earthenware potsherd. Level IV was almost entirely sand with a few brickbats and some charcoal. As indicated, this was the original hole with Level III intruded into it. The artifacts included a Dutch gunflint, a mortar bomb fragment, a Type D-1 button, ten Type 1a porcelain potsherds, 21 Type 1b porcelain potsherds, a Type 1c porcelain potsherd, a Type 2 porcelain potsherd, eight Type 1a stoneware potsherds, two Type 1b stoneware potsherds, two Type 1b earthenware potsherds and a Type 4 earthenware potsherd. The Type 2 porcelain potsherd and the Type 1b stoneware potsherd crossmended with fragments from Level II above and just south of Feature 52.

Feature 69 was a clay-lined cellar hole 41.5 feet from the north wall and against the east wall (fig. 16). It measured 15.5 feet north-south and 13.5 feet across and was slightly assymetrical. It was 3.5 feet deep and the clay lining was .6 to 2 feet thick. There were three levels. Level I was the fill adjacent to an intrusive stone and concrete foundation built between 1839 and 1851 (Waite, 1972, p. 61) (city map). Level II was a layer of brickbats, mortar and charcoal extending down to the floor. Artifacts found on the clay floor were designated Level III. Artifacts in Level II included two Type 4a axes, a Type 4c axe, a Type 3 spade, a Type 1 file, 1742 Dutch gunflints, 1002 French gunflints, a complete 4.5-inch mortar bomb, 56 mortar bomb fragments, a kettle fragment, three tin can fragments, two Type A-1a buttons, a Type B-2 button, a Type C-1 button, a Type D-1 button, a Type D-2 button, a Type E-1 button, a Type F-2 button, a Type H-1 button, seven Type 1b porcelain potsherds, a Type 1d porcelain potsherd, six Type 1a stoneware potsherds, a Type 1b stoneware potsherd, a Type 1d stoneware potsherd, two Type 1a earthenware potsherds, seven Type 1b earthenware potsherds, ten Type 2a earthenware potsherds and a Type 4 earthenware potsherd. Level III contained four Dutch gunflints, two Type

A-1a buttons, a Type A-1b button, a Type E-1 button, a Type F-2 button, a Type 1a porcelain potsherd, three Type 1b porcelain potsherds, four Type 1a stoneware potsherds, a Type 1b stoneware potsherd, a Type 1d stoneware potsherd, four Type 1a earthenware potsherds, five Type 1b earthenware potsherds, a Type 1d earthenware potsherd and four Type 2a earthenware potsherds.

Feature 72 was another clay-lined cellar hole 65 feet from the north wall and 1.5 feet from the east wall. It measured 15 feet north-south, 14 feet across and 4 feet deep. The clay lining had largely eroded away or been destroyed by modern intrusions, including the ca. 1839-1851 foundation noted under Feature 69 and an oil storage tank. Level I was largely disturbed by intrusions and contained brickbats, charcoal, mortar and loam. Level II lacked the loam and did not appear to have been disturbed by post-1781 intrusions. Level III was confined to artifacts on the clay floor of the cellar. Artifacts in Level II included a French(?) jetton dated 1700, a 1752 British halfpenny, five Dutch gunflints, two French gunflints, a 4.5-inch mortar bomb, a mortar bomb fragment, a Type A-1a button, a Type A-4 button, two Type B-1 buttons, a Type D-1 button, five Type 1a porcelain potsherds, three Type 1b porcelain potsherds, ten Type 1a stoneware potsherds, three Type 1b stoneware potsherds, four Type 1a earthenware potsherds, four Type 1b earthenware potsherds, a Type 2a earthenware potsherd, a Type 2e earthenware potsherd and a Type 4 earthenware potsherd. Level III contained three Dutch gunflints, a Type A-1a button, a Type B-1 button, eight Type 1a stoneware potsherds, two Type 1b stoneware potsherds and a Type 1b earthenware potsherd.

West Barracks

This structure measured 120 feet long and 20 feet wide (figs. 14, 15). Only fragments of the wall sleepers remained. Two samples were identified as eastern white pine (*Pinus strobus*). These were 1 foot wide, charred and resting on sterile soil. There were fragments of charred sleepers across the structure at distances of 5, 8, 10.5, 14, 19, 30, 33.5 and 36.5 feet from the south end. The best preserved of these butted against the east wall sleeper and were 1 foot wide. A plank floor running lengthwise to the structure was probably nailed to the sleepers.

A brick chimney base (without a hearth) was

found in the south wall, 11.5 feet from the east wall. It was 3 feet wide and 1.5 feet thick. Only a couple of courses of badly deteriorated brick, bonded with a sandy gray lime mortar were found. A fragment of a mortar bed was found in Level II of Feature 56, just north of this brick.

Level I was a gray loam over the whole area containing post-1781 artifacts. There were six cellar holes beneath this barracks. Three were lined with 1-foot-wide vertical wood planks and three were lined with clay. The contents of these cellars, brick rubble, charcoal and burned artifacts, indicated deliberate filling after one or more fires (fig. 17).

Figure 17. Profile, looking north, of the rubble filling a clay-lined cellar (Feature 57) in the west barracks. Width of the cellar is 11 feet.

Feature 60 was a wood-lined cellar 1 foot from the north wall and 13 feet from the east wall. It measured 10 feet from north to south, approximately 7 feet across and 4.5 feet deep. Level I was a sand and cobblestone layer 2 feet deep which contained 19th-century ceramics. Below this was a layer of brickbats, mortar, a lime deposit and charcoal (Level II). In the lime deposit were 2,145 wrought iron nails 1 to 3 inches long. Level III was those artifacts resting on the wood plank floor in what appeared to be burned straw. The 1-foot-wide plank flooring ran north-south with 6-inch-wide plank sleepers under it. The sides of the cellar were shored up with vertical planks 1 foot wide but the framing which must have held these upright was not found. The south end of this cellar was destroyed during demolition work on the site in 1970. There was a trench 3 feet wide along the west side that extended 4 feet beyond the north

wall and terminated at a circular wood-lined hole 3 feet in diameter and 2.5 feet deep (not a buried barrel). This may have been an intrusive 19th-century feature, but this could not be determined stratigraphically in the field and there were no artifacts in it. Level II contained a tool kit consisting of five files, a punch, an iron bar and a nail wrapped in coarse cloth and tied with a string, two Dutch gunflints, eight Type B-1 buttons, a Type D-1 button, two Type E-1 buttons, a Type 1a porcelain potsherd, five Type 1b porcelain potsherds two Type 1d porcelain potsherds, three Type 1a stoneware potsherds, two Type 1b stoneware potsherds, four Type 1a earthenware potsherds, three Type 1b earthenware potsherds, eight Type 2a earthenware potsherds, a Type 2d earthenware potsherd and a Type 2e earthenware potsherd. Artifacts in Level III included a Type 5a axe, two inkwells, three Type B-1 buttons, two Type B-3 buttons, a Type 1c stoneware potsherd and a Type 1a earthenware potsherd.

Feature 3, a clay-lined cellar, lay approximately 46 feet from the north wall and 7 feet from the east wall. It was approximately 13 feet long north-south, 10 feet across, and 4 feet deep with a 1-foot-thick clay lining. It was badly disturbed by demolition in 1970 and by two pipelines. Level II was a disturbed layer of gray loam and brick rubble with post-1781 artifacts in it. Level III included the disturbed fill over the two 6-inch pipelines below the top of the clay lining. Level IV was largely brickbats, mortar and charcoal but also contained some post-1781 artifacts. Level V was confined to those pre-1781 artifacts on the remaining portions of the clay floor. An *in situ* fragment of a pine beam (*Pinus strobus*) was collected from the top of a remaining section of the clay lining in Level II. In the fill of Level II was a 1766 Spanish 2 reales coin, two French gunflints, a Type 1a porcelain potsherd, four Type 1b porcelain potsherds, 14 Type 1a stoneware potsherds, two Type 1a earthenware potsherds, two Type 1b earthenware potsherds, a Type 1d earthenware potsherd, three Type 2a earthenware potsherds and a Type 2e earthenware potsherd. Level IV contained two kettle fragments, a Dutch gunflint, two Type A-1a buttons, a Type B-3 button and two Type D-3 buttons. Artifacts in Level V included three Dutch gunflints, a French gunflint, a Type 1a porcelain potsherd, a Type 1b porcelain potsherd, four Type 1a stoneware potsherds and two Type 1a earthenware potsherds.

Feature 63, a wood-lined cellar, lay 42 feet from the south wall and 1.5 feet from the east wall. It was 8 feet north-south, approximately 7 feet across and 4 feet deep. There were vertical planks 1 foot wide along the east side but preservation was poor on the other sides. Feature 64, a clay-lined cellar, had been dug through the west side of this feature, destroying a part of it. Level II contained brickbats, mortar and charcoal but had been disturbed by a 1910 foundation which made it impossible to see the outline of Feature 64 until we reached a depth of 6 inches below the foundation so that this level contained artifacts from both features as well as later material. Level III was undisturbed and contained brickbats mortar and charcoal. Level IV was restricted to those artifacts on the floor. Artifacts in Level III included a balance beam from a scale, a Dutch gunflint, two Type 1b stoneware potsherds, a Type 1a earthenware potsherd, two Type 1b earthenware potsherds and seven Type 2a earthenware potsherds. Level IV contained a Type 1a stoneware potsherd and a Type 2a earthenware potsherd.

Feature 64, a clay-lined cellar hole was 37 feet from the south wall and 9 feet from the east wall. It was 13 feet north-south, 10.5 feet across and 3.5 feet deep. As noted, it cut into the lining and fill of Feature 63 and, as a result of an intrusive 1910 wall, Level II was included with Level II of Feature 63. Level III contained brickbats, mortar and charcoal, and Level IV was restricted to the floor of the cellar. Level III contained a Type 3b file, six French gunflints, a Type 1a stoneware potsherd, a Type 1b stoneware potsherd and 12 Type 2a earthenware potsherds. Level IV produced a Dutch gunflint, a French gunflint, a Type 1b stoneware potsherd and nine Type 2a earthenware potsherds.

Feature 57 was a clay-lined cellar hole 12.5 feet from the south wall and 7 feet from the east wall (fig. 17). It measured 14.5 feet north-south, 11 feet across and 4 feet deep. The clay lining was .7 to 2.0 feet thick but broken on the east side for a distance of 3.5 feet (entry?). The south end of this cellar intruded the north end of Feature 56. Level II contained brickbats, mortar and charcoal but had been disturbed by a 1910 foundation. Level III also contained brickbats, mortar and charcoal but was undisturbed. Level IV was restricted to artifacts on the floor. Artifacts in Level III included a George I halfpenny (date illegible), a 1722 British halfpenny, two Dutch gunflints, nine French gunflints, a Type A-1a button, a Type B-1 button, two Type 1b porcelain potsherds, two Type 1d porcelain potsherds, six Type 1a stoneware potsherds, two Type 1a earthenware potsherds, five Type 1b earthenware potsherds and seven Type 2a earthenware potsherds. Level IV contained a kettle fragment, a brass pot lid, a Type 3 spade, three Dutch gunflints, a French gunflint, two Type A-1a buttons, two Type B-3 buttons, a Type D-1 button, four Type E-1 buttons, a Type F-3 button, a Type 1a porcelain potsherd, six Type 1b porcelain potsherds, three Type 1c porcelain potsherds, a Type 1b stoneware potsherd, three Type 1a earthenware potsherds, five Type 1b earthenware potsherds, three Type 2a earthenware potsherds, three Type 2d earthenware potsherds and a Type 2e earthenware potsherd.

Feature 56 was a wood-lined cellar hole 2 feet from the south wall and 10.5 feet from the east wall. It was 10.5 feet long, north-south, 7 feet wide and 5 feet deep. There was an earth bench 2 feet wide and 1.5 feet high along the east and north sides with two planks laid on this on the east side. The upper half of the northwest corner had been destroyed by the clay lining of Feature 57. The walls were lined with charred vertical planks, 1 foot wide, with vertical posts in the corners 6 inches in diameter. Level II contained brickbats, a fragment of a mortar bed, slate and burned earth. It was separated from Level III by a layer of wood planks ranging from .5 to 1.5 feet wide. The mortar bed probably came from a hearth associated with the chimney base found at the south end of the west barracks and the whole level represented material in a depression caused by settling of the lower fill. Level III was a layer of brickbats, mortar and charcoal down to the level of the bench. Level IV was largely sand and gravel with some brickbats to a depth of 1.5 feet below the bench surface. If it were not for the artifacts and a slightly darker color this level would have looked like the sterile soil underlying the fort. Level II contained a 1768 Spanish 1 real coin, a Type 4 spade, two Dutch gunflints, a Type B-1 button, a Type D-6 button, a Type G-1b button, a Type I-1 button, a Type 1a porcelain potsherd, eight Type 1b porcelain potsherds, ten Type 1a stoneware potsherds, two Type 1b stoneware potsherds, 17 Type 1a earthenware potsherds, 11 Type 1b earthenware potsherds, and four Type 2a earthenware potsherds. The Type G-1b button is evidence of a post-1776 date for this level. Level III included two kettle fragments, two wooden buckets, three sacks of wheat and oats, a Type 4a axe, two Type E-1 buttons, a Type 1a porcelain potsherd, a Type 1b porcelain potsherd, nine Type 1a stoneware potsherds, three Type 1b stoneware potsherds, two Type 1d stoneware potsherds, ten Type 1a earthenware potsherds, eight Type 1b earthenware potsherds and a Type 2a earthenware potsherd. Level IV contained a glass beaker, a Type 1a stoneware potsherd and a Type 1a earthenware potsherd.

We know that the barracks burned twice, in 1774 (Duncan, 1969) and in May 1781 (Lauber, 1932, p. 581). Either of these fires could have produced the rubble in the fill of these cellars. The problem to be resolved is whether all the cellars were filled after one of these fires, and if so which fire, or whether some were filled after one fire and some after the other. Stratigraphically, Feature 57 intruded Feature 56, destroying part of the latter's wood lining and Feature 64 intruded Feature 63 destroying the west side of Feature 63. It is impossible, therefore, for Features 56 and 63 to be contemporaneous with Features 57 and 64 and they must be earlier in time. It is logical to assume that Features 56 and 63 were filled *ca.* 1774 and Features 57 and 64 filled *ca.* 1781. As the former pair were wood-lined and the latter clay-lined, we sought evidence from the fill of these cellars which would corroborate these dates and allow us to state that all the wood-lined cellars were filled *ca.* 1774 and all the clay-lined cellars *ca.* 1781. To do this we resorted to a null hypothesis that there was no temporal difference between the cellars. If this were true they should have the same types of artifacts in the same proportions. No coins were found dating after 1774 in these cellars but there were two post-1776 American buttons, one in Level II over Feature 56 and the other in Level III of Feature 69. Gunflints, buttons, ceramics and pipestems were deemed the most useful artifacts for comparison because work has been done on providing dates for the various types. Lyle Stone (1972, p. 47) has suggested that French gunflints were introduced after 1740. Table 8 illustrates that the frequency of French gunflints relative to Dutch gunflints increased with time. No French gunflints were found in the wood-lined cellars but half of the 44 specimens in the clay-lined cellars (excluding the concentration of 3,412

in Level II of Feature 69) were French. This high a percentage (if we use the Valley Forge sample for comparison) should indicate a post-1775 date. Unfortunately, the sample for the clay-lined cellar holes is quite small and not consistent except that all have French gunflints in them.

The buttons are less instructive. All the types found in the wood-lined cellars were also found in clay-lined cellars although nine types, including one Revolutionary War button, were found only in clay-lined cellars, primarily Feature 69. Type A-1 buttons were more prevalent in clay-lined cellars (11 in four as opposed to two in Feature 52) but, again, the sample size is small. The high number of Type B-1 buttons in Feature 60 could have originated from a single garment although they were not found in a cluster.

The ceramics were also scarce. We applied Stanley South's mean ceramic date formula (South, 1972) to what we had with a singular lack of success, even after eliminating the Oriental porcelain (Type 1 porcelain) and Delftware (Type 1 earthenware), because of the small samples. Lumping together the cellars to increase the sample size produced mean dates of 1770.8 ± 13.7 years for the wood-lined cellars (67 sherds) and 1774.1 ± 14.3 years for the clay-lined cellars (124 sherds). This indicated that the clay-lined cellars were filled later than the wood-lined cellars but that the fill contained material nearly as early in time as the latter (1759.8 and 1757.1, respectively).

The pipestem bore diameters were no help because the sample sizes were too small. Lumping the samples together and applying the Harrington principle (Harrington, 1954) indicates that the clay-lined cellars might be somewhat earlier than the wood-lined cellars. However, the clay-lined cellar combined sample (36 specimens) is barely adequate, and the difference of the two means is only .05/64th of an inch, not statistically significant for the size of the sample.

We are left with only the stratigraphy, one button and logic for the statement that the wood-lined cellars were dug *ca.* 1764 and filled *ca.* 1774, while the clay-lined cellers were dug *ca.* 1776 and filled *ca.* 1781. The fill of the cellars does not vary sufficiently for us to separate them in time. This is probably due to (a) only a 7-year time interval between the two periods of filling in which artifacts did not change sufficiently to allow us to measure that change and (b) the nature of the fill itself. The compactness of the brickbats, etc. in the holes, the absence of brickbats beyond the limits of the holes, and the absence of lensing, indicate deliberate and rapid filling. If there was any pre-1776 debris left on the site after the fort was rebuilt it could have been shoveled into the clay-lined cellars along with any post-1776 artifacts. The finding of similar button and ceramic types in the two kinds of cellars supports the null hypothesis. That French gunflints and some button types occur only in clay-lined cellars could be accidental, and are not sufficient by themselves to disprove the hypothesis. As we cannot distinguish between the artifacts in the two kinds of cellar holes then we must conclude that the contents date from 1758 to 1781 since they could contain material which was on the parade ground before the barracks were built and the earliest cellars dug (1764).

Bastions

. . . a part of the inner inclosure of a fortification, making an angle towards the field, and consists of 2 faces, 2 flanks, and an opening towards the centre of the place, called the gorge: or it is rather a large mass of earth, usually faced with sods . . . (G. Smith, 1779, p. 99)

All sources agree that Fort Stanwix had four bastions located at the corners of the square fort. The archeological record was not too helpful; the information derived from the excavations had to be augmented with what was supposed to have been built. The northwest bastion was the most intact and yielded the most information. We were able to outline the right flank, part of the right face and part of the left flank. This enabled us to determine the following dimensions and angles at parade ground level: flank length, 35 feet; face length, 108 feet; reentry angle, 111 degrees; flank angle, 125 degrees; salient angle, 62 degrees. The angles and measurements were probably the same for all the bastions and checked out when we projected a plan of the fort (fig. 10).

In the original 1758 fort, there was a powder magazine in the southeast bastion (fig. 4), and the bastions are shown as earth-filled structures revetted with logs on the exterior. The magazine will be described under the section to follow entitled "Bombproofs."

When the Americans occupied the fort, they rebuilt the bastions and incorporated in them a bakehouse and three bombproofs. These will be described separately. The passage leading into these greatly constricted the gorge, or throat, of each bastion, thus hampering movement of troops or cannons.

Berm

. . . a little space, or path of 6 or 8 feet broad, between the ditch and talus of the parapet; it is to prevent the earth from rolling into the ditch, and serves likewise to pass and repass. As it is in some degree advantageous to the enemy, in getting footing, most of the modern engineers reject it. (G. Smith, 1779, p. 99)

The only evidence of a berm at Fort Stanwix came from the north and east curtains. Along the north curtain a beam .5 foot wide was found lying parallel to the scarp of the ditch, 5.5 feet from the edge. We believe this beam was part of the rampart, although much smaller in diameter than expected. It may have served as a brace to keep the rampart logs from slipping. On the east curtain were a pair of large posts flanking the sally port, 7.5 feet from the edge of the scarp. These two posts formed part of the revetment where the sally port cut through the curtain wall. Based upon this, the berm on the east side was 7.5 feet wide. A 1764 plan (fig. 5) shows a 6-foot berm around three sides and a 5-foot berm on the south side. The latter was probably constructed to increase the thickness of the south curtain wall. Another 1764 plan (Crown Collection CXXI, 103) shows pickets on the berm on the east side, but no archeological evidence for these was found.

Bombproofs

MAGAZINE, a place in which stores are kept, or arms, ammunition, provisions, &c. . . . . Powder-Magazine . . . ought to be . . . bombproof. In fortifications they are frequently placed in the rampart . . . (G. Smith, 1779, p. 155)

Four bombproofs were located at Fort Stanwix, one inside each bastion. The one beneath the southeast bastion was built in 1758, but the others were probably in use during the Revolution. The southwest bombproof also served as a hospital and repository for valuables during the siege in 1777 (Reid, 1905, p. 99).

Northeast Bombproof

Although we have no written reference to this structure, the symmetry of the fort is completed with a bombproof under each bastion. The main chamber of the structure was approximately 16 feet square, although much of it was destroyed by tree roots and a cistern (figs. 18, 19). A single layer of thick roof planks, 1 to 1.5 feet wide, that collapsed after fire desroyed the structure, ran east-west. No evidence of a floor was found.

Presumably, it was a dirt floor at an elevation of about 448 feet, 3 feet below the parade ground. Most of the floor was fill, apparently used to build out the hill on which Fort Stanwix stood, and this made it impossible to define since it did not differ from the surrounding soil.

The entrance to the bombproof was a passage, 6 feet wide on the west side with an interior width of 4.5 feet. The passage ran for 12.5 feet, then turned 35 degrees north and continued for another 12.5 feet. It increased in exterior width

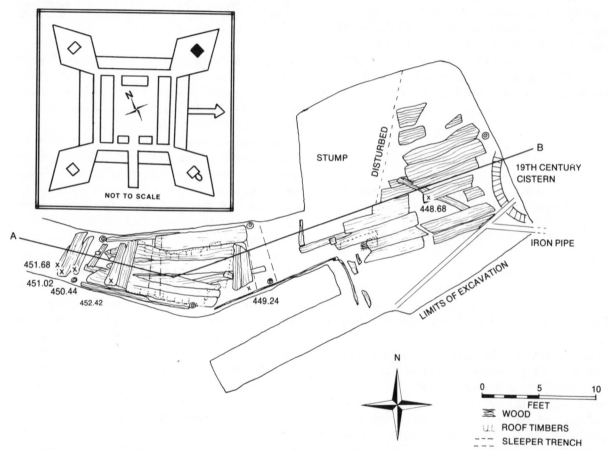

Figure 18.   Ground plan of the northeast bombproof. See figure 19 for section along the A-B line.

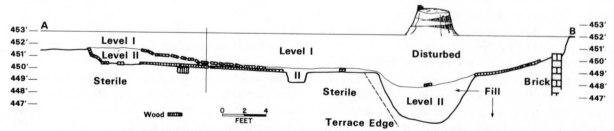

Figure 19. Section through the northeast bombproof and passageway.

to 7 feet at the turn. The walls of the passage were revetted with horizontal planks .7 foot wide, held in place by randomly spaced vertical posts. In one area nine of these planks were crushed together giving the passageway a height of at least 6 feet. Trenches for two sleepers .8 foot high were spaced along the passage. Three layers of planks .6 to 1.2 feet wide and 1 inch thick were found on the floor of the passage. A few of these may have fallen from the walls but some of them were definitely floor planks under which lines of musket balls and canister shot were found where they had fallen through cracks. Level I consisted of a gray loam above the roof planks in the passageway and main chamber. It contained some post-1781 artifacts. Level II was a brown sandy loam beneath the roof planks and on the floor. It was undisturbed. One large deposit of 45 cannister shot found under the floor at the widest point in the passage may have fallen through a substantial gap along the wall. All the artifacts ascribed in the next chapter to this structure were found in Level II of the passageway except a Dutch gunflint, two French gunflints, a scabbard hook, both buckles, a .69 cal. musket ball, a Type 1a porcelain potsherd, three Type 1b porcelain potsherds, seven Type 1a stoneware potsherds, two Type 1b stoneware potsherds and two Type 1a earthenware potsherds. The dirt beneath the floor boards was at an elevation of 449.24 feet.

At the west end of the passageway two steps led to an elevation of 451.88 feet. The steps of hewn beams had .6-foot risers, .8-foot treads and were 4 feet wide. The top step, above the parade ground elevation, probably served as a curb to keep water out of the passageway. Two iron pintles were found on the steps and a door was probably at the top of the steps on the north side. The passage was roofed with planks .5 to 1.2 feet wide which lay across the passageway and were supported by the walls.

Northwest Bombproof

. . . the engineer had neglected to build a magazine, though he knew there was no secure place for the ammunition. The garrison, in order to remedy this difficulty, took the seven spare feet which were left of the pickets, . . . and having framed them, so as to form a square inclosure, the whole was placed within the body of one of the bastions, and being covered with earth, formed a safe deposit for the powder. (W. Willett, 1831, p. 49)

This trapezoidal structure met the description of the magazine constructed in 1777 (figs. 20, 21). The walls of the main chamber and the passageway were tightly spaced vertical logs .4 to 1.2 feet in diameter with .5 feet being the most common size. Seven logs were identified as eastern hemlock (*Tsuga canadensis*). There was some evidence for a frame to keep the log walls upright. Lengths of the walls in feet were: north, 16; south, 13; west, 21 and east, 21 (including the doorway). The roof was made of a single layer of .5-foot-thick planks running east-west, .6 to 1.5 feet wide. The floor had eight hewn .5-foot square sleepers running east-west, resting on sterile soil with another beam across the west wall and short round beams connecting the hewn sleepers down the midline. Nailed to these were ten 1-inch-thick planks 1.2 to 1.5 feet wide. Both the sleepers and floor boards were identified as eastern white pine (*Pinus strobus*). The floor was at an elevation of 449.84 feet while the sterile soil below was 449.22 feet. The highest point on the bombproof was 452.04 feet, but if we use Willett's account, the ceiling was probably 7 feet above the sterile soil at an elevation of 456 feet. The thickness of the roof would add .5 foot leaving 4.5 feet of dirt on top of the roof if the bastion were raised 10 feet above the parade ground. Although the interior was burned, the top of the roof was not, indicating that it was covered with earth.

The passageway ran to the east 12.5 feet and then made a 43 degree turn to the south, continuing for another 45 feet. It was 6 feet wide with an interior width of 4.5 feet, widening 1 foot at the turn. Vertical hemlock posts about .7 foot in diameter lined both sides of the passageway. Sleepers were located along the base of the interior of the walls with perpendicular sleepers irregularly spaced along the passageway. To these were nailed eastern white pine planks 1.5 feet wide and three abreast.

The roof was formed of planks .6 to 1.2 feet wide lying across the passageway and resting on the walls. The door was located at the outer end of the passageway where two large strap hinges and pintles were found (fig. 40c). It probably opened out toward the east.

Level I was a gray loam above the roofs of the bombproof and passageway. Level II was burned brown sandy loam between the partially collapsed roofs and the floor. This material washed

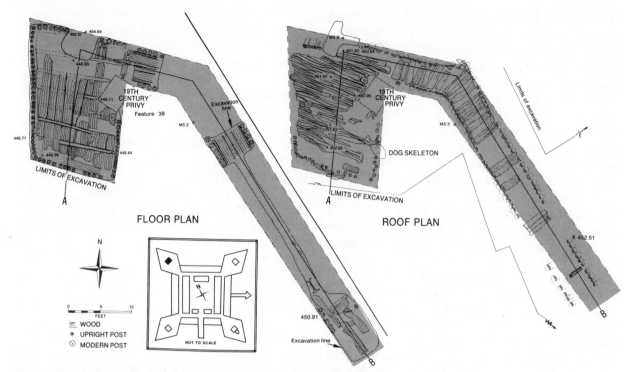

Figure 20. Roof and floor plans of the northwest bombproof. See figure 21 for section along the A-B line. See figure 10 for excavation limits.

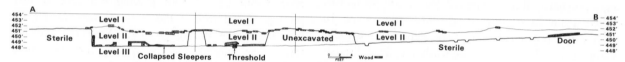

Figure 21. Section through the northwest bombproof and passageway.

in after the roofs collapsed judging by the lensing of the deposit and hollow spaces beneath some roof planks. Level III was confined to objects on the floor or beneath it. All of the material listed in the chapter on artifacts for this structure came from the passageway except the musket balls, a Type 1c strap hinge, two Type 2b pintles, two bayonet fragments, six iron spear tips, a Type 1a earthenware potsherd, a Type 1b earthenware potsherd and a Type 2a earthenware potsherd. The last three were in Level II and the remainder in Level III. All the musket balls listed in the chapter for the northwest bombproof came from the floor (Level III) of the main chamber just inside the entrance from the passageway.

Southwest Bombproof

. . . This Day the Col. Ordered . . . all the public papers and money in the Hands of Mr Hanson & the papers in the Hands of Mr Van Veghten belonging to the Paymaster to be lodged in the Bombproof in the S W Bastion . . . (Reid, 1905, p. 99).

This structure was definitely in use during the siege of Fort Stanwix.

The main chamber was nearly square, approximately 20 feet long east-west and 19.5 feet across (figs. 22, 23). Like all the other structures, this was destroyed by fire. The walls were greatly disturbed by modern intrusions; accurate measurements were not possible. The walls rested on narrow pine sleepers (*Pinus strobus*) laid on sterile soil. There was a single sleeper 9 feet long, 1 foot wide and .5 foot thick, below the floor. This was located 9.5 feet west of the entrance, running north-south. The floor was composed of pine planks resting on sterile soil. These were 1.1 to 1.5 feet thick, but may have been thicker before burning. They ran east-west except along the west wall where there were four planks running

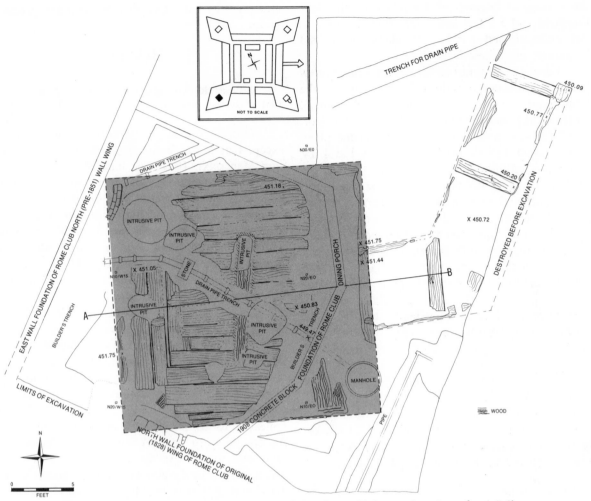

Figure 22. Plan of the southwest bombproof. See figure 23 for section along the A-B line.

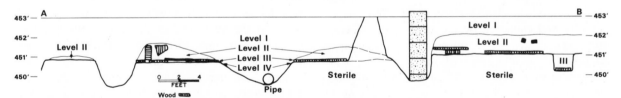

Figure 23. Section through the southwest bombproof.

north-south, some of which lay under the ends of east-west planks. These were laid loose and not nailed down. The floor was at an elevation of 451.20 feet. Only a few fragments of the roof were found. These measured 1.1 to 1.3 feet wide and .4 to .85 feet thick. The planks appeared to run north-south and probably rested on the walls. There was a 4.7-foot wide doorway in the east wall, 7.2 feet from the northeast corner. Vertical door jambs, .8 foot square, were morticed into a threshold .8 foot wide. A passageway 6.5 feet wide with an interior width of 5.5 feet extended east 5 feet where it made a 60 degree turn to the north, then continued for at least 17 feet more before it was obliterated by intrusions. Beyond the turn it narrowed to 6 feet in exterior width. The walls were not found, but they were probably horizontal planks held up by framing since there were several planks in the fill which could not be related to the floor. The elevation of the floor of the passage was 450.77 feet above mean sea level. Three sleepers, 1 foot wide, were found across the passage at intervals of 4.5 feet from the door threshold and 5.5 feet and 7 feet from each other. An undetermined number of planks were laid lengthwise over these for a floor.

Level I was disturbed fill over the bombproof including trenches cut through the floor of the bombproof. Level II was undisturbed charcoal (after 1781) and burned earth fill over the floor. Level III was those artifacts directly on the plank floor and in the sleeper trench while Level IV was those artifacts beneath the floor. All of the artifacts listed in the next chapter for the southwest bombproof were in the main chamber except for a French gunflint and two 3-pounder cannonballs. Level II contained two 3-pounder cannonballs, a mortar bomb fragment, a cannister shot, a Type 1b buckle fragment, a door latch, a door pull, a steel axe bit, six straight pins, three round-cornered staples, a Type 1b porcelain potsherd, four Type 1a stoneware potsherds, two Type 1a earthenware potsherds, three Type 1b earthenware potsherds, two Type 2a earthenware potsherds, two Type 2a earthenware potsherds and a Type 5c earthenware potsherd. Level III contained a Dutch gunflint, a screw, a 3-pounder cannonball, two musketballs and three miscast musketballs. Level IV contained three cannister shot, 23 musket balls, three miscast musketballs, lead waste, a round-cornered staple and a Type E-1 button.

1758 Magazine

This magazine was shown in the southeast bastion on all the British plans up to 1764 but apparently had collapsed by the time of the Revolution since it was never referred to in documents relating to the rebuilding of the fort. The bakehouse was built over the fill of the hole in which the magazine was placed. Because of intrusions we were able to locate only a part of the structure. Finding no artifacts in the part we excavated to the floor level, we did not complete the excavation because of its low priority. The magazine measured 16 feet in width—narrower than shown on the 1758 elevation (fig. 4). Only 25 feet of the original length was uncovered, the ends having been destroyed by an 1842 cellar (Waite, 1972, p. 40) and a street. The floor was at an elevation of 442.76 feet, with the highest remaining wood from the roof at an elevation of 448.63 feet. Two samples of this roof wood were identified as eastern white pine (*Pinus strobus*). Fill below the roof

shows lensing indicating abandonment and gradual decay.

Bridge

. . . the outside Gate and the Draw Bridge are to be shut at Retreat Beating . . . (Lauber, 1932, p. 541).

Information on this drawbridge was scanty, except that it was built *ca.* 1764 (Crown Collection Map cxxi, 103). The method of raising and lowering the bridge is unknown and our excavations did not shed much light on the subject. A large pintle and a matching hinge (fig. 41) which showed much wear, were found in the southeast casemate (Level II) and at the north end of the bridge (Level XIII) respectively. Along with the footings, these artifacts are interpreted as the only solid evidence for a drawbridge.

Level I was a gray loam layer about 2 feet thick over the entire area. Levels II-X were 19th-century strata above the bridge (judging by the presence of post-1781 ceramics). Level XI encompassed the bridge decking at the north end of the bridge. Two dark gray clay lenses at the south end were labled Levels XII and XIV. These appeared to be buried sod layers washed down the counterscarp and separated by graded sterile sand and gravel. At the north end Level XIII was a burned sandy clay beneath the bridge decking. Level XV was two layers of clay separated by sterile wash similar to that found at the south end of the bridge. Artifacts from Levels XI-XV were all secondary deposits and dated *ca.* 1764-1781. At the north end of the bridge, the rampart had a 12-foot indentation, approximately 13 feet wide. The scarp below this had an angle of 45 degrees from vertical. In the bottom of the ditch at a distance of 12 feet from the berm stood two large vertical pine posts (*Pinus strobus*) 9 feet apart which ended slightly above the floor of the ditch. Although too badly decayed to measure accurately, these appeared to be at least 1.5 feet square. Fifty-two feet south of these were another pair of posts .5 feet in diameter and 9.5 feet apart set in the counterscarp which had an angle of 37 degrees from horizontal. Allowing for a 4-foot overlap on the counterscarp, the bridge was 74 feet long. On the floor of the ditch (Level XIII) were two .8-foot-square white cedar sleepers (*Thuja occidentalis*) 8 feet apart. The best preserved specimen was over 39 feet long and exhibited one square mortice hole 28.6 feet from the north end which ended against one of the large vertical posts at the base of the scarp. The space between the sleepers was filled with sand to an elevation of 442.18 feet. A few cross planks were found under the sleeper, probably to shim it up.

Little of the superstructure was found. At the north end, extending 5 to 19 feet from the north end of the bridge, were planks at a 90-degree angle to the axis of the bridge (Level XI) which may have been decking. They ranged in width from .7 to 1 foot wide; none were more than 7.5 feet long. Under these at a distance of 3 to 10 feet from the north end were the large hinge and 97 large spikes.

No details on how the drawbridge was raised were found but the indentation in the scarp could have served as a well for counterweights.

Casemates

. . . a work made under the rampart, like a cellar or cave with loopholes, to place guns in it. (Muller, 1746, p. 214).

Common usage of the term "casemate" on military plans in late 18th-century North America meant structures under the ramparts which offered shelter from artillery fire. They may have been used for troops' quarters as well. Loopholes were not feasible in earth-and-log forts. All of the casemates at Fort Stanwix were log structures built into the ramparts with the roofs serving as the terrepleine of the curtain walls. Casemates were a consistent feature of the fort and, although they may have been rebuilt several times, they retained the same general shape and size on the plans.

North Casemate

This structure was approximately 144 feet long on the back wall, approximately 120 feet in length on the front wall with the west end wall 25 feet long (figs. 24, 25). The east end was not found and length was projected from the midline of the fort. The angle formed by the back and west end walls was 60 degrees, producing a total depth to the structure of 22 feet. The sill beams were 1 foot wide and rested on sterile soil. One

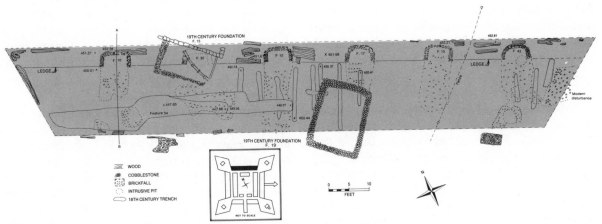

Figure 24. Plan of the north casemate. See figure 25 for section along the A-B line. See figure 10 for excavation limits.

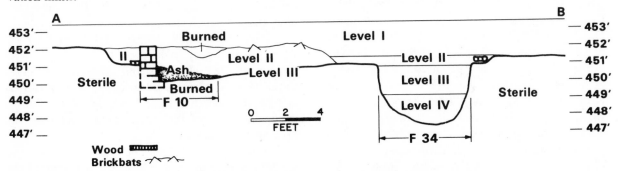

Figure 25. Section across the north casemate.

of these specimens was identified as eastern white pine (*Pinus strobus*). Two possible doorway areas were uncovered in the form of cobblestone paved areas centered 10 feet and 90 feet from the southeast corner along the front wall. Two stone foundations, Features 15 and 19 intruded the north casemate along with a drain pipe, sump and water line associated with the former. Feature 15 was actually two foundations, one dating from *ca.* 1873 (city map) and the other from *ca.* 1878 (city map). Feature 19 dated from *ca.* 1878 and represented the moving of a small structure from the 1873 foundation. The east end of the casemate for about 30 feet was disturbed by gardening activities; plow scars and bush holes intruded the floor of the structure.

There were six single-hearth fireplaces (features 10, 12, 13, 17, 30 and 42) along the rear wall which measured 7.5 feet wide except the westernmost (fig. 26) which was 7.8 feet wide. They were 3 feet deep, with 1-foot-thick jambs at an angle of about 85 degrees from the back wall. None of the fireplaces were aligned to the rear wall, indicating that they were not a part of the original structure, having been added after the wall was built. The jambs were one and one-half bricks thick and the rear wall one brick length thick in alternating courses of headers and stretchers. The hearths were all composed of sterile soil projecting only a short distance in front of the fireplace. Rubble from the collapsed chimneys extended to the front of the casemate but not beyond. Feature 10 contained 13 wrought iron nails, a .58 cal musket ball, a .69 cal. musket ball, a dark green bottle fragment, a blob of lead weighing 237 grams, a Type 1a porcelain potsherd and some calcined bone. Feature 12 contained 5 wrought iron nails, a round-cornered staple, a Type 3 knife fragment, a Type 1b porcelain potsherd, a Type 1b porcelain potsherd, a Type 1a earthenware potsherd and a Type 2a earthenware potsherd. Feature 13 contained three wrought iron nails, a Dutch gunflint, a .69 cal. musket ball, five case bottle fragments, a Type 1a stoneware potsherd, a Type 1b earthenware potsherd, and a Type 2a earthenware potsherd. Feature 17 contained three wrought iron nails, two Type 1a porcelain potsherds, a Type 1b stoneware potsherd, a Type 1a earthenware potsherd, a Type 1b earthenware potsherd and three Type 2a earthenware potsherds. This fireplace was badly disturbed, probably by a garden. Feature 30 contained a lead game counter,

Figure 26. View of the westernmost fireplace (Feature 10) in the north casemate before excavation, looking north. Note the brick fall from the chimney. Width of the fireplace is 7.8 feet.

a Type 1a stoneware potsherd, a Type 2a earthenware potsherd, a Type 6b earthenware potsherd and a Type 6g earthenware potsherd. This fireplace was largely destroyed by an 1873 foundation, Feature 15. Feature 42 contained 12 wrought iron nails, a 1745 British halfpenny, two Type 1b shoe buckle fragments, a Type 1c shoe buckle fragment, a scabbard hook, a .69 cal. musket ball, four dark green bottle fragments, a case bottle fragment and a Type 1b stoneware potsherd. All of this material is included in the north casemate artifacts listed in the next chapter.

Between the fireplaces, along the rear wall, was a bench of sterile soil 4.5 feet wide at an average elevation of 451 feet. In front of this were occasional sleeper trenches at a 90-degree angle to the rear wall and about .5 foot deep. The sterile soil was quite uneven and many of the sleepers may have rested on top of it with no trench. At the west end, floor planks were found running parallel with the back wall. They were too badly decomposed to measure. Over the floor and running perpendicular to the rear wall were planks 1 to 2 feet wide which probably fell from the roof. Level I was a gray loam over the entire area with some post-1781 ceramics and other objects in it. Level II was a series of brickbat concentrations in front of each fireplace. Level III was a brown sandy loam under the brick rubble and over the floor of the casemate.

Starting near the midline of the casemate and reaching a maximum depth of 3.5 feet toward the west wall, where it stopped, was a trench below the floor level. This was designated Feature 34 and was filled with sand but no function for it could be determined except possibly drainage. It was definitely a pre-1781 feature. Two artificial Levels (III and IV) were designated, but no difference was noted between them except that most of the artifacts were in Level IV (more than 2 feet below the floor or 3 feet below datum). Feature 34 contained 42 wrought iron nails, a rivet, a Dutch gunflint, a French gunflint, a piece of buckshot, 11 mortar bomb fragments, a bone handle fragment, five Type 1b porcelain potsherds, a Type 1d porcelain potsherd, eight Type 1a stoneware potsherds, a Type 1b stoneware potsherd, a Type 1d stoneware potsherd, nine Type 1a earthenware potsherds, ten Type 1b earthenware potsherds, 64 Type 2a earthenware potsherds, a Type 2e earthenware potsherd, 14 dark green glass bottle fragments, 31 case bottle fragments, 24 green pharmaceutical bottle fragments, two clear table glass fragments and 288 pipestem fragments with a mean bore diameter of 4.05/64th of an inch.

The even spacing of the fireplaces suggests that the structure was divided into 20-foot-square rooms, probably for use as officers' quarters.

West Casemate

Only the north end of this structure was found (fig. 10). The middle section was destroyed by a swimming pool and utility lines while test trenches dug where the south end should have been failed to find any trace of the building. The footings for the rear and north end walls were 1-foot-wide eastern white pine beams (*Pinus strobus*) at an angle of 52 degrees, resting on sterile soil. The rear wall sill extended over the end wall, suggesting dovetailing of the joint. The front wall had been removed by a large modern pit with a concentration of late 19th-century bottles. Parallel to the rear wall, 9.5 feet in from it, was a sleeper 1 foot wide set in a trench 1 foot deep. The sterile soil beneath the floor was at an elevation of 451.84 feet. There was a 1-foot-deep trench 8.5 feet long and 2 feet wide in the northwest corner running parallel to the rear wall and 3 feet from it. Level I was a gray loam containing a large lens of cement such as one might find at a construction site, and probably dates from the building of the swimming pool *ca.* 1930 (Waite 1972, p. 30). There was also a concentration of post-1781 animal bones with saw marks typical of bones found in 19th-

century privies on the site. There was some evidence of gardening in the form of bush holes. Level II was a brown sandy loam over the casemate floor and in the trenches. In the test trenches at the south end of this casemate Level I extended down to sterile soil confirming an account that this area had been scraped to level the fort for a house built in 1828 (Wager, 1896, p. 52).

The remains of a plank floor parallel to the rear wall were found in the back half of the casemate. On top of this, confined primarily to the front half, were planks at a 90-degree angle to the rear wall. These were 1 to 1.5 feet in width. On top of one of these was the remains of a brick pillar .8 foot square and at least 6 courses high (approximately 1.5 feet) which had fallen on its side. This may have been a footing for a roof support. It lay 10 feet from the back wall and 10 feet from the north end wall. No fireplaces were found, but there was a burned area in the floor beginning 25 feet from the northwest corner and 5 feet from the rear wall which extended into the area disturbed by the swimming pool. Projected from the midline, the approximate length of the rear wall was 144 feet; front wall, 117 feet; and the north end wall, 28 feet. The angle of the south end wall could not be determined.

Southwest Casemate

This building was one of the better preserved ones (figs. 27, 28) although the southwest corner was destroyed by a 1910 cellar (city directory). The front or north wall was 56 feet long marked by a trench (Feature 48) 1-foot wide and .8-foot deep. Some wood was found in the east end of the trench. The east wall was marked by a .6-foot-wide beam at a 90-degree angle to the front wall. Although most of the beam was missing, it probably measured 22.5 feet long. The rear wall beam was 1.5 feet wide and approximately 69 feet long. It was made of eastern white pine (*Pinus strobus*). The west wall beam was 1.5 feet wide and set at an angle of 60 degrees to the rear wall. It was approximately 25.5 feet long. These sill beams rested on sterile soil.

Level I was a gray loam over the area which included some post-1781 ceramics. Level II was a layer of ash, mortar, brickbats and brown sandy loam over the floor of the casemate. The floor (Level III) was composed of a mixture of hard-packed earth, ash and mortar. At the ends of the

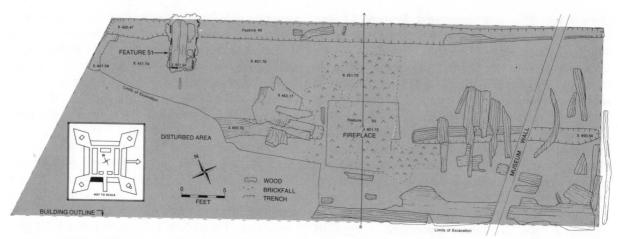

Figure 27. Plan of the southwest casemate. See figure 28 for section along the A-B line.

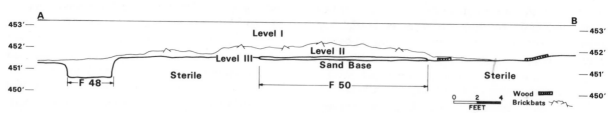

Figure 28. Section across the southwest casemate.

casemate and along the rear wall there seemed to be no prepared floor, only sterile soil. Running the length of the structure, 9.5 feet from the rear wall, was a wood sleeper 1 foot wide set in a trench 1 foot deep. This was interrupted in the center by the foundation of a fireplace (Feature 50). The fireplace was set on a yellow sand layer 8.5 feet long and 7.5 feet wide located 6 feet from the rear wall and 23.5 feet from the east wall. Only the mortar bed of the fireplace remained. It had back-to-back hearths that faced the ends of the building. The rubble from the chimney lay over the center of the structure. In the fill above the fireplace there was a cluster of four Type 4 spades. The roof consisted of 1 to 1.2-foot-wide planks at a 90-degree angle to the rear wall. The central sleeper may have served as a foundation for posts to support the roof.

Buried to a depth of .7 foot in the floor, 6 feet from the northwest corner, was a wood-lined box 6 feet long and 3 feet wide (Feature 51) (figs. 29, 30, 31). This was floored with three .9-foot-wide planks. The walls were vertical planks 1.1 to 1.5 feet wide. There were two rows of six staples each driven into the floor .7 foot from each end and spaced .4 foot apart. Their purpose is not

Figure 29. View of the brick rubble on top of Feature 51, a wooden box in the floor of the southwest casemate, looking south-southwest. See also figures 27, 30, and 31.

known. The box was filled with brickbats to a height of 1.6 feet and contained 385 wrought iron nails, 24 brass tacks, a cannon primer, two 3-pounder cannonballs, a .56 cal. musketball, a .64 cal. musketball, four .69 cal. musketballs, a sad iron, coarse cloth, a Type F-2 button, a Type 2 bead, a Type 1e buckle, a Type 5a buckle, 9 brass straight pins, a brass pot, an axle hub, a Type 6 knife, a Type 6b axe, a claw hammer, a Type 1 ruler fragment, a protractor fragment and a plumb bob. We strongly suspect that it was a carpenter's tool box.

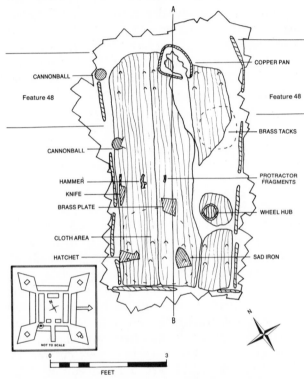

Figure 30. Plan of the box in the floor of the southwest casemate (Feature 51). See figure 31 for section along the A-B line.

Southeast Casemate

Most of this structure was destroyed prior to our excavations. In 1965 Campbell found a 1-foot-wide sill beam located where the east end wall should have been. We uncovered a 1-foot-wide white cedar beam (*Thuja occidentalis*) which was part of the front wall at the northwest corner, and a fragment of a 1-foot-wide beam 12 feet south of this down the center of the floor. Projecting dimensions from these, we arrived at the following approximations: front wall, 60 feet long; rear wall, 68 feet long; west end wall, 22.5 feet long and east end wall, 23.5 feet long. The west wall was at a 90-degree angle and the east wall at a 70 degree angle to the rear wall. Beyond this, there was no information on the structure. It probably was a mirror image of the southwest casemate except that it was longer. Level I was a gray loam with post-1781 ceramics in it over the entire area which extended down to sterile soil over the eastern three-fourths of the structure. Only on the west end could we find evidence of undisturbed Level II. This was a brown sandy loam. Features 14, 24, 25, 26 and 27 were small post-1900 rubbish pits dug into the sterile subsoil.

East Casemate

We know the least about this structure. All we found was a fragment of a 1-foot-wide beam for the rear wall and a large trench 30 feet long, 5 feet wide and 3 feet deep which was 10 feet from the rear wall in the northern half of the structure. Running through the approximate center of the casemate on an angle of 6 degrees south of the rear wall was a drainage trench which is described under the section to follow entitled "Drain." This

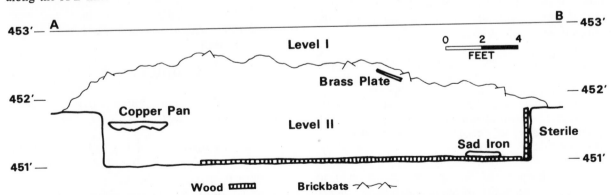

Figure 31. Section through wooden box (Feature 51) in the southwest casemate.

ended where the front wall of the casemate should have been, 22 feet from the rear wall, the only dimension we could determine for this structure. Level I was a gray loam with post-1781 ceramics in it over the entire area extending down to sterile soil. Two pipelines and a deep stone-lined cellar (ice house?) (Feature 55) built before 1851 (city map) and not closed until the early 20th century accounted for some of the destruction. Level II was a brown sandy loam and was confined to the 30-foot-long trench.

Communication

. . . trenches that unite one work to another, so that men may pass between them without being exposed in the enemy's fire . . . (G. Smith, 1779, p. 149)

See section to follow entitled "Sally Port."

Covered Way

. . . is a space of 6 fathom broad (36 feet), going quite around the works, and is adjoined to the counterscarp of the ditches, covered by a parapet 7¼ feet high, including a banquette of 2½ feet . . . (G. Smith, 1779, p. 101)

The covered way at Fort Stanwix was never this broad except at the corners of the ditch where the salient angles of the glacis went beyond the rounded corners of the ditch. At the only point where the covered way was located it was 10 feet broad. This was opposite the west face of the southwest basion. Level I was a gray loam with post-1781 ceramics. At the point where we located the covered way we found a burned hearth area 1.7 feet in diameter (Feature 47) with two wrought iron nails, a strike-a-light flint made from a Dutch gunflint and a pipe stem. This probably represented a temporary guardpost from the 1777 period when a quarter Guard was mounted on the covered way (M. Willett, 9/10/77).

. . . the quarter-guard . . . is to maintain good order in the camp. This guard now fronts outwards, though it was formerly the custom to front inwards . . . and as this guard is merely to maintain good order in the camp the present alteration seems improper. The *quarter-guards* of all Foreign troops front inwards . . . (G. Smith, 1779, p. 311)

The purpose of the quarter guard at Fort Stanwix was probably to prevent desertions; hence

their post on the covered way enabled them to observe anyone climbing over the walls.

At the base of the glacis on the covered way was a trench 2 feet wide and 2.5 feet deep (Level III). There were traces of postmolds in the trench about .5 to .7 feet in diameter and set only a few inches apart. We know that in 1777, a line of pickets was placed on the covered way and that the posts were 10 feet long (W. Willett, 1831, p. 44). This would mean that they portruded 7.5 feet above the covered way. It appeared to us that these posts had been pulled out at some time in the past since some of the postholes had collapsed and others were filled with debris from Level I including a blue transfer-printed pearlware potsherd matching specimens from Level I. The pickets were still standing after the fire of 1781 (G. Clinton, 1900, Vol. XI, p. 878) and some were still visible as late as 1828 (Wager, 1896, p. 52).

Curtain

. . . is that part of the body of the place, which joins the flank of one bastion to that of another. (G. Smith, 1779, p. 101)

The curtains at Fort Stanwix were earth-filled log structures (Carroll, 1973, pp. 103–106). On the inner side they were revetted up to the level of the terrepleine (7.5 feet) as the rear walls of the casemates. The thickness of the curtain walls was determined by measuring the distance from the rear of the casemates to the edge of the ditch and then subtracting the probable width of the berm. We arrived at the following dimensions: north curtain thickness, 16 feet; west curtain, 19 feet; south curtain 12 feet and east curtain, 16.5 feet. It should be noted that the thickest walls face the most probable direction of enemy attack. Wood that lay on the scarp of the northwest bastion in Level X has been identified as northern white cedar (*Thuja occidentalis*) and was probably from the rampart wall.

Counterscarp

. . . is the outside of a ditch, opposite to the parapet of the work behind the ditch . . . (Muller, 1746, p. 215)

Two measurements on the sterile soil of the counterscarp produced angles of 43 degrees and 37 degrees from horizontal. An average of 40 degrees would mean that the foot of the counterscarp would have been 12 feet out from the top at a depth of 10 feet.

Ditch

In 1758, the British attempted to put a ditch completely around the fort (fig. 4). The ditch on the east side was abandoned and, by 1764, the ends of the ditch were closed at the southeast and northeast corners of the fort (Crown Collection Map cxxi, 103). At the same time, a causeway before the main gate was replaced by a wooden bridge. The bottom of the ditch was at an elevation of 441.08 feet at the north face of the northwest bastion, 440.78 feet at the west face of the south-west bastion and 440.80 feet below the bridge on the south side of the fort. We projected the angles of the scarp and counterscarp and found the following widths of the ditch: top of north (fig. 32) and south ditches at the center of the curtain, 59 feet; at the bastions, 42 feet; bottom of north and south ditches, 35 feet and 18 feet, respectively; top of west ditch at the center of the curtain, 54 feet; at the bastions, 39 feet; bottom of west ditch, 30 feet and 15 feet respectively. The bottom of the ditch was dug into sterile graded sand. For this reason it drains very well and was probably dry most of the time. Levels I-X in the ditch contained post-1781 ceramics and constituted the fill put in the ditch to landscape the area. Some of this fill was undoubtedly the walls of the fort (Wager, 1896, p. 52). Level XI at the bottom of the ditch was fort related and dated *ca.* 1758-1781. In the bridge area the complexity of the stratigraphy led us to divide Level XI into Levels XI-XV.

Drain

A wooden drain 1 foot wide ran through the east casemate and beneath the sally port at an angle of 6 degrees to the long axis at the east casemate (figs. 33, 34). This drain was a wood-lined box type judging by the nails found. It was set in a trench and covered with sterile soil. It apparently served to keep water from the east bar-racks roof from running through the sally port and ruining the footing. We lost track of it at the edge of the berm but a trench through the glacis of the communication at an angle of 64 degrees north of the communication to the redout, and 15 feet out from the edge of the berm, probably was a continuation of the drain. This indicated that the drain angled over to the north side of the com-munication below the steps and continued out un-der a wooden banquette. It probably emptied into the creek east of the redout. The drain began at the front of the east casemate. No grill was found but it may have been simply a barrel top with holes drilled through it. The elevations of the bottom of the drain are 447.74 feet at the beginning, 446.75 feet at the berm and 443.72 feet where it left the communication.

Drawbridge

See section entitled "Bridge."

Gateway

The main entrance to the fort lay behind the drawbridge between the southwest and southeast

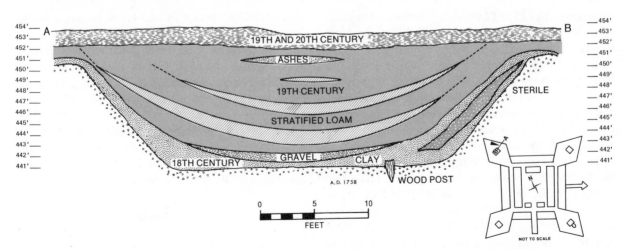

Figure 32. Cross section of the north ditch showing natural stratigraphy.

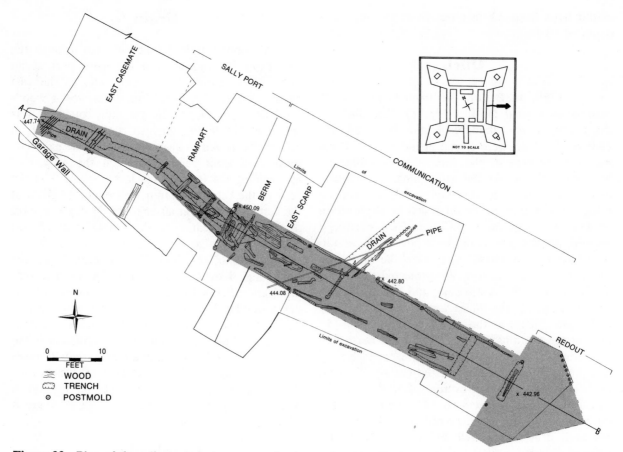

Figure 33. Plan of the sally port, drain, communication and redout. See figure 34 for section along the A-B line.

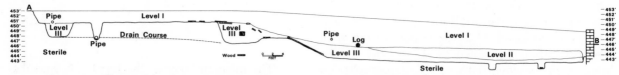

Figure 34. Section through the sally port, drain, communication and redout.

casemates (fig. 35). The distance between the case-mate walls was 13.5 feet. Inside of this was a large wooden frame which probably supported the gate and the lifting mechanism of the drawbridge. The sills of the frame were 1.5 feet wide and rested on sterile soil. They were 18 feet long and projected 5 feet south of the casemates onto the edge of the indentation of the scarp below the bridge.

Along the east side of the gateway was a brick drain, one brick length wide with a line of bricks on edge along the western side. The drain dropped from an elevation of 450.60 feet above mean sea level to 450.36 feet about 4 feet from the edge of the scarp where it ended. The northern end had been destroyed by a test trench dug in 1965 (Campbell, 1965). Level I was a gray loam

with post-1781 ceramics and Level II was a brown sandy loam layer over sterile soil.

No remains of the main gate itself were found. Spikes found in Level XIII of the ditch under the bridge probably were used to stud the gate. If so, the gate was 7 inches thick, since the spikes were clinched at 7 inches. Considering the width of the frame, it was probably a double-hung gate. It probably hung at the rear of the frame and swung inward into niches created by the frame and the casemates to leave the gateway unimpeded.

Glacis

. . . is the part beyond the covert-way, to which it serves as a parapet and terminates toward the Field

Figure 35. View of the main gate excavation area, looking north-northeast. Note the brick drain on the right side. Rubble fill in the foreground is from two 19th-century outhouses disturbed by Campbell's 1965 test trench. Width of the gateway is 10.5 feet.

in an easy slope at about 20 fathom distance [120 feet] . . . (G. Smith, 1779, p. 102)

The glacis at Fort Stanwix appears never to have been 120 feet broad. No two historic plans agree as to its actual width but none show it wider than 75 feet. We were unable to get an angle of the slope from which to project its width. We did uncover the base of part of the parapet of the glacis opposite the west face of the southwest bastion. Its slope measured 40 degrees. Projecting a height of 6 feet (see "Parapet") and allowing a slope of 5 degrees for the face of the glacis, the width of the glacis would be 75 feet. At the southeast and northeast ends it should have been 10 feet narrower (Crown Collection cxxi, 102 & 103). A slope of 5 degrees was selected inasmuch as this would project the face of the glacis to the sole of the embrasures on the parapet, giving the maximum field of fire to the fort's defenders.

Laboratory

. . . signifies that place where all sorts of fire-works are prepared, both for actual service, and for pleasure,

vic. quick-matches, fuzes, portfires, grape-shot, case-shot, carcasses, hand-grenades, cartridges, shells filled, and fuzes fixed, wads &c. &c. (G. Smith, 1779, p. 135)

In a plan prepared *ca.* 1778, Defleury identified the west barracks as a laboratory (W. Stone, 1838, p. 230). Nothing found in the excavation confirmed that identification. The material found in Feature 69 suggests that if there were a laboratory, it was in the east barracks.

Magazine

See section entitled "Bombproofs."

Main Gate

See section entitled "Gateway."

Necessary

A necessary was a privy or outhouse. On the 1758 plan of Fort Stanwix (fig. 4) and the Gansevoort Plan (*ca.* 1777, fig. 7), large wooden necessaries were depicted off the east face of the southeast bastion, standing on stilts over the small creek that ran along the east side of the fort. Passage to the privy was accomplished by a catwalk from the bastion. The orderly book for the Third New York Regiment (M. Willett, 1777-1778) mentioned building new necessaries from time to time in the ditch and elsewhere. The site of the necessaries off the southeast bastion was occupied by modern buildings and could not be excavated.

We found three pits on the parade ground, two of which we interpreted as necessaries (fig. 10). Feature 73 was 14 feet north of the center of the fort along the midline, and consisted of a rectangular pit 9 feet long, 5 feet wide and 4 feet deep. A northern white cedar post (*Thuja occidentalis*) was found in the upper part of the fill, 18 feet from the center of the fort on the midline (See "Whipping Post"). This contained sand to a depth of 4 feet with a layer of gray loam on the bottom of the pit. Artifacts included a Type B-3 button, 20 mortar bomb fragments, seven pieces of birdshot, a .53 cal. musketball, a .58 cal. musketball, a .63 cal. musketball, three .69 cal. musketballs, two brass pins, a Type 4a pipe bowl, four Type 1b porcelain potsherds, two Type 1d porcelain potsherds, seven Type 1a stoneware potsherds, two Type 1b stoneware potsherds, two Type 1a earthenware potsherds, two Type 1b earthenware potsherds and two Type 2a earthenware potsherds.

Feature 58 was 5.5 feet in diameter and 4.5 feet deep located 24 feet north of the southwest casemate and 27 feet east of the west barracks. There was some charred wood around it which may have been related to the guard house. The fill was sand except for a thin layer of gray loam on the bottom of the pit. It contained a Type D-3 button, eight mortar bomb fragments, two .63 cal. musketballs, a .69 cal. musketball, a brass pin, a Type 1d stoneware potsherd, a Type 1a earthenware potsherd and a Type 2a earthenware potsherd.

Feature 70 was only 1 foot east of Feature 58 and was approximately 8.5 feet in diameter and 2.5 feet deep. It was filled with sand and there was only eleven badly corroded nail fragments and a Type 5c earthenware potsherd.

Parade Ground

. . . the place where troops assemble, before they go on duty. (G. Smith, 1779, p. 310)

The parade at Fort Stanwix was only 90 feet long, 85 feet wide and located in the center of the fortifications. The parade ground elevation was established as the top of the sterile soil zone where there was a faint trace of a living surface (Level II) in the form of bits of charcoal, bone splinters and pipe stems. Level I was a gray loam with post-1781 ceramics. Elevations taken around the site resulted in an average elevation of 451 feet to the parade ground with a variation of less than 6 inches above or below this reading.

Parapet

. . . an elevation of earth, designed for covering the soldiers from the enemy's cannon, or small shot . . . its height 6 (feet) on the inside . . . of the covert-way, is what covers that way from the sight of the enemy . . . (G. Smith, 1779, p. 199)

No evidence of the parapet was found on the rampart. For the parapet on the glacis see the section entitled "Glacis."

Palisades

. . . are a kind of stakes made of strong split wood of about 9 feet long, fixed 3 feet deep in the ground, in rows about 6 inches asunder: they are placed in the covert-way, at 3 feet from, and parallel to the parapet of the glacis . . . (G. Smith, 1779, p. 103)

. . . stakes made of strong split wood, about 9 feet long, 6 or 7 inches square, 3 feet deep in the ground, in rows about 2½ or 3 inches asunder, placed in the covert-way . . . (G. Smith, 1779, P. 198)

When Fort Stanwix was initially constructed, a palisade was placed around the fort in the ditch (fig. 4). The posts were about 11 feet long and sunk 3 feet in the ground. We found part of this palisade line in the north ditch at the base of the northwest bastion (fig. 10). The posts were badly decomposed and there were gaps in the line where some had apparently rotted away without a trace. The sections most intact were posts spaced 1 foot apart, center to center, and were about .5 to .7 foot in diameter.

In 1777, the palisade line was moved to the covered way (W. Willett, 1831, pp. 44, 49). Here we found a trench 2 feet wide and 2.5 feet deep along the base of the glacis into which the posts had been set. Inasmuch as these posts were 10 feet long (W. Willett, 1831, p. 44) they must have projected 7.5 feet above the covered way and 1.5 feet above the glacis. It was difficult to discern postmolds, but a few were found about .5 to .7 feet in diameter. When the fort burned in 1781 the palisade apparently remained intact (G. Clinton, 1900, Vol. XI, p. 878). At some later date, these posts were probably pulled out and used for other purposes as the fill in the postmolds differed from the trench in which they were set. They contained more man-made debris including one blue transfer-printed pearlware potsherd, matching sherds in Level I. Some pickets in this area were still visible in 1828 (Wager, 1896, p. 52). If the northwest bombproof walls were made from the remains of these pickets as Willett reported (1831, p. 49), the posts were probably eastern hemlock (*Tsuga canadensis*) since this was the type of wood used to construct the northwest bombproof.

Rampart

. . . an elevation of earth raised along the faces of any work, of 10 or 15 feet high, to cover the inner part of that work against the fire of an enemy . . . (G. Smith, 1779, p. 103)

See section entitled "Curtain" for the thickness of the ramparts at Fort Stanwix.

Ravelin

... works raised on the counterscarp before the curtain of the place, and serve to cover the gates of a Town, and the bridges. They consist of two faces forming a saliant [sic.] angle, and are defended by the faces of the neighboring bastions ... (G. Smith, 1779, p. 221)

There was a ravelin before the bridge in 1764, (fig. 5); repaired to some extent by the Americans (W. Willett, 1831, p. 45). Archeologically, the only evidence was a trench (Feature 76) 33+ feet long, 8 feet wide and 5 deep deep across the east face of the ravelin and a disturbed deposit of trash in the area where the outer gate should have passed through the ravelin. Level I was a gray loam containing post-1781 ceramics. Level II was the trash deposit. The purpose of the trench was not ascertained, although it was probably defensive. It would have necessitated a bridge before the outer gate and we suspect it was used only a short time. It was steep sided, the walls having slumped from erosion. The original width may have been closer to 6 feet. The trench fill contained a 1732 British halfpenny, four Type A-1a buttons, five Type B-2 buttons, a Type B-3 button, two Type D-1 buttons, eight Dutch gunflints, a French gunflint, a Type 1 gun cock, two bayonet fragments, a frow, a Type 1b axe, a Type 3b axe, a Type 4d axe, a Type 4 spade, three pairs of scissors, a Type 1a key, four Type 1b porcelain potsherds, 42 Type 1a stoneware potsheds, 14 Type 1b stoneware potsherds, a Type 1d stoneware potsherd, 47 Type 1a earthenware potsherds, 40 Type 1b earthenware potsherds, 14 Type 1d earthenware potsherds, three Type 2a earthenware potsherds, a Type 2d earthenware potsherd, and a Type 2e earthenware potsherd. We found nothing in the trench to indicate it was in use during the Revolution, and it was probably filled prior to that date.

Assuming that the trench was parallel to the face of the ravelin, the faces of the ravelin would have been at an angle of 55 degrees to the midline of the fort, and at least 60 feet long. From the 1764 plan (fig. 5) they would have been 66 feet long but inasmuch as the salient angle we found was more obtuse than that depicted, the faces would have had to have been 77 feet to extend as far into the covered way as they did on the 1764 plan, and give maximum protection to the main gate. On the 1764 plan, the center of the outer gateway was 30 feet from the salient angle while our trash deposit was 36 feet from the salient angle.

The deposit included a Type A-1b button, a Type A-1j button, two Type D-3 buttons, two Type F-2 buttons, a Type F-4 button, four Dutch gunflints, three French gunflints, a Type 1 pick, a Type 3 key, two Type 1a porcelain potsherds, seven Type 1b porcelain potsherds, five Type 1a stoneware potsherds, six Type 1b stoneware potsherds, a Type 2a stoneware potsherd, eight Type 1a earthenware potsherds, two Type 1b earthenware potsherds, a Type 1c earthenware potsherd, a Type 1d earthenware potsherd, four Type 2a earthenware potsherds, a Type 2c earthenware potsherd and five Type 2d earthenware potsherds.

The elevation of the works was 448 feet. This made it possible for the ravelin to contain a 10-foot-high gateway and still be low enough for defenders on the curtain wall behind it to fire over the top. This elevation also made it necessary for a ramp to be built at the south end of the bridge to compensate for the 3 feet difference in elevation.

Redout

... a kind of work placed beyond the glacis, and is of various forms ... (G. Smith, 1779, p. 103)

The one redout at Fort Stanwix covered the sally port entrance on the east side of the fort (figs. 33, 34). It was pentagonal and the body of the work stood at an elevation of 443 feet above mean sea level. It was fortified with a row of posts surrounded by an earthen parapet or glacis. Those found were .4 to .5 foot in diameter and set .7 to 1.0 foot apart, center to center. Only 11 of these postmolds of the redout were found. There was a banquette 3.5 feet wide and 1.5 feet high around the inside of the posts and an earthen parapet outside the palisade line. The angle of the one line of posts was 43 degrees from the midline, while the banquette base on the other side was 40 degrees from the midline. The approximate interior lengths: east flank, 5.5 feet; east face, 14 feet; south face, 18 feet; south flank, 4.5 feet and northwest face, 21 feet. The northwest face was joined to the sally port by a covered communication 9.5 feet wide. The southwest corner extended 2.5 feet beyond the corner of the communication with a gate approximately 3 feet wide on this side for access to the small creek on the east side of the fort.

Level I was a gray loam with post-1781 ceramics. Level II was a deposit of garbage described under the section "Sally Port," which was disturbed by tree roots along a retaining wall on the east side. Level III was a brown sandy loam on the floor of the redout. It contained two Dutch gunflints, a cannon primer, a wheel hub, a Type A-1a button, a Type A-1i button, a Type B-1 button, a Type B-2 button, a Type 1a porcelain potsherd, a Type 1b porcelain potsherd, five Type 1a stoneware potsherds, four Type 1b stoneware potsherds, a Type 2b stoneware potsherd, seven Type 1b earthenware potsherds, four Type 1d earthenware potsherds, two Type 2a earthenware potsherds and a Type 4 earthenware potsherd.

Revetment

. . . a strong wall built on the outside of the rampart and parapet, to support the earth, and prevent its rolling into the ditch . . . (G. Smith, 1779, p. 103)

The only revetment found at Fort Stanwix was on the scarp of the north ditch which had been sodded to keep the earth in place. The sod was apparently laid on flat, rather than cut and stacked like bricks. To hold it in place, wooden stakes .5 to 1.5 feet long were driven into the scarp at 1-foot intervals in rows .7 foot apart. The rows tended to drop slightly in elevation from east to west.

Sally Port

. . . are those under-ground passages, which lead from the inner works to the outward ones . . . When they are made for men to go through only, they are made with steps at the entrance, and going out. They are about 6 feet wide, and 8½ feet high. There is also a gutter or shore made under the sally-ports, which are in the middle of the curtains, for the water which runs down the streets to pass into the ditch; but this can only be done when there are wet ditches. (G. Smith, 1779, p. 312)

The sally port at Fort Stanwix was located in the east curtain wall of the fort (figs. 33, 34). No trace of it was found through the east casemate except the drain that ran through, 6 degrees south of a right angle to the rear wall of the casemate (see section entitled "Drain"). Through the rampart and out onto the berm it was also marked by charred sill beams and sleepers. This indicated a passageway 5 feet wide on the exterior with .5 foot thick walls. The first arm of the sally port, through the casemate, was 22 feet long and the second arm, through the rampart, 21 feet long. The angle between the two arms was 24 degrees.

The sally port at the berm entered a communication 61 feet long which ran down the scarp and out to a redout. This was 9.5 feet wide with .5-foot thick white pine sleepers (*Pinus strobus*). The remains of three steps were found at the western end of the communication on the scarp. The end of the sally port projected 3 feet into the communication on the berm. The communication was anchored by two 9-inch squared uprights in the exterior of the rampart. At the eastern end there was a sleeper with two nails driven vertically into it 2 feet apart. They probably had something to do with a threshold since the door at the end of the communication must have been wider than this. This sleeper, and another one 10 feet west of it, were 1 foot wide.

Above the floor of the communication and the redout was a deposit of dark gray loam containing numerous artifacts. The presence of a number of Revolutionary War period buttons in this midden (Level II) indicated a date of deposit between 1776 and 1781. Since the deposit would have interferred with access through the communication, this must have been abandoned and torn down sometime after 1776. The upper surface of this deposit was slightly concave, indicating that it formed the base of a trail from the sally port to the redout. Artifacts in this deposit included a 1732 British halfpenny, a signet inset, a Type 4b axe, a Type 4c axe, a Type 2 spade, a saw fragment, two scissor fragments, a bone button bit with unfinished blanks, a .62 cal. two-pronged gun worm, an escutcheon plate marked "17th R^t.", a Type 2 lock plate, 21 Dutch gunflints, 23 French gunflints, a cannon primer, ten mortar bomb fragments, 13 Type A-1a buttons, three Type A-1b buttons, two Type A-1c buttons, a Type A-1d button, a Type A-1e button, a Type A-1g button, four Type A-1i buttons, a Type A-1j button, a Type A-1k button, a Type A-11 button, a Type A-1z button, a Type A-3 button, a Type A-4 button, a Type B-1 button, five Type B-3 buttons, a Type D-2 button, two Type D-3 buttons, a Type D-4 button, eight Type E-1 buttons, two Type F-2 buttons, seven Type 1a porcelain potsherds, 24 Type 1b porcelain potsherds, two Type 1d stoneware potsherds, 53 Type 1a stoneware potsherds, ten Type 1b stoneware potsherds, two Type 1d stoneware potsherds, 32 Type 1a earthenware potsherds, 39 Type 1b earthenware potsherds, a Type 1d earthenware potsherd, 57 Type 2a earthenware potsherds, five Type 2b earthenware potsherds, a Type

2c earthenware potsherd, three Type 2d earthenware potsherds, seven Type 2e earthenware potsherds, two Type 2f earthenware potsherds and a Type 2g earthenware potsherd. Some ceramics from this deposit could be cross-mended with sherds from the west end of the north casemate. On the floor of the communication and the scarp below the sally port (Level III) there was a brown sandy loam which contained three Dutch gunflints, a French gunflint, a Type A-1a button, a Type A-1b button, a Type A-1e button, a Type B-3 button, a Type D-2 button, a Type E-1 button, a Type F-2 button, a white oak (*Quercus*) scrub brush, two Type 1a porcelain potsherds, nine Type 1b porcelain potsherds, four Type 1d porcelain potsherds, thirty-six Type 1a stoneware potsherds, seven Type 1b stoneware potsherds, a Type 1d stoneware potsherd, 22 Type 1a earthenware potsherds, 20 Type 1b earthenware potsherds, four Type 1d earthenware potsherds, four Type 2e earthenware potsherds and a Type 4 earthenware potsherd.

The floor elevation of the sally port was 451.10 feet. The communication dropped from 450.09 feet on the berm to 444.08 feet at the base of the scarp and 442.96 feet at the eastern end. Banked against both sides of the communication was a ramp of earth or glacis. The top was about 4.5 feet above the floor level and sloped at an angle of 10 degrees. This produced a width of 25 feet to the embankment.

Scarp

. . . the interior talus or slope of the ditch next [to] the place, at the foot of the rampart. (G. Smith, 1779, p. 228)

The scarp at Fort Stanwix was measured at several points and averaged 40 degrees in slope. Below the bridge, on the south curtain it was 45 degrees.

On the east side of the fort a deposit of pre-1781 artifacts was found on the scarp. Level I was a gray loam over some lenses of brown loam which were post-1781 deposits used to landscape the area and build out the slope to a *ca.* 1839 retaining wall along Spring Street. Level II was a deposit of pre-1781 artifacts lying on the slope of the scarp north of the communication at the angle of the glacis of the communication. Artifacts found include a George II halfpenny, a Type 2 axe, a Type 7 axe, a Category 1 hammer, a sad iron, a 4-pounder cannonball, a 6-pounder cannonball

with a broad arrow, five mortar bomb fragments, twenty-two Dutch gunflints, nine French gunflints, a "Jesuit" ring, five Type A-1a buttons, a Type A-1b button, a Type A-1f button, a Type A-1i button, a Type A-1k button, a Type A-1z button, a Type A-4 button, six Type B-1 buttons, 15 Type B-2 buttons, three Type B-3 buttons, two Type D-3 buttons, a Type D-4 button, a Type E-1 button, a Type E-2 button, a Type F-2 button, a Type G-1 button, 12 Type 1a porcelain potsherds, 38 Type 1b porcelain potsherds, three Type 1d porcelain potsherds, 55 Type 1a stoneware potsherds, 30 Type 1b stoneware potsherds, a Type 2a stoneware potsherd, a Type 3 stoneware potsherd, 82 Type 1a earthenware potsherds, 67 Type 1b earthenware potsherds, 13 Type 1c earthenware potsherds, ten Type 1d earthenware potsherds, 48 Type 2a earthenware potsherds, two Type 2b earthenware potsherds, seven Type 2e earthenware potsherds and two Type 4 earthenware potsherds.

The presence of Revolutionary War buttons indicated that this deposit was made between 1776 and 1781. Despite the presence of a few military objects this was predominantly a deposit of household trash and cross-mends of a few potsherds indicate that it came from the east end of the north casemate. Higher up on the east scarp just below the berm and 4 feet north of the sally port communication, stood a brick fireplace (Feature 68) (fig. 36). The jambs and back wall were .8-foot thick and were made from alternating courses of

Figure 36. View of the brick hearth on the east scarp, looking west-northwest. Note the barrel hoop broiler fragments on the floor. The front edge has eroded away. The back wall of the fireplace is 4.8 feet wide.

headers and stretchers. It measured 4.8 feet wide at the back and was 3 feet deep. The jambs expanded to a thickness of 1.2 feet at the ends and were at an angle of 93 degrees to the back wall. The hearth was paved with bricks laid at right angles to the back wall at an elevation of 449.32 feet. It projected 1.3 feet beyond the front of the fireplace and was approximately 7.8 feet wide. Its position is a mystery, but there may have been some temporary shelter erected in this relatively protected area between the rampart and the communication. There was a "USA" button (Type A-1b) on the hearth indicating it was used during or after 1776 and a broiler made from a folded iron strap (barrel hoop?).

Terrepleine

. . . the top platform, or horizontal surface of the rampart, whereon the cannon are placed, as well as the troops that defend the place . . . (G. Smith, 1779, p. 243)

The terrepleine of the curtains at Fort Stanwix was formed by the roofs of the casemates. The bastions had solid earth-filled terrepleines which sloped down slightly toward the parapet to take up the recoil of the cannon. For this reason the casemate roofs must have been lower on the rampart side.

Whipping Post

The stump of a white cedar post (*Thuja occidentalis*) was found 18 feet from the center of the fort along the midline. Its position, which would be approximately 28 feet in front of the headquarters building, suggests that it was the remains of a whipping post. The fort is known to have had one capable of holding four men at once (Elmer, 1848, p. 138).

Summary

Fort Stanwix was a highly organized military post with all available space used for quarters or some other purpose. Our excavations were facilitated by this organization, and the resulting symmetry and the existence of a number of British and American plans of the fort (Luzader, 1969) made while it was in use. We took advantage of this information in planning our excavations, and attempted to excavate each structure as an entity in the hope that we would be able to tell from the artifacts recovered just how the buildings were used, draw inferences about the social and economic status of the occupants, and separate British and American components. For a variety of reasons, principally disturbance and the short time frame of the 18th-century components, 1758-1781, the data was not what we had hoped for. Because of the disturbance, few of the buildings were intact enough that they could be thoroughly excavated. With rare exceptions what was excavated in terms of the artifacts was rather homogeneous; approximately the same types of artifacts in nearly the same frequencies showed up in all the structures. Finally, our efforts to separate documented British and American components came to naught. The only structural evidence which supports the documentation is: the presence of clay-lined and wood-lined cellar holes with two of the former intruding two of the latter, six single-hearth fireplaces in the north casemate where the British plans show three double-hearth "H-shaped" fireplaces, and a bakehouse built over a 1758 powder magazine which had collapsed prior to the building of the bakehouse. None of these really gave us any clear-cut distinction between the two components, because we could not document exactly when these changes took place except that they occurred after 1764, the date of the last British plan for the fort, and 1781, when the fort was destroyed and abandoned. This time span overlaps both periods of occupation. Trash deposits on the east scarp, in the sally port communication, and in Feature 69 clearly date after 1776, but we strongly suspect that earlier material is included in the deposits and application of the South mean ceramic date formula confirms this (South, 1972).

The documentation on the fort shows that it was being repaired constantly and, in some cases, modified. The major changes were made in 1763-64 when the east and west barracks and headquarters were constructed. Sometime later, by 1777, a guardhouse and storehouse were added and three bombproofs and a bakehouse were put into the bastions. From the excavated remains, it is hard to escape the conclusion that the Americans either completely eradicated the British foundations when they rebuilt the fort, or found substantial parts of it intact and merely made repairs. The fact that the rebuilding was done in a relatively short time favors the latter conclusion. Although the British barracks burned in 1774 (Duncan, 1969) there was still habitable space occupied by a trader, probably in one of the casemates.

Poor preservation prevented us from making any detailed study of construction methods. It was noted that the six fireplaces in the north casemate were not squared to the rear wall, and that the entire east barracks was slightly out of line (2 degrees) with the rest of the fort. This is just not enough evidence to generalize on the abilities of the workmen who built the fort. Basically, the archeological work enhanced our knowledge of the location, size and shape of Fort Stanwix and its component structures, assisted us in identifying some of the materials used in its construction (Wood, bricks, mortar and hardware) and provided additional information on the distribution of certain artifact types in the period 1758-1781. Figure 10 depicts a plan of Fort Stanwix as projected from the archeological evidence, incorporating documentary evidence to fill in the holes. Figure 8 shows how the fort would look based on archeological evidence, historic plans, contemporary descriptions and comparable forts.

Chapter 4

Artifacts

For the reasons summarized at the end of the last chapter, the artifacts from the fort cannot be separated stratigraphically into two components, and must be considered to date between 1758 and 1781 except where datable artifacts narrow this time range. Examples include Type 2a earthenware pottery (creamware) which was introduced after 1762 (Noël Hume, 1970, p. 125) and American uniform buttons which date post-1775. The vast majority of the artifacts were manufactured during a period that spanned the entire time range of the occupation of the fort. The few pieces that can be identified positively as of English manufacture mean little because captured military goods were redistributed to the American army, or sold at public auction (Willet, 8/31/77).

Another method that can be used to identify the artifacts associated with each component of a long term occupation is comparison with other short-term occupations or single component sites in the same time period. The only comparable site for which we found published data was Fort Ligonier (Grimm, 1970). Other sites either have not been published on or were occupied longer than Fort Stanwix. General references were of limited use for the same reason as that cited by Stanley South concerning buttons at Brunswick Town and Fort Fisher ". . . none gave the type of detailed information which would prove of value in a typological analysis such as would be most useful to the archeologist . . ." (South, 1964, p. 113).

The first step in analyzing the artifacts from a site is a description of the material. Because the Fort Stanwix collection numbered nearly 42,000 specimens (not counting the post-1781 material) serving a wide range of functions, we found it necessary to resort to a classification system in order to handle the data. In this report we have used a system based on the function and form of the artifact. We have used a graduated breakdown into series, type and variety levels adapted from L. Stone (1970). Series are divided on the basis of function and/or place of origin. Types are defined on the basis of observable manufacturing techniques or major variations in form. Varieties are generally divided on the basis of decoration or minor variation in form. Like all classifications, this one does not encompass the full range of artifacts recovered. Although it is flexible to a degree, we have abandoned it when the need dictated so as not to obscure what we consider significant attributes by too rigid an adherence to the system. It should be stressed that this classification was adopted solely for the purpose of grouping similar artifacts in order to facilitate their description. This description may seem unncessarily complex to some and non-productive in terms of generating new data, but we feel that a less detailed description along strictly functional lines might not meet the needs of future researchers. Although we cannot predict those needs, it is logical to assume that when a larger corpus of data is available, patterns will show up which are not now apparent. We hope, in fact, that this report will lead others to look for such patterns.

To some extent our approach implies levels of relationship between varieties within types and types within series, as opposed to other classifications such as that by South (1964) which imply no relationship between types. Anyone familiar with the data will recognize that neither of these implications are wholly true or false and the two methods are both valid approaches depending upon the aims of the classifier. Again, our aim here is to describe the artifacts found at Fort Stanwix with as little repetition as possible.

One problem encountered in the description and classification of artifacts involves the ravages of time. Everyone knows that wood decomposes and iron rusts, but few consider how much of an artifact inventory is perishable. Thus, under normal conditions, my desk would be reduced in time to eight drawer pulls, a lock, a few screws and a handful of paper clips, provided it was not disturbed and some items carried off. Someone excavating my desk would be hard pressed to identify it except by the presence of paper clips. An accurate reconstruction would be impossible if there existed no drawings or identical desks to work from. This is the problem we faced at Fort Stanwix, and the reader should know that we have occasionally been reduced to making educated guesses preceded by the words "probably" and "possibly" or have put certain artifacts into "categories" because we could not type them due to poor preservation and breakage.

Because there was post-1781 occupations of the site, one of our first problems was to separate the later material from the fort artifacts. The bulk of the fort-related artifacts was found in the undisturbed strata described in the previous chapter. We also included those artifacts in the upper disturbed zones which could be clearly identified as pre-1781 by comparison with artifacts found in pre-1781 context or reference to published descriptions. For example, a sad iron found on the surface was identical to two found in pre-1781 contexts, and was included with them for descriptive purposes because none of this type were found in post-1781 features such as privies and cellars. On the other hand, pearlware, perfected by 1779 (Noël Hume, 1970, p. 128) was not found in a pre-1781 context, but was common in early 19th-century privies. This led us to omit pearlware from this report on the basis that an association with Fort Stanwix could not be established even though it was temporally possible. This task was made easier by the 20-year hiatus in the occupation after the destruction of the fort, during which there were modifications in artifacts. The association of most of the post-1781 artifacts were with privies, house foundations and utility lines. Where a separation is not possible, it is so noted. In general, the only instances where we allude to post-1781 artifacts is to make a comparison with the fort-related material.

The spatial distribution of artifacts was handled on two levels, within the site and with other sites. With most types of artifacts, we compared the relative amounts in the various buildings of the fort, the ditch, the parade ground (which included the gateway), the ravelin and the dumps on the east scarp and in the sally port complex (actually, in the communication and redout). As noted, we hoped to achieve a better understanding of the function of each building by its contents. We included the artifacts in the Campbell collection of 1965, material not identified by provenience, although most of it apparently came from the bakehouse and southeast casemate. For purposes of comparison we converted the actual number of specimens found to a standard ratio per 100 square feet of excavated area per structure. This is a crude technique in that it lumps *in situ* artifacts along with artifacts from the fill, but an examination of the *in situ* artifacts alone which formed a preliminary study for this report did not generate any testable hypotheses, primarily because there were not many *in situ* artifacts compared to the total collection. It is assumed that there was little lateral movement in the artifacts, an assumption that is borne out by the relative absence of midden outside the structures except on the east scarp. We were thus able to treat each structure as an entity for quantitative analysis. In some cases, as in the barracks, it was feasible to break down the artifacts by the various cellar holes. By and large, there were too few comparable artifacts to make any meaningful comparisons above the presence or absence level in the various buildings and dumps, but the figures are included for the record in the event that someone else wants to compare their buildings and trash deposits with ours. Comparisons with other sites by us were hampered by a lack of published material, and the inability of the authors to examine comparable collections due to a lack of travel funds and time. Through the courtesy of Mr. Horace Wilcox and staff, we were able to look at some of the material from Valley Forge and Dr. Lyle Stone permitted us to use his Ph.D. dissertation on Fort Michilimackinac. The quality of the published data varied considerably. Thus, it was possible to make definitive statements about the pipes and gunflints, but we found ourselves in virgin territory with such items as window glass and shovels.

An attempt to cross-mend potsherds from the site showed that a significant number of vessels (6.7 percent) from the north casemate had sherds in the dumps on the east scarp and in the sally port. Material from the west end of the north case-mate (Levels II and III) was dumped in the sally port (Level II) and material from the east end of the north casemate (Level I) was dumped on the east scarp (Level II). There was one cross-mend between the sally port (Level II) and the south end of the east barracks (Level I) and another between Level II of the west end of the southwest casemate and Level I of the south end of the west barracks.

The artifact descriptions that follow are grouped under general headings so that function-ally similar objects are described together. There are a few items at the end which could not be fitted in and the best way to find these is to refer to the index. A summary of the artifacts is incorporated in the last chapter.

Building Hardware

The structures at Fort Stanwix were of wood, either of log or frame construction. The casemates and northwest bombproof were constructed of logs; the buildings on the parade ground, and prob-ably the northeast and southwest bombproofs and the bakehouse, were frame buildings. All the frame buildings were quite flimsy as this report of a fire in the guardhouse at midnight on April 13, 1780, suggests:

. . . we were necessitated [in order to save the rest of the garrison from being consumed] to also haull down part of the rist of the Barracks, immediately in the morning I had all the Carpenters collected & employed who have now nearly again repaired the barracks that were knock's down . . . (Van Dyck to Van Schaick, April 17, 1780)

It is likely that the buildings were probably quite simple with wooden walls, floor and roof and interior partitions to set off rooms. Judging from documents, each had a door and at least one win-dow and fireplace. Building hardware was kept to a minimum: nails, rivets and staples for joining wood; pintles and hinges for hanging doors and shutters; locks and latches for securing the doors and gates; and hooks and bricks for the fireplaces. Bricks and nails are the most common artifacts of this class. The general absence of hardware may be attributed to the collection of iron that was made just prior to the fort's abandonment in 1781 (Lauber 1932 p. 582).

If any generalization can be made about the building hardware it is that there was a lack of uniformity. This may be interpreted as a result of the low level of technology in America, no one manufactory having been capable of supplying all the needs for a particular item, even in such a small area as the Mohawk Valley. As a conse-quence, hardware was supplied by a number of small forges and may even have been scavenged from existing buildings in the Valley. Colonial furnaces produced 14 percent of the world's iron supply at the outbreak of the American Revolu-tion (Ransom, 1966, p. 6). Most of this iron went to England to be made into finished products, but there were American forges capable of producing goods. Bridenbaugh (1950, p. 61) lists eight iron furnaces, one steel furnace, 42 forges, one plating mill and one slitting mill for New Jersey alone in 1767. We know that the *Type 4* axes discussed under the section entitled "Tools" were invented and made in America. Prior to the war most nail rods were imported to the Colonies with the fin-ished nails turned out as a sort of cottage industry (Clark, 1929, p. 222). The war forced Americans to produce their own finished products although conscription and the unsettled conditions greatly lowered the productivity of the furnaces (Ransom, 1966, p. 6). Robert Erskine was probably the best known American iron manufacturer in the Revo-lution (Ransom, 1966, p. 36). Except for cast items such as cannonballs, shot and shells, he was shipping most of his pig iron to the American army where it was apparently being forged into tools and hardware as needed (Clinton, 1900, Vol. I, pp. 225-226, p. 666).

Five series of metal fasteners were used at the fort for jointing wood and metal to other woods and/or metals. These were: nails, staples, screws, rivets and bolts. Nails were the most common be-cause they were the easiest to manufacture and use. Essentially, rivets were nails with a large head at both ends of the shank; they were apparently used in place of a clinched nail.

Bolts and nuts were sometimes used when clinched nails or rivets were not strong enough (Mercer, 1960, p. 248). The advantage of the bolt and nut was that adjustments could easily be made by tightening or loosening as the need arose. More initial work had to be done when using a bolt because a hole had to be drilled. Many blacksmiths did not have the dies to make bolts and nuts and, although various inventions in the 17th and 18th centuries increased the production of these items, they were not common (Mercer, 1960, pp. 250-251). The same limitations applied to screws.

Nails

Approximately 24,600 wrought iron nails were found in pre-1781 context. Of these, 8,005 were measurable and the other 16,600+ were fragmentary. The military occupation of the site as a whole ended in 1781, nearly a decade before cut nails were introduced (Nelson, 1968; Noël Hume, 1970, p. 252). Therefore, only hand wrought nails will be discussed in this report, although cut nails were found in post-1781 contexts. Of the 8,005 measurable wrought nails, 871 may not have been associated with the fort since they were found in association with 19th century material or in disturbed areas.

A few of the wrought nails were well preserved because they had been burned, but most were badly corroded. Because of the great number of specimens, only a small number were treated for preservation. These were not randomly selected; we only attempted to clean fairly well preserved or unusual specimens. This precluded any attempts to make any percentage studies of the functional types of nails based upon head, shank and point shape.

The lengths of a large sample of nails were measured to the nearest ⅛ inch and plotted on a graph. They did not fit into the modern penny sizes, but clustered into the following inch-range groups: 0-1, 1-1½, 1½-3, 3-3½, 3½-4, 4-4½, 4½-5, 5-6, 6-7, 7-8, 8-9 and 9-10. The 1½-3 inches category spanned the 4d-10d sizes, but there were as many specimens falling between the pence sizes as in them, and the curve was a normal distribution (fig. 37). Few specimens were found above 6 inches in length and the upper divisions were arbitrary.

The barracks and guardhouse were frame structures with board siding, plank floors and shingle roofs. These buildings should have had a larger number of nails than the casemates which were constructed of logs with plank floors. Floor planks were probably the thickest pieces, about 1 to 2 inches thick. Most of the framing was probably mortised or dovetailed in some fashion, which explains why 85 percent of all measured nails were from ½ to 4 inches long (table 1).

The barracks were constructed more than

once. The British built the first barracks in 1764. These burned in 1774. The Americans rebuilt on the same locations in 1776. In 1780, as noted, the guardhouse burned and part of the west barracks was pulled down to prevent the spread of the fire. Both were rebuilt shortly after the fire, and in 1781 the fort burned again. Since the majority of the nails found were in the fill of the cellars, the nails probably were from the barracks in which the cellars were located. One lens in Feature 60 (Level II) of the west barracks contained 2,145 nails, many of them bent. The debris probably came from an area of about 1,200 square feet, or half the barracks. The same may be true to a lesser degree of all the cellars. After the barracks burned in 1774 and 1781, debris from them may have been used to fill the cellars in order to level the parade ground. An effort was made to plot all the nails found in the excavation that might have been *in situ* but this proved a futile endeavor, as no pattern could be discerned.

All the common types of hand wrought nails of the period described by Nelson (1968, p. 6) are present (fig. 38). All the types include both sharp and flattened points.

Rose-head (fig. 38a). Rose-head nails appear in all sizes but not all specimens of this type have rounded heads; many were flat with only short slopes near the edges.

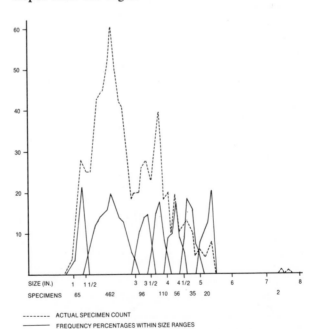

Figure 37. Iron nail sizes.

Table 1.

Distribution of iron nails at Fort Stanwix by length in inches. (Ratios given are the number of nails per 10 square feet of excavated area within the structure; U = unmeasurable specimens; ST = subtotals; T = totals.)

	0-1	1-1½	1½-3	3-3½	3½-4	4-4½	4½-5	5-6	6-7	7-8	8-9	9-10	ST	U	T
Casemates															
North															
Number		36	281	154	129	91	58	17	3	5	1		775	2,144	2,919
Ratio		1.1	8.8	4.2	4.0	2.8	1.8	.5	.1	.2	.1			67.0	91.2
West															
Number		1	10	2	4	4	2	2		.3			26	77	103
Ratio		.3	2.5	.5	1.0	1.0	.5	.5		.3				19.3	25.8
Southwest [1]															
Number		18	332	48	40	37	30	20	2	4	1		531	3,243	3,775
Ratio		1.8	33.2	4.8	4.0	3.7	3.0	2.0	.2	.4	.1			324.3	377.5
Southeast															
Number		1	8	3	1	1							14	266	280
Ratio		.7	5.3	2.0	.7	.7								177.3	186.7
East															
Number		12	121	19	17	10	15	10	4	3			211	537	748
Ratio		1.1	11.0	1.7	1.5	.9	1.4	6.9	.4	.3				48.9	68.0
Barracks															
East															
Number		28	417	79	75	15	12	3	1	2			632	2,302	2,934
Ratio		2.0	29.6	5.6	5.3	1.1	.9	.2	.1	.1				163.3	208.1
West															
Number	1	27	3,031[2]	81	69	39	46	40	2	5		1	3,342	3,654	6,996
Ratio	.1	2.1	238.7	6.4	5.4	3.1	3.6	3.2	.2	.4		.1		287.7	550.9
Guardhouse															
Number		3	137	31	19	7	6	2	1		1		207	1,298	1,505
Ratio		.3	11.4	2.6	1.6	.6	.5	.2	.8		.8			108.2	125.4
Headquarters															
Number			6	1	1								8	50	58
Ratio			.9	.2	.2									7.7	8.9
Parade Ground															
Number		3	3	1				1			2		10	102	112
Ratio		.3	.3	.1				.1			.2			11.3	12.4
Bombproofs															
Northeast															
Number		2	34	12	13	7	15	5			1		89	294	383
Ratio		.4	6.2	2.2	2.4	1.3	2.7	.9			.2			53.5	69.6
Northwest															
Number			7	8	8	10	7	4	1	1			46	275	1,321
Ratio			1.4	1.6	1.6	2.0	1.4	.8	.2	.2				56.1	65.5
Southwest															
Number			24	12	14	11	15	5	1	3	7		92	335	427
Ratio			4.4	2.2	2.5	2.0	2.7	.9	.2	.5	1.3			60.9	77.6
Bakehouse															
Number			8	3	4	3	3	2	1		1		25	129	154
Ratio															
Ditch															
Number	1	7	66	35	42	22	14	17	1	28	55	3	291	752	1,043
Ratio	.1	.2	2.3	1.2	1.5	.8	5	.6	.1	1.0	1.9	.1		26.3	36.5
Ravelin															
Number		8	132	27	22	20	13	12		2			236	299	535
Ratio		1.8	29.3	6.0	4.9	4.4	2.9	2.7		.4				66.4	118.9
East Scarp															
Number		31	274	38	32	24	25	10	1	1			436	662	1,098
Ratio		4.6	40.9	5.7	4.8	3.6	3.7	1.5	.1	.1				98.8	163.9
Sally Port															
Number		75	730	118	116	52	43	42	6	8	4		1,194	1,700	2,894
Ratio		8.7	84.9	13.7	13.5	6.0	5.0	4.9	.7	.9	.5			197.7	336.5
Totals															
Number	2	250	5,517	657	583	338	303	191	24	63	71	4	8,005	16,615	24,620
Ratio		1.3	28.2	3.4	3.0	1.7	1.5	1.0	.1	.3	.4			84.9	125.8

[1] Includes 1,665 nails in a wooden box in the floor.
[2] Includes 2,145 nails from a single deposit in a wood lined cellar.

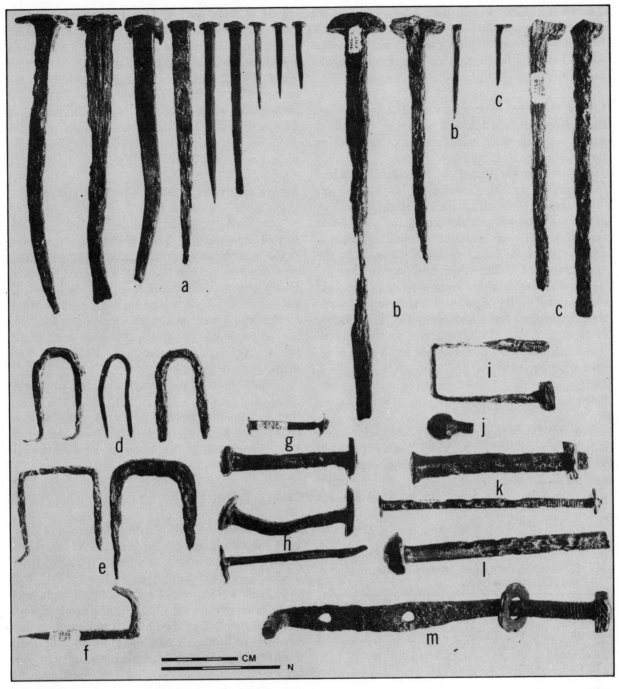

Figure 38. **a,** rose-head nails from Feature 76, Level II, the sally port, Level II, the west casemate, Level II, the sally port, Level II, the west casemate, Level II, Feature 60, Level II, the bridge area, Level XI, the west barracks, Level II and Feature 56, Level II; **b,** T-head nails from Feature 56, Level III, the bridge area, Level XII and the west barracks, Level II; **c,** L-head nails from Feature 56, Level III and Feature 69, Level II (2); **d,** round cornered staples from the southwest bombproof, Level III, the southeast casemate, Level I (2); **e,** square cornered staples from the southwest casemate, Level II and the guardhouse area, Level II; **f,** piton from the southwest bombproof, Level III; **g,** Type I rivets from the east scarp, Level II and the sally port, Level II; **h,** Type 2 rivets from the guardhouse area, Level I and the north casemate, Level II; **i,** U-bolt from the north casemate, Level I; **j,** Type 4a bolt from the sally port, Level II; **k,** Type 1a bolts from the southwest casemate, Level II and Feature 48; **l,** Type 4b bolt from the sally port, Level II; **m,** Type 3 bolt from the west barracks, Level I.

T-head (fig. 38b). T-head nails also appear in all sizes. Some were obviously rose-head nails with two sides flattened to form the "T" but the large spikes have flat heads and are not reshaped rose-heads.

L-head (fig. 38c). The L-head nails appear in all sizes. However, most are 3 inches or shorter in length as they were used primarily as finishing nails (Nelson, 1968, p. 6).

There are no records of nails being received or requested by the garrison. A blacksmith was listed as one of the artificers during the American occupation, but he probably could not have made enough to keep up with the demand. Therefore, most of the nails found probably came from the lower Mohawk Valley area. It is known that pig iron was being shipped from American furnaces to the army on the Hudson where it was presumably forged into tools and hardware (G. Clinton, 1900, Vol. I, pp. 225–226). Prior to the Revolution most nails were probably imported from England (Nelson, 1968, p. 2).

Staples

Forty-five metal staples (fig. 38) of various lengths and thicknesses were found scattered widely around the site with no large clusters in any particular area (table 2). Most of the staples were probably made from nail rods, as 21 are square in cross section, 15 are rectangular and the remaining nine are round. All the staples, whether made from a round or four-sided rod, were pounded either to a tapered point or to a chisel point. The staples varied in length from ⅝ to 6⅝ inches, with the majority ranging from 1½ to 3¼ inches, the widths falling primarily in the ¾ to 1½-inch range. The largest was ½ inch in diameter and the smallest was 3/16 by ¼ inch while most were in the ¼ to ⅜ range.

Square cornered (fig. 38e). There are nine of these made from four-sided rods.

Round cornered (fig. 38d). U-shaped staples were made from both round and four-sided rods. This was contrary to the findings and conclusions at Fort Ligonier (Grimm, 1970, p. 147) where all U-shaped staples were round in cross section. Some staples show wear in the interior of the "U" but not on the sides, suggesting that they were driven into the ceiling and objects were suspended from them.

Six round-topped staples have both ends clinched, some with the ends in the same direction and some in opposite directions. None of these could have been driven into a plank more than 1½ inches thick if they were to be used to suspend objects.

Chain

On the east scarp (Level II) there was found a U-shaped bracket with out-turned flat ends pierced for attachment to a wall. Hanging from this are two chain links, 2 inches long and ½ inch wide, and a 3½ inch long wire with bent ends made to attach it to the chain and provide a hook end. The function of the object is unknown. It may have served to keep a chest lid from opening more than 90 degrees. The U-shaped portion and wire are round in cross section and 5/32 inch in diameter, while the chain links are rectangular and measure 5/32 by 3/32 inch. Two more U-shaped brackets were found in the east barracks (Level II) and the sally port (Level III). This was the only chain found at Fort Stanwix.

Piton?

One unique fastener was found in the southwest bombproof (Level III), a J-shaped nail prob-

Table 2.

Distribution of staples, screws, rivets, nuts and bolts, and washers.

	Staples	Screws	Rivets	Nuts and Bolts	Washers
Casemates					
North	7		4	4	
Southwest	3		2	2	2
Southeast	2			2	
East	2				
Barracks					
East	3			1	
West	5			4	2
Guardhouse	3		1		1
Bombproofs					
Northeast	1				
Northwest	1		1	1	
Southwest	5				
Bakehouse	2				
Ditch	5				1
Ravelin	2		1		
East Scarp	2	1	3	1	
Sally Port	2	1	4	2	2
Totals	45	2	16	27	8

ably used for suspending objects (fig. 38f). It is made from a rod ¼ inch square; the shank is 3 inches long and all four sides taper to the point. The rod is bent 90 degrees to form the bottom of the "J" which is 1 inch long. The curved portion is ¾ inch long and hammered flat. This may have been used as a rafter spike. Its shape is not similar to one illustrated in Watson (1968, p. 12) but corresponds very well to pitons used as climbing equipment, even though there are no cliffs close by.

Screws

Two wood screws were found (table 2). One found in the east casemate (Level III) is 1¼ inch long, ¼ inch in diameter and tapered. The head is oval with a slot and the threads stop ½ inch below the head. The other, found in the sally port (Level II), is probably identical but the tip and part of the shank are missing.

Rivets

Rivets were a compromise between nails and bolts (fig. 38). They were easier to make than nails because they had blunt ends, but, as with bolts, holes had to be bored through the objects to be fastened before rivets could be used. A rove, or washer, was often used with a rivet if two pieces of wood or other soft materials were being joined; the rove could be omitted if the material was hard (Mercer, 1960, p. 246). The distribution of rivets is shown in table 2.

The rivets were made from nail rods and round rods of several sizes, and were made to order rather than to a set size standard. The tip was not pointed, but often was split so that it would spread more easily when struck (Mercer, 1960, p. 246). Roves were also made to order, their size dependent upon the diameter of the rivet and material of the objects being joined. In general, the ones found are larger than the heads, but only one half as thick and are cut from flattened sheets of iron. All rivets found exhibit rose-heads of one variation or another. They range in length from 2 to 3¾ inches and in diameter from 3/16 to ½ inch.

Type 1 (fig. 38g). The heads of 15 specimens were formed by enlarging the end of the rod. Roves are still attached to 12 specimens.

Type 2 (fig. 38h). One specimen has a separate head welded to the shank.

Nuts and Bolts

A total of 15 bolts and 11 nuts, nine of which are still attached to bolts, were recovered (fig. 38). All except one were found within the limits of fort buildings (table 2).

Type 1. Bolts made from round rods, the shank hammered square above the threads to the head.

Variety a. Flat, square heads (fig. 38k). The heads of eight specimens are slightly larger on all sides than the shank. On some, the underside of the head is at a 90-degree angle from the shank; on others the head tapers down to the size of the shank which has a diameter from ¼ to ⅝ inch. The shanks are approximately 5 to 6 inches long, approximately one-fourth of which is threaded. Three smaller specimens came from the north casemate (Level II), east casemate (Level III) and southwest bombproof (Level V). They are fragmentary pieces, missing parts of the head or shank, or both. All are ¼ inch in diameter. These average slightly thinner than Fort Ligonier bolts (Grimm, 1970, p. 51) but just as long.

Variety b. T-head slightly convex rather than flat. One specimen is 5 inches long, shaped from a rod 5/16 inch in diameter. The head is 1½ inches long and 5/16 inch wide. The tip is tapered. The threads began ¼ inch above the tip, and continued for a distance of 1¼ inches.

Type 2. U-bolt (fig. 38i). One U-bolt has a 5/16 inch diameter round shank pounded flat with squared corners to form the "U." The "U" is 3½ inches long and 1¼ inches wide with a 1-inch threaded section on both arms. One nut is still attached. It came from the north casemate (Level I).

Type 3. L-shaped (fig. 38m). Two bolts are modified pintles; at least the end of one specimen was serviceable as such. One was fashioned from a rod ½ inch in diameter. The hinge pin, at 90 degrees from the shank, is ¾ inch long, the shank is 8 inches long and has two distinct portions. The half toward the hinge pin was beaten flat and exhibits two holes drilled 1 inch and 3 inches from the pin to receive nails or other fastening devices. The other half of the shank is round and the end is threaded for 1½ inches of its length. A washer 1¼ inches in diameter and a nut are attached. They were found in the west barracks (Level I) and the southeast casemate (Level I). These may date post-1781.

Type 4. Hemispherical heads and round shanks.

Variety a. One-piece construction (fig. 38j). The head is approximately ¾ inch in diameter and flattened on the sides to facilitate turning. The shank is ¼ inch in diameter. It is broken, and the original length cannot be determined. Threads run the entire length of the shank to the base of the head. The specimen came from the sally port (Level II).

Variety b. Two-piece construction (fig. 38l). The shank was welded onto a preformed hemispherical head. Both specimens are missing part of their shanks, and have no threads on the remaining portion. Their identification is, therefore, tentative. Their heads both measure 1¼ inches in diameter; one shank is ½ inch in diameter, and the other ¼ inch in diameter. The larger specimen is from the sally port (Level II) and the smaller from Feature 60 (Level II) in the west barracks.

Category 1, nuts. Two nuts, both 1¼ inches square, with flat top and bottom surfaces were found, one in the east barracks (Level I) and the other on the east scarp (Level II). They are ¼ inch thick and one fitted a 9/16 inch diameter bolt and the other a ⅜ inch diameter bolt.

Washers

Eight flat metal washers were found (fig. 39a). One from the west barracks (Feature 63, Level III) is a 1-inch square piece of sheet metal with an irregular hole cut in it; the remainder are doughnut-shaped. The smallest specimen is ¾ inch in diameter with a 5/16 inch hole and may be the only one to have been stamped out. All the other circular washers are irregular in thickness and symmetry between the outside and bore rims. These measure from 1 to 4½ inches in diameter, ⅜ to 1¼ inches in hole diameter, and 1/16 to ½ inch in thickness.

Metal Supports

These were used to reinforce and/or fasten two pieces of wood. Some may have been used on wagons or gun carriages.

Three L-shaped braces were found, one in the south ditch (Level XIII), one in the ravelin (Level II) and one in Feature 3 (Level IV) in the west barracks. They are strips of iron bent 90 degrees, one leg of which is two to three times

longer than the other, and with one or two attachment holes (fig. 39h). They range in length from 4 to 5⅜ inches and from ⅛ to ¼ inch in thickness.

A brass strap was found on the east scarp (Level I). It is 8 inches long, ⅞ inch wide and 3/16 inch thick. A hole has been bored ¼ inch from each end and partially countersunk.

A large wrought strap was found in the northwest bombproof (Level II). Each end is split into two flat prongs approximately 3 inches long, 1 inch wide and tapering from ¼ inch down to ⅛ inch thick at the tips. The total length is 29 inches and the main stem is 1¼ inches wide and ½ inch

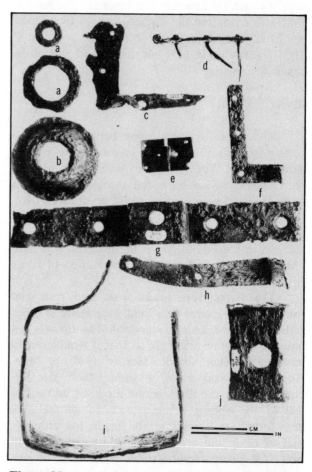

Figure 39. **a,** washers from the southwest casemate, Level I and the bridge area, Level XIII; **b,** flange from the sally port, Level II; **c,** Type 7 hinge from Feature 76; **d,** Type 2b hinge from Feature 60, Level II; **e,** Type 5 hinge from Feature 48; **f,** Type 4 hinge from the southwest casemate, Level II; **g-j,** metal supports from the east casemate, Level II, the ravelin, Level II, Feature 57, Level III and the bridge area, Level X.

thick. Two countersunk holes are bored in each prong for attachment and one screw was still in a hole.

A wrought iron strap found in Feature 57 (Level III) in the west barracks may have been a reinforcing band around a timber up to 4½ by 5 inches in diameter (fig. 39i). The strap is 1¾ inches wide and 3/16 inch thick. The band is broken so the length cannot be determined. The ends of the straps were bent away from the beam and were either riveted or bolted together or to another beam. One U-shaped bracket found in the south ditch (Level X) was a wrought iron strap 5½ inches long, 2 inches wide and 3/16 inch thick (fig. 39j). The arms of the "U" are 1¼ inches long and the bottom 4 inches long. Two attachment holes are bored in each arm approximately ½ inch from the ends, while one hole, ¾ inch in diameter, is in the approximate center of the bottom. This may have been a pivot plate for a light, four-wheel wagon.

One support with a raised center found in the east casemate (Level II) was a metal strap with a squared U-shaped offset (fig. 39g). It is 10¼ inches long. Each arm is approximately 4¼ inches long, while the offset is 1½ inches long and ¾ inch above the arms. The strap is 1½ inches wide and ¼ inch thick. Two countersunk holes are bored through each arm and another through the center of the offset.

Hinges

Hinges were nailed or screwed to a shutter or door that swung open (see also the section entitled "Pintles"). The size and shape of the hinge depended upon the size, shape and weight of the object to which it was attached and also whether the hinge was to add a decorative effect (table 3).

Type 1. Strap hinges that worked in conjunction with a pintle. One end of the strap was wound around a mandrel and welded to form an O-ring that fitted over the pin of the pintle.

Variety a. Flat, with straight sides for half the length, then tapered to a point. One specimen measures 8¼ inches long, 1¼ inches wide at the pin, ⅛ inch thick and has two attachment holes 1½ and 4½ inches from the pintle end.

Variety b. Similar to Variety a, with the exception of an expanded disc end. They range in length from 6¾ to 11 inches, width from 1 to ⅜ inches and are ⅛ inch thick (fig. 40f). Each hinge has three holes for attachment, two along the strap and one at the tip.

Variety c. Similar to Variety b, with the exception of a spear-shaped tip rather than a disc. These range in length from 10½ to 18 inches, width from 1 to 1½ inches and have a thickness of ⅛ inch (fig. 40c, e). The number of attachment holes varies from three to six; there is no correlation between the length and the number of holes.

Table 3.

Distribution of hinges, pintles, hasps and keys.

Type Variety	Hinges 1a	1b	1c	1d	1e	2a	2b	3	4	5	6	7	Pintles 1a	1b	1c	2a	2b	2c	3	4	Hasps 1	2a	2b	Keys 1a	1b	2	3	Unidentifiable keys
Casemates																												
North			1		1									1											1			1
Southwest		2	2			1	1						1								1							
East		1																										
Barracks																												
East																1												
West				1				1					1											1				2
Guardhouse																												
Parade Ground											1																	
Bombproofs																												
Northeast													3			1										1		
Northwest			2	1												2	2											
Southwest																1	1					1		1				
Ditch	1			1						1					1	3	1					1	1				1	
Ravelin												1																2
Sally Port		2									1					1	1	1					1				1	
Variety totals	1	5	5	3	1	1	1						5	1	1	10	4	1				1	2	2	2			
Type totals	15					2		1	1	2	2	1	7			15			1	1	1	3		4		1	2	5

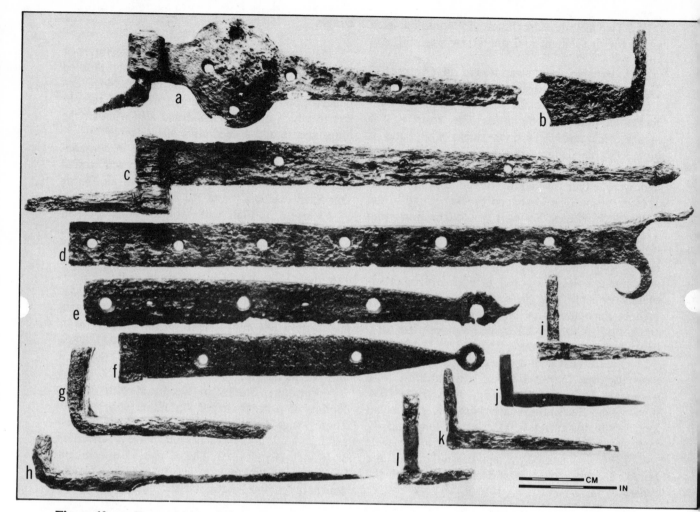

Figure 40. **a,** Type 1d hinge from the bridge area, Level I; **b,** Type 4 pintle from the northeast bombproof, Level III; **c,** Type 1c hinge from the northwest bombproof, Level II; **d,** Type 1e hinge from the southwest casemate, Level II; **e,** Type 1c hinge from the southwest casemate, Level I; **f,** Type 1b hinge from the southwest casemate, Level II; **g,** Type 2c pintle from the sally port, Level III; **h,** Type 2b pintle from Feature 57, Level III; **i,** Type 1a pintle from Feature 72, Level II; **j,** Type 1b pintle from the sally port, Level II; **k,** Type 2a pintle from the bridge area, Level XIII; **l,** Type 3 pintle from the northeast bombproof, Level II.

One specimen from the northwest bombproof passageway (Level III) has five nails still attached. They were clinched through wood 1½ inches thick.

Variety d. A bulbous expansion in the strap approximately 1 inch from the pintle end, then tapered gradually to a point. Specimens measure 11½ to 16 inches in length, 1¼ inches in width on the strap, 2¼ to 3 inches on the expansion and ⅛ inch thick (fig. 40a). Each has five attachment holes, two near the outer edges of the expansion and three along the midline of the strap. The holes extend from the pin ring along two-thirds of the length of the strap and there are no holes in the last one-third of the strap.

Variety e. Parallel sides along the entire length and the end split into two prongs. One prong continues in an upward curve ending in a point, while the other prong curves downward to form a hook pointed back toward the strap (fig. 40d). This specimen is missing the pintle ring and a short section of strap. The remaining portion measures 18½ inches long, 1⅜ inches wide and ⅛ inch thick. Six holes are bored approximately 2½ inches apart along the strap. It came from the southwest casemate (Level II).

Type 2. One-piece strap hinge with a fixed pin.

Variety a. Straps shaped like isosceles triangles with the widest part at the pin. About one-third of one section is missing. The projected length is 3 inches; width, ⅝ inch; and thickness, 1/16 inch. Two holes were bored near the pin in one section. One hole was bored approximately in the middle of the other section. This came from the north casemate (Level I). It may be post-1781.

Variety b. Rectangular straps (fig. 39d). One specimen measures 3½ inches long, 1⅛ inches wide and ⅛ inch thick; the pin being 3/16 inch in diameter. Five nails, the longest being 1¾ inches, were still through it. It was found in Feature 60 (Level II).

Type 3. A special hinge designed to work with the Type 1c Pintle to hinge the drawbridge (fig. 41a). One was found at the bottom of the south ditch (Level XIII) where the bridge once stood. It was driven into a piece of wood like the pintle instead of being attached by nails or bolts. The shank is wedge-shaped with a 1-inch diameter hole bored through the thickness of the shank, 5 inches from the tip; it is barbed on two opposite edges to grip the wood. It measures 15½ inches long, 1⅞ inches wide, 1⅛ inches thick and has a ring diameter of 2 by 3 inches.

Type 4. An L-shaped hinge designed to work with a pintle (fig. 39f). This has a vertical leg 3⅝ inches long, ⅝ inch wide and ⅛ inch thick with three attachment holes. The ⅜-inch-diameter pintle ring is at the end of the horizontal leg which is 1¼ inches long, ⅝ inch wide and ⅛ inch thick, with no attachment holes. It came from the southwest casemate (Level II).

Type 5. Brass box hinge (fig. 39e). The patterns were stamped out of thin sheets of brass and folded over to form one half of the hinge. There were two patterns, differing only at the fold, so that the two parts would interlock and a pin, a separate piece, could pass through. Each section has three attachment holes in a triangular pattern similar to modern box hinges. It came from Feature 57 (Level III).

Type 6. Butterfly hinge. The narrowest part of the hinge is at the pin. The two sides flare out like the wings of a butterfly, and measure 1½ and 2½ inches maximum width, ¾ and 1¼ inches minimum width, 2+ and 3+ inches in length and 1/16 and ⅛ inch in thickness. They came from Feature 58 and the sally port (Level II) respectively.

Type 7. Hook and eye hinge (fig. 39c). One half of the hinge is flaring, and the other half is a tapered strap with a hook attached through the eye. The eye section is 4 inches long, ⅞ to 2 inches

wide, and ⅛ inch thick. The strap is 3½+ inches long, ¾ inch wide, tapering to a point, and ⅛ inch thick. The flaring half has three attachment holes and the strap, two. It came from Feature 76 (Level II).

Category 1. Three speimens with their tips missing belong to Varieties 1a, 1b, or 1c. They were found in the ditch (Level XV), north casemate (Level II) and a cellar Feature 56 (Level III) in the west barracks.

Category 2. Seven pintle rings with 1 inch or less of a Type 1 strap were found. They came from widely separated areas. The range of the diameters of the rings of all Type 1 hinges is from ⅜ to ⅞ inch which corresponds well to the range of diameters of ¼ to ¾ inch for the pins.

All the pintles and hinges, except the brass box hinge, were forged from wrought iron. The only unusual specimens are the two that we presume belonged to the drawbridge which were made by special design and the Type 7 hinge. The remainder are typical of that period and were made in large numbers.

All Type 1 hinges were capable of carrying considerable weight. They probably were used for doors, heavy shutters and lids to large storage boxes. Types 2 through 6 are rather light, and were probably used on cupboards, trunks and small chests for personal effects. Type 7 is quite unusual, its use is unknown.

Pintles

Pintles were attached to the immovable frames of doors or windows to support hinges (table 3). They were made of two constituent parts: the shank driven into the frame, and the pin on which the hinge pivoted. All but one of the pintles found at Fort Stanwix correspond to Stone's Series B at Fort Michilimackinac (L. Stone, 1970, p. 487).

Type 1. Two-piece construction with the shank wrapped around and welded to the pin (L. Stone's Series B, Type 1; L. Stone, 1970, p. 488). The pin was made from a round rod and the shank from a rectanguar strap forged to the desired shape.

Variety a. Shank with square cross section at the pin (Stone's Series B, Type 1, Variety c; L. Stone, 1970, p. 488). The top and two sides are tapered to the tip (fig. 40i). These range in length from 4½ to 7½ inches and are ½ to ¾ inch square at the pin. The pins are ½ inch in diameter and protrude 1½ to 1¾ inches above the shank.

Variety b. Shank rectangular in cross section. The thickness is uniform from in front of the weld to the tip; the top tapers from the weld to the tip (fig. 40j). The pin is ½ inch in diameter and beaten to a rectangular shape where the shank is welded to it. It protrudes 1¾ inches above the shank.

Variety c. Very large (fig. 41b). This specimen was found in the southeast casemate (Level II) near the area of the drawbridge. Judging from its size and location, it probably hinged the drawbridge. The shank is 13½ inches long and flares in width from 1⅛ inches at the pin to 1¾ inches at the tip, and tapers in thickness from 1¼ inches at the front of the pin to a point. A hole 1 inch in diameter was drilled through the thickness of the shank 3 inches from the tip. Barbs were cut on the edges to help keep the pintle from sliding out of the wood. The pin is 1½ inches in diameter and rises 2½ inches above the shank.

Type 2. One-piece construction (Stone's Series B, Type 2; L. Stone, 1970, p. 488). All are fashioned from rectangular rods. One end of the rod is hammered to a circular shape, then bent 90 degrees to form the pin. Varieties a and b are beveled at the base of the shank below the pin.

Variety a. Shank rectangular in cross section. The maximum size is at the juncture with the pin, and it tapers on the top and two sides to the point (fig. 40k). One specimen from the bridge area (Level I) is still attached to a hinge. The length of the shanks range from 3¼ to 6 inches; maximum widths range from ½ to 1 inch, maximum thickness ranges from ⅜ to 1½ inches; pin lengths range from 1¼ to 1½ inches; pin diameters are the same measurements as the maximum thickness of the shank.

Variety b. Shanks that were beaten flat. The top of the shank tapers to make the point, while the sides and bottom are parallel (fig. 40h). These range in length from 4¾ to 5¾ inches; in maximum width from ½ to ⅝ inch; in maximum thickness and pin diameter from ⅜ to ½ inch, and in pin length from 1⅛ to 1¾ inches.

Variety c. Very crude with a blunt point (fig. 40g). The tip is missing but there is no taper to any of the shank; consequently, it probably had a blunt end. The one specimen is over 6 inches

long, ½ inch wide, ¾ inch thick and has a 2-inch-high pin. It came from the sally port (Level II).

Type 3. Two-piece construction with the pin welded to the shank (fig. 40l). The pin of this specimen is ½ inch in diameter and 2¼ inches long. The shank was made from a square rod ½ inch thick. Part of the shank and point are missing, but it appears that the top and sides taper to a point.

Type 4. One-piece construction with the shank pounded flat to a triangular shape (Stone's Series A, Type 1; L. Stone, 1970, p. 487). This pintle was attached to the frame with three nails or screws (fig. 40b). The pin is offset from the shank by ½ inch and is ⅜ inch in diameter and 1½ inches high. The tip of the shank is missing but its projected length is 3½ inches. It is 1 inch wide at the pin, about 2 inches wide at the tip and ⅛ inch thick. It came from Level III in the northeast bombproof.

The hinges that were attached to the pintles were so constructed that all were capable of supporting doors to structures. Except for the Type 4 pintle, they would appear to have been driven into wood. Generally, a hole slightly smaller than the pintle was bored in the wood and then the pintle driven in (Orville Carroll, personal communication). This is particularly true of the large pintle for the drawbridge. In addition, a hole perpendicular to the length of the drawbridge pintle had to be bored to pass a pin through the hole in the shank to lock it in.

Hasps

Two type of hasps were found: a two-part hinge type and a one-piece hasp secured by a staple (table 3). The one-piece specimens were more crude in appearance and were probably used to secure doors and shutters rather than box or chest lids.

Type 1. Hinged (fig. 42c). This elaborate specimen is made of steel, and has the configuration of a spear point. The hasp is 4½ inches long. 1⅛ inches in maximum width where the eye was cut, and ⅛-inch thick. The eye is ⅞ inch long, 3/16 inch wide and 2½ inches from the pivot. It came from Level II in the southwest casemate.

Type 2. Slit strap.

Variety a. Strap with cut slit (fig. 42a). This is an iron strap 3/16 by ⅜ inch in which a large

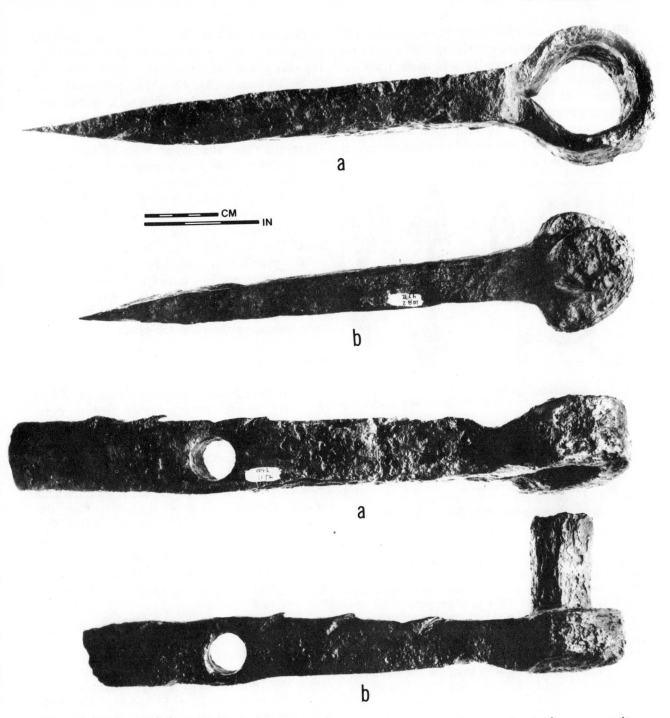

Figure 41. a, Type 3 hinge from the bridge area, LevelXIII; **b,** Type 1c pintle from the southeast casemate, Level II.

slit was cut and spread to form the eye, and a smaller slit cut at the other end for attachment. It is approximately 9 inches long, 1¼ inches in maximum width, and has a 90-degree bend. The eye is 2 inches long and ½ inch wide. A U-shaped

fastener was used to secure the hasp and to give it the mobility necessary to slip on and off the catch. It came from the southwest bombproof (Level II).

Variety b. Two rods welded together (fig.

42b). These were constructed of two square rods bent and welded together. The specimen from the guardhouse area (Level II) was made from ¼-inch-square rods welded immediately in front of the eye. The eye is 2 inches long 9/16 inch wide. It was broken behind the eye. The second hasp was made of ⅛ by ¼ inch rods. It also was broken just behind the eye. The elliptical eye is 2¾ inches long and ⅝ inch wide.

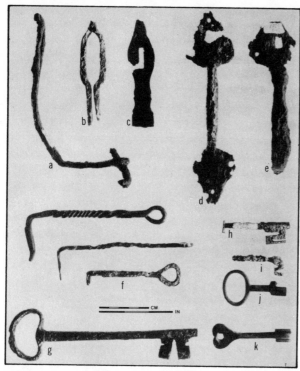

Figure 42. **a.** Type 2a hasp from the southwest bombproof, Level II; **b,** Type 2b hasp from the guardhouse area, Level II; **c,** Type 1 hasp from the southwest casemate, Level II; **d-e,** door pulls from the northeast bombproof, Level I and the southwest bombproof, Level III; **f,** door hooks from Feature 60, Level II, the north casemate, Level I and the east barracks, Level I; **g-h,** Type 1a keys from Feature 76 and the sally port, Level II; **i,** Type 1b key from the southwest bombproof, Level II; **j,** Type 3 key from Feature 76; **k,** Type 2 key from Feature 60, Level III.

Door Pulls

Three door pulls were found, one each from the southwest bombproof (Level III), northeast bombproof (Level I), and the ditch (Level XI). The first two have spear-shaped plates with a rectangular latch hole in one plate. One specimen was made from a round rod ½ inch in diameter (fig. 42d), and the other from a rectangular strip ½ by 3/16 inch (fig. 42e). The pull made from the round rod is approximately 8 inches long with plates 2½ inches long and 2 inches wide. The handle is 3 inches long and offset 1¼ inches. There are three attachment holes in each plate. The specimen made from a strap is approximately 9 inches long with one plate approximately 2¼ inches long and 2 inches wide. The other plate has rusted away. The handle is 4 inches long and offset 1¾ inches. The plate has three attachment holes. The third pull, from the ditch, has semicircular plates. It is made from a strap ¼ by ½ inch. It measures 7⅞ inches long with plates 2 inches wide and 1¼ inches long. The handle is 4 inches long and offset 1¾ inches. There are three attachment holes in the plates.

Door Hooks

Five door hooks without eyes were excavated (fig. 42f). Staples were probably used as eyes, and also to secure the hooks to either the door or frame. Square rods were used to form the hooks. One end was wound around a mandrel to form an eye, the shank has been twisted a number of times to give it a decorative effect, and the end opposite the eye is bent 90 degrees to form the hook, which is tapered to a point. Of the five specimens, two are from the north casemate (Levels I and II), two from the west barracks (Level I and Feature 60, Level II) and one from the east scarp (Level II). They range in length from 3¾ to 5½ inches.

Locks

Stock locks were commonly used for doors during the 18th century. A large specimen from the guardhouse area (Level I) and one small lock each from the southwest casemate (Level II) and east scarp (Level II) were found. The large lock has a cover plate 7 inches long and 4 inches wide. The arms of the U-shaped spring are 3 inches and 3¾ inches long. The ward and bolt are missing. The small locks are fragmentary and badly corroded. They are approximately one half the size of the large specimen. No 18th-century padlocks were found.

Keys

The keys of the Gates to be delivered to the Captain of the Day as soon as Tattooe beating is over, who is to be carefull in observing that the Gates are well locked . . . (M. Willett, 9/2/77)

In addition to the gates, all chests, trunks and probably some building entrances were under lock and key. Eleven whole and fragmentary keys were found (table 3). Three specimens are made of brass, seven of wrought iron and one of steel.

Type 1. A large and fairly complex web which extends in one direction from the pin.

Variety a. Solid pin with no collar (fig. 42g, h). A large specimen from Feature 76 is 7¼ inches long, and may have been used with a gate lock. The semicircular bow is 1⅛ by 2 inches, the stem is 4½ inches long, the web 1¼ by 1 inch, and the pin 1⅜ inches long, extending ⅜ inch in front of the web. A smaller specimen from the sally port (Level II) is missing the bow; the stem is 1½ inches long, the web ¾ by ½ inch and the pin 1 inch long, extending ¼ inch in front of the web.

Variety b. Hollow pin (fig. 42i). This key revolved on a pin in the lock. Two incomplete specimens were found, both about 3½ inches long. One came from the southwest bombproof (Level II) and the other from the north casemate (Level I).

Type 2. Narrow web expanding in two directions from the pin (fig. 42k). One brass specimen has a heart-shaped bow with a round hole cut in the center. The key is 3⅛ inches long, the stem 1⅛ inches long with no collar. The pin is hollow, ⅝ inch long, and does not extend in front of the web. The web is ⅛ inch wide on both sides of the pin. It came from Feature 60 (Level III).

Type 3. No web. The stem has a specially shaped hollow pin (fig. 42j). Two similar specimens were found, one of cast brass from Feature 76 and one of iron from Feature 63 (Level II). The iron key has a longer stem but otherwise is identical to the brass specimen. The keys measure 2½ and 3 inches in length; the bows are oval shaped, 1 by 1½ inches. The stems are ¾ and 1⅜ inches long, ending in diamond shaped pins ⅝ inch long and ⅜ inch wide on a side.

Category 1. Five additional iron specimens are too fragmentary to type.

Window Glass

Window glass was found scattered over most of the site but clearly much was of 19th- and 20th-century origin. A total of 3,076 fragments were found in pre-1781 context. These range in thickness from .8 to 3.2 mm. The mean and standard deviation for this sample is 1.59 mm. and .4079 respectively. A "refined" sample restricted to the undisturbed cellar holes of the two

Table 4.

Distribution of thicknesses of window glass in wood and clay lined cellar holes.

	East Barracks			West Barracks				
	Wood	Clay	Clay	Wood	Wood	Wood	Clay	Clay [1]
.8-.9 mm.		5	1			1		1
1-1.1 mm.	25	36	4	3	8	6	3	5
1.2-1.3 mm.	23	36	8	10	16	12	5	3
1.4-1.5 mm.	29	41	18	11	21	5	5	4
1.6-1.7 mm.	15	24	8	12	26	16	13	6
1.8-1.9 mm.	13	14	6	14	19	9	20	2
2-2.1 mm.	9	10	6	23	9	5	12	2
2.2-2.3 mm.	3	6		3	3			
2.4-2.5 mm.		2			1		2	
2.6-2.7 mm.		2			2			4
2.8-2.9 mm.	1			1	1			
3-3.1 mm.	1	1						5
3.2-3.3 mm.								3
Total	119	177	51	77	106	54	60	35
Mean	1.48	1.47	1.52	1.74	1.63	1.53	1.74	1.88
Standard Deviation	.3810	.3919	.2993	.3486	.3600	.3400	.3066	.7375

[1] Distributed by utility lines.

barracks (644 specimens) has a mean thickness of 1.57 mm. and a standard deviation of .3736. There is a statistical significance at a level of .01 in the thickness of the glass between several of the cellars and trash dumps of the fort (table 4) but this cannot be explained in terms of time, spatial distribution, or the type of cellar in which the glass was found. John Walker (J. Walker, 1971, p. 78), has suggested that window glass in the 19th century was made thicker with the passage of time. The window glass at Fort Stanwix supports his conclusions but does not refine his method since there is obviously a minimum thickness for window glass which was still in use until ca. 1840 (J. Walker, 1971, p. 78). A conversion to means instead of ranges as used by Walker might enable us to extend the utility of the hypothesis but we lack the data from other sites necessary to develop this. By presenting our data in some detail we hope to stimulate such a development.

No clustering of glass fragments was found which might indicate the location of windows in the structures. Two panes, one in the north casemate (Level III) and one in the west barracks (Level II), were 7 inches along one edge and at least 3 inches in the other dimension. The Thomas DeWitt powderhorn (dated 1778), shows windows with cross pieces suggesting four panes of glass for all the buildings on the parade ground, but this may have been artistic license.

During the siege, St. Leger sent emissaries to the fort. These were "conducted blindfolded into the fort, and received by Colonel Gansevoort in his dining room. The windows of the room were shut, and candles lighted . . ." (W. Willett, 1831, p. 55). This room was probably darkened by shutters over the windows. Such shutters would have been necessary in the winter to conserve heat, and probably served incidentally to protect the glass from breakage during a siege.

Bricks

At Fort Stanwix in 1758, the British had ". . . got 40000 Bricks ready to Burn for the Chimneys & propose another kiln of 100000" . . . (Abercromby Papers: Stanwix to Abercromby, Sept. 5, 1758). It is very probable that all the bricks used in constructing the fort were produced locally. There are no comparable American records to verify this, however. The bricks were fired

an orange-red; a few were over-fired and glazed on one side. All were hand made, and contained a large amount of sand. X's were scratched on one side of four bricks, and another was impressed by the paw of a large dog.

Dimensions of the measured bricks: length, 6⅞ to 8½ inches, median 8¼ inches; standard deviation, .4575; width, 3¼ to 4⅜ inches, median 3⅞ inches, standard deviation, .1969; thickness, 1⅝ to 2½ inches, median, 2⅛ inches, standard deviation, .1546. Although they average slightly longer and narrower than 19th-century bricks from the site, it should be noted that the difference is not statistically significant at a level of .05.

Bricks were concentrated in the cellars of the east and west barracks and on the parade ground side of fireplaces in the casemates. The latter were probably pushed over by the weight of the collapsing curtain walls, and the former were apparently dumped into the cellars while clearing the site since they were not found in the fill adjacent to the cellars.

Mortar

All mortar found in the fort consisted of burned lime with a high percentage of sand. Color was generally a light cream white. Samples were saved for comparative purposes, and as models for the reconstruction. "Lyme-stone" was sent to the fort along with boards for the 1777 reconstruction (Gansevoort-Lansing Papers, May 14, 1777).

Weapons

Only scattered parts of weapons were found (table 5). Most appear to have been broken and then discarded. Several pieces of brass furniture from guns had been burned in a fire, probably one of those that destroyed the fort in 1774 or 1781. Most of the brass furniture was marked on the back with engraved Roman numerals. The greatest concentration of musket parts was recovered in the west barracks. Sources used in identifying parts are Darling (1970), Neumann (1967) and Peterson (1968).

Muskets

Sling Swivels. Nine sling swivels were excavated, one of brass from the ravelin (Level II), the re-

Table 5.

Distribution of weapons, weapon parts and accouterments. (Ratios given are the number of specimens per 10 square feet of excavated area within the structure.)

	N	W	SW (Casemates)	SE (Casemates)	E (Casemates)	E (Barracks)	W (Barracks)	Guard-house	Head-quarters	Bomb-proofs NE	Bake-house NW	Ditch	Ravelin	East Scarp	Sally Port	Camp'l Coll.	Totals
Sling swivels				1	4									2	2		9
Triggers					1			1					2		1	1	6
Trigger plates					1									1			2
Trigger guards	5			1		1	8						3	1	4	1	24
Lock plates	2					1										1	4
Cocks	1		1		1	1		2						1	1	1	9
Frizzen														1			1
Frizzen springs	1		1														2
Main springs			2														2
Side plates	1			1			7	2								2	13
Escutcheon plates					1		1								1		3
Screws		1	1			1								1			4
Butt plates	1			1	1							1	1	1	1	1	8
Nose caps	1						2										3
Gun barrels						1	1						2	1		1	6
Forward Band																1	1
Ramrod pipes	1		1	1	2	2	3					1	2	1	2	2	18
Ramrod tips			1	1			1							1	1	1	6
Gun worms	2															1	3
Vent picks	2		1					1							2	1	7
Bayonets	5	1	2	1	1	3	3	1			2	1	3	4	1	3	31
Scabbard hooks	6	2	1	3	3	3				1			1	4	3	1	28
Scabbard tips			2		1				2					2	2	2	11
Spear tips											7		2				9
Total weapon parts	28	5	12	6	14	15	30	8	1	1	9	2	13	13	16	22	15 → 210
Ratios		.875	1.250	1.200	4.000	1.272	1.064	2.362	.667	.154	.182	1.837	.455	2.889	2.389	2.558	.811 → 1.073

mainder of iron (fig. 43a). Dimensions: length: 26 to 30 mm., average 29.5 mm.; width, 52 to 59 mm., average, 55.4 mm.; thickness, 4 to 5.5 mm., average, 4.5 mm. These were probably from British Land Pattern-like (Brown Bess) muskets.

Triggers. All specimens were of iron (fig. 43b), and all but one were fragmentary. The complete specimen is 53 mm. high, 25 mm. long and 14 mm. wide. Two others are 14 mm. wide also. These were probably from British Land Pattern-like muskets.

Trigger Plates. Two brass trigger plates with slots 35 mm. long, off-center to the right (fig. 43c) are 19 mm. and 18 mm. wide; one is 9.1 cm. long. One specimen, from Feature 57 (Level IV), is marked on the back with "VIII" and the other, from Level II on the east scarp, "VIIII." These would be from British Land Pattern muskets.

Trigger Guards. All were made of brass and so fragmentary that complete measurements are not possible (fig. 43e). Four specimens are marked: one from Level XI below the bridge with two stamped "W's" and an "XIIIII"; one from Feature 69 (Level II) with a stamped "Y"; one from the east casemate with "VIII" and "VIIII" and one from Feature 57 (Level III) simply "VIII." All were from British Long Land Pattern muskets.

Lock Plates. All were made of iron and contained the firing mechanism of flint lock firearms. None are marked and all are badly corroded.

Type 1. One specimen (fig. 43g) is 14.5 cm. long and 2.8 cm. high with a flash pan 2.5 cm. wide. It has five screw holes and still retains the cock with a French gunflint, sear, sear spring, tumbler and frizzen spring. Judging by its size, it was probably from a large pistol or American rifle. It was found in Level I of the north casemate.

Type 2. Three specimens, all with 10 screw holes, are 17.2 cm. long and 3.2 cm. high with a flash pan 3.0 cm. wide (fig. 43h). All had been stripped of parts. The curvature suggests early British Long Land Pattern muskets, but these may have been American copies. They were found in

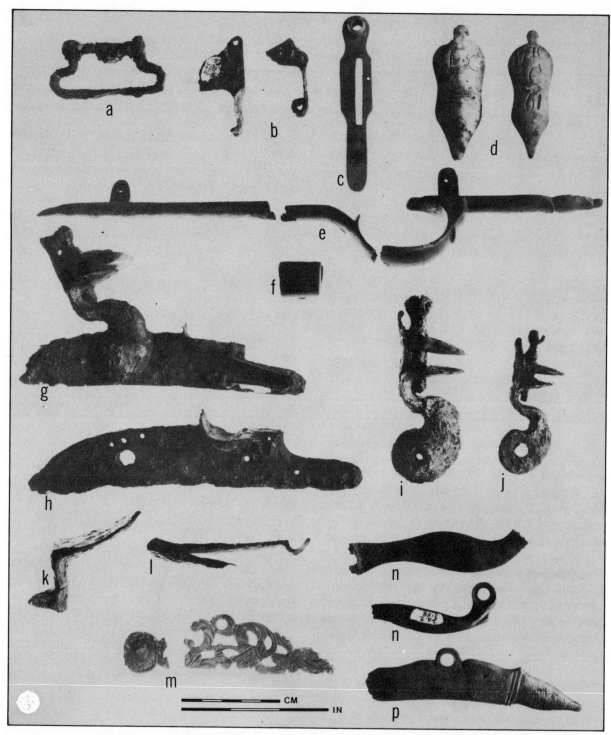

Figure 43. a, sling swivel from the sally port, Level II; **b,** triggers from the east casemate, Level II and the east scarp, Level II; **c,** trigger plate from the east scarp, Level II; **d,** escutcheon plates from Feature 57, Level IV and the sally port, Level II; **e,** trigger guard fragments from the bridge area. Level XI and Feature 57, Level III (2); **f,** nose cap from Feature 57, Level III; **g,** Type 1 lock plate from the north casemate, Level I; **h,** Type 2 lock plate from the north casemate, Level II; **i,** Type 1 gun cock from the guardhouse area, Level II; **j,** Type 2 gun cock from Feature 69, Level II; **k,** frizzen from ravelin, Level I; **l,** main spring from the southwest casemate, Level I; **m,** Type 1 side plate from Feature 3, Level III; **n,** Type 2 side plates from Feature 57, Level III and the north casemate, Level II; **p,** Type 3 side plate from Feature 57, Level III.

the north casemate (Level II), Feature 69 (Level II) and the sally port (Level II). Two found at Fort Ligonier (Grimm, 1970, p. 91) are 18.1 and 18.3 cm. long and are more likely from British issue weapons.

Cocks. All specimens are of iron; only three are complete. They held the gunflint which struck a steel frizzen to ignite a priming charge in the flash pan. All are from British Land Pattern muskets, except Types 2 and 4, which are probably pistol or rifle cocks.

Type 1. Four specimens have a height of 90 mm.; jaw widths of 26 to 27 mm. and a jaw screw length of 49 mm. (fig. 43i). Three jaws have hollows and two have teeth for gripping gunflints. They were found in the east casemate (Level I), in the guardhouse area (Level II) and in Features 48 and 76.

Type 2. Two specimens have a height of 70 mm., jaw widths of 18 to 19 mm. and a jaw screw length of 36 mm. (fig. 43j). One was broken and repaired by brazing. They were found in the guardhouse area (Level II) and Feature 69 (Level II).

Type 3. One fragment with a jaw screw length of 45 mm. was recovered. This specimen had been broken and repaired by brazing. It came from the sally port (Level II).

Type 4. One specimen with a height of 84 mm., jaw width of 23 mm. and jaw screw length of 42 mm. (fig. 43g). This is the cock on the lock plate found in the north casemate (Level I).

Frizzen. One steel frizzen fragment was found in the ravelin (Level I) (fig. 43k). It is 32 mm. wide, and was probably from a British Land Pattern musket.

Frizzen Springs. Two steel frizzen springs were recovered. One from Feature 50 measurements 7.0 cm. long. It is probably from a British Land Pattern musket; the second is 4.7 cm. long and on the lock plate found in the north casemate. These specimens held the frizzen in place over the flash pan to receive the blow of the gunflint.

Main Springs. Two steel main springs 82 mm. long were found (fig. 43l). These forced the cock forward when the trigger was pulled. The specimens are probably from British Land Pattern muskets. They were found in the southwest casemate (Level I and Feature 48).

Side Plates. All were made of brass and all were fragmentary. They were mounted on the stock opposite the lock plate and were fastened to it with screws.

Type 1. A thin excised brass plate, probably from a pistol, came from Feature 3 (Level III) (fig. 43m). It is over 10 cm. long but broken.

Type 2. Ten plano-convex "serpentine" plates, probably with two screw holes (fig. 43n). Five are marked on the back. One specimen from the north casemate (Level I) has a broad arrow and the number "1" stamped on it, and the engraved Roman numeral "XV." Two others from Feature 57 (Level III) were stamped "XIII." One, from Feature 57 (Level III), has a stamped "G," and part of a Roman numeral is stamped on another from Feature 60 (Level II). These were from British Land Pattern muskets.

Type 3. One specimen is a flat plate, probably with two screw holes (fig. 43p). This has been identified as from a 1751 Spanish infantry musket by an arms collector, but we have doubts about this identification. It came from Feature 57 (Level II).

Escutcheon Plates. Brass plates mounted on top of the stock and fastened with screws to the trigger guards (fig. 43d). One measures 62 by 28 mm. and is engraved on the front with "L x C". On the back it has an "XIII" and a stamped "C". It came from Feature 57 (Level IV). Another, from the sally port (Level II). measures 65 by 24 mm. and is engraved on the front with "17 R^t". "C", "61". A stamped broad arrow appears on the back. This specimen is probably part of a musket taken from the British 17th Regiment of Foot in 1779 at Stony Point, New York since it was in a post-1776 context. Two companies of the 17th were stationed at Fort Stanwix in 1763 (Gage, 1931, p. 210). The third specimen, from the east casemate (Level II), is partially melted, but has a Roman numeral on the front. These were from British Land Pattern muskets.

Screws. Four brass screws, 24 mm. long, probably came from weapons. Two are 4 mm. in diameter and two are 5 mm. in diameter. The heads range in diameter from 10 to 15 mm. These were probably from British Land Pattern muskets.

Butt Plates. These specimens are all made of brass.
Type 1. Three plates made from sheet brass

were nailed to the butt of the stock (fig. 44q). Length, 12.8 cm. (one specimen); width, 3.4 cm., 4.4 cm. and 5.0 cm.; thickness, 1 mm. These were probably American made. They came from the north casemate (Level III), Feature 72 (Level II) and the west ditch (backfill).

Type 2. Five specimens cast with a tang projecting over the stock, and held on by screws (fig. 44p). Length, 12.3 cm. (one specimen); width, 4.9 to 5.0 cm.; thickness, 2 to 3 mm. These were from British Land Pattern muskets. They were found in the east casemate (Level I), on the east scarp (Level II), in Feature 76, in the bakehouse area (Level I) and in the Campbell collection.

Nose Caps. Made of brass and fitted over the end of the stock near the muzzle of the weapon (fig. 43f). They were probably from British Land Pattern muskets.

Type 1. Two specimens are 22 to 25 mm. long. These had a single hole for mounting; one retained a brass rivet in place. They were found in Feature 57 (Level III) and the north casemate (Level I).

Type 2. One specimen, 23 mm. long, with two mounting holes and a groove on the underside for the ramroad came from Feature 57 (Level III).

Gun Barrels. These specimens were made of wrought iron.

Type 1. Two specimens were from .75 cal. smoothbore muskets. Both are fragmentary, but one from the north ditch (Level II) still retained the breech plug. It tapers from 3.2 to 2.3 cm. in diameter. The other, 2.3 cm. in diameter, is a short fragment with an iron bayonet stud brazed onto it 5.0 cm. from the muzzle. This came from Feature 72 (Level II). These were from British Land Pattern-like muskets.

Type 2. One specimen from Feature 76 is a .69 cal. smoothbore musket barrel with an exterior diameter of 2.3 cm. A mounting notch for a ramrod pipe is situated 20 cm. from the muzzle. The grain of this barrel makes a complete turn every 13 cm. One end was hammered flat and the other showed pounding from use as a tent peg. Origin is uncertain.

Type 3. One specimen from the north ditch (Level VIII) is a .66 cal. smoothbore pistol barrel 14.9 cm. long, with the breech plug intact (fig.

45c). It tapers from 2.9 to 2.0 cm. at the muzzle and has a mounting notch for a ramrod pipe 6.2 cm. from the muzzle.

Type 4. Two specimens are .44 cal. smoothbore musket barrels with an exterior diameter of 1.8 cm. One specimen from Feature 57 (Level III) has a notch for a ramrod pipe 11 cm. from the muzzle. One end has been flattened and a hole punched through it. The other came from the Campbell collection. These were probably American made.

Forward Band. A single iron forward band, probably from a French weapon, was found by Campbell.

Ramrod Pipes. These specimens secured the ramrod to the bottom of the stock and were fastened to the stock by pins. All were made of brass.

Type 1. Cast forward pipe with two mounting lugs. One specimen, 10.3 cm. long, (fig. 44d), was from a British Land Pattern musket with a steel ramrod. It came from the sally port (Level II).

Type 2. Cast forward pipes with one mounting lug. Four specimens were broken or partly melted, but are about 6.0 cm. long. These were probably from British Land Pattern muskets. They were found in the east barracks (Level I) the bakehouse hearth and Feature 57 (one in Level III and one in Level IV).

Type 3. Cast 2d pipes with one mounting lug. Nine specimens are from 3.1 to 4.0 cm. long (fig. 44b). These were from British Land Pattern muskets.

Type 4. Cast tail pipe with one mounting lug. Length, 74 mm. (fig. 44a). This was from a British Land Pattern musket and was found in the south ditch (Level XI).

Type 5. Sheet 2d pipes bent to form a mounting lug. Three specimens are from 2.8 to 3.7 cm. long (fig. 44c). These were almost certainly of American origin (Neumann, 1967, p. 96). They came from the north ditch (Level X), the sally port (Level II) and the southeast casemate (Level I).

Ramrod Tips. No iron "button-tipped" ramrods were found, but six brass tips for wooden ramrods were recovered (fig. 44e). Two from the sally port (Level II) and Feature 76 are marked with stamped broad arrows. All are truncated brass

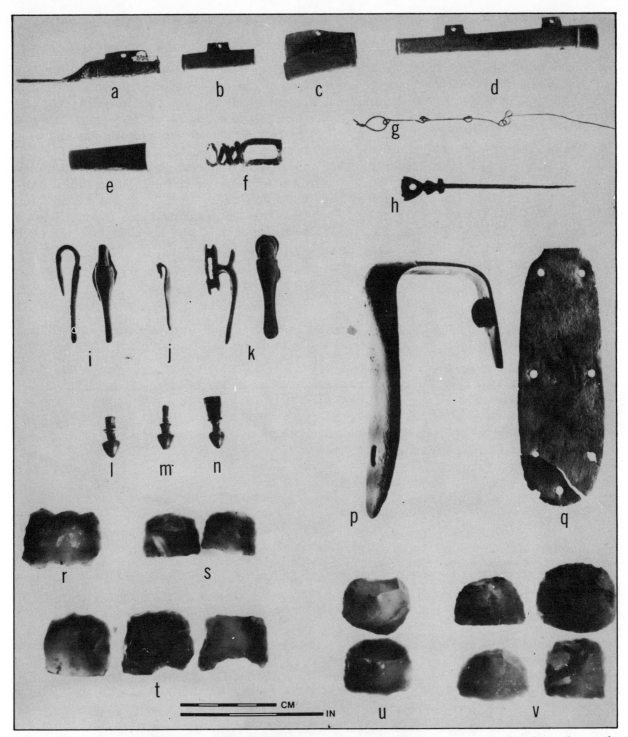

Figure 44. **a,** Type 4 ramrod pipe from the bridge area, Level XI; **b,** Type 3 ramrod pipe from the north casemate, Level III; **c,** Type 5 ramrod pipe from the sally port, Level II; **d,** Type 1 ramrod pipe from the sally port, Level II; **e,** ramrod tip from the southeast casemate, Level I; **f,** Type 2 gun worm from the sally port, Level II; **g,** Type 1 vent pick from the sally port, Level II; **h,** Type 2 vent pick from the southwest casemate, Level II; **i,** Type 1 scabbard hooks from the west casemate, Level III and Feature 60, Level II; **j,** Type 2 scabbard hook from the north casemate, Level II; **k,** Type 3 scabbard hooks from the east casemate, Level I and the sally port. Level III; **l,** Type 2a scabbard tip from the guardhouse area, Level II; **m,** Type 2b scabbard tip from the sally port, Level II; **n,** Type 2c scabbard tip from the ravelin, Level II; **p,** Type 2 butt plate from the east scarp, Level III; **q,** Type 1 butt plate from Feature 72, Level III; **r,** Type 1 French gunflint from the southwest casemate, Level II; **s,** Type 3 French gunflints from Feature 69, Level II and the southwest casemate, Level III; **t,** Type 2 French gunflints from the west barracks, Level I, the east barracks, Level I and Feature 69, Level II; **u,** Type 1 Dutch gunflints from Feature 69, Level III and the sally port, Level II; **v,** Type 2 Dutch gunflints from Feature 52, Level III; Feature 60, Level III, the bridge area, Level XI and the east casemate, Level II.

cones with an end brazed onto them. The following calibers were found: one .70 cal., two .64 cal. and three .63 cal. These undoubtedly served larger caliber weapons, probably .75 cal. British Land Pattern muskets.

Gun Worms. These specimens were made of iron and designed to extract lead balls from a musket to unload it.

Type 1. Single prong. One specimen from the north casemate (Level I) measures .31 cal.

Type 2. Double prong (fig. 44f). Two specimens measure .56 cal. and .62 cal. They came from the sally port (Level II) and the north casemate (Level I) respectively.

Vent Picks. These were used to clean the vent hole from the flash pan through the barrel of the weapon.

Type 1. Brass wire picks on brass chains (fig. 44g). Five specimens had a wire pick with a loop at one end to attach it to the chain. Three consist of chains only. One from the sally port (Level II) measures 14 cm. long from the tip of the pick to a loop that probably fastened to a button hole on a soldier's waistcoat.

Type 2. Cast brass picks (fig. 44h). Two specimens were cast or stamped with a drilled decorative finial. They are 9.2 cm. and 6.7 cm. long. One from the guardhouse area (Level II) has a heart-shaped finial and the other from the south west casemate (Level II) appears to be a thistle.

Bayonets

Steel bayonet fragments were scattered over the entire site. All had triangular blades and were

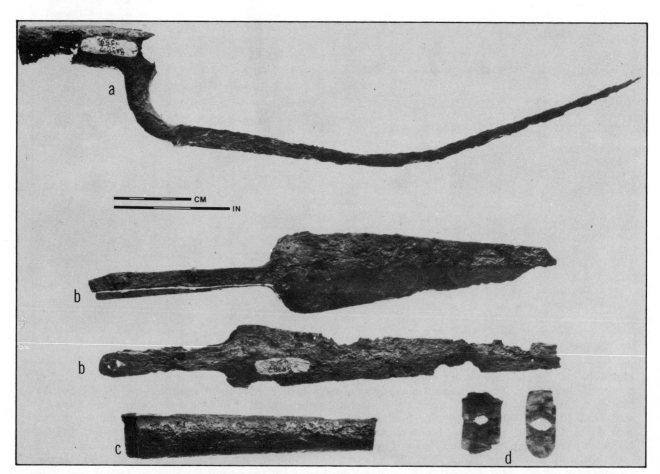

Figure 45. a, bayonet from the northwest bombproof, Level II; **b,** spear tips from the northwest bombproof, Level II; **c,** Type 3 pistol barrel from the north ditch, Level VIII; **d,** gunflint pads from the main gate area, Level II (2).

probably of a British pattern (Peterson, 1968, p. 85), including one from the northwest bombproof (Level II) which is stamped "US" on the blade (fig. 45a). Another from the west casemate (Level II) is stamped with what appears to be a rampant lion, but not the British East India Company mark (Darling, 1970, p. 54). The most complete blades are 36.5 cm. long (14.4 inches) with a maximum width of 3.0 to 3.5 cm. The sockets have an interior diameter of 2.2 to 2.5 cm., and none have a clasp to secure the bayonet to the musket. The blade edges of two fragments from Feature 69 (Level II) were hammered together until they touched, but the function of these is unknown.

Scabbard Hooks

These brass hooks were used to attach scabbards to a belt. Apparently they pulled out of the leather quite easily, as several were intact and leather was still attached to two specimens. A scabbard hook similar to Type 1, but made of iron, was found at Fort Ligonier, 1758-1766 (Grimm, 1970, p. 127). Type 3 was also the most common type at Fort Ligonier (Grimm, 1970, p. 127).

Type 1. Three specimens, 51 to 52 mm. long (fig. 44i), were attached by inserting a triangular projection through the leather. They were found in the west casemate (Level II), Feature 60 (Level I) and a disturbed area of the west barracks.

Type 2. One specimen from the north casemate (Level II) is 35 mm. long (fig. 44j). It appears to have been soldered on to another plate which was then attached to the leather.

Type 3. Twenty-four specimens (table 5) are from 47 to 57 mm. long with an average of 53.2 mm. (fig. 44k). They were attached by two rivets and a backing plate to the leather. The leather was 2 to 4 mm. thick.

Scabbard Tips

Type 1. A folded brass sheath with a brazed seam and a finial in the end was identified as a scabbard tip. It came from the east scarp (Level II) and is 56 mm. long and 23 mm. wide.

Type 2. These specimens are made of solid brass and three varieties were recovered.

Variety a. Short solid post (fig. 44l). Four of these specimens have the following dimensions: length, 21 mm.; diameter, 10 to 12 mm. One still had leather adhering to it. They were found

in the southwest casemate (Level II), the east casemate (Level I), Feature 76 and the sally port (Level II).

Variety b. Long solid post (fig. 44m). Three of these have the following dimensions: length, 24 to 32 mm.; diameter, 9 to 11 mm. They came from the southwest casemate (Level II), the guardhouse area (Level I) and Feature 76.

Variety c. Hollow post (fig. 44n). Three of these have the following dimensions: length, 27 to 43 mm.; diameter 9 to 10 mm. The largest from the sally port (Level II) may have been a Type 2 specimen with a brass sheath around the post. The others came from the guardhouse area (Level II) and the east scarp (Level II).

Spear Tips

These specimens were concentrated in the northwest bombproof (Level II) and the south ditch (Levels I and XV). They are made of wrought iron and none are identical (fig. 45b). All have two tangs between which the wooden shaft was seated. Iron rivets were driven through the tangs and shaft. Blade length: 17 to 29+ cm., average, 20.7 cm.; blade width: 3 to 5 cm.; total length: 21+ to 38.5+ cm., average, 30.4+ cm.; spear shaft diameter: 2 to 3 cm. On August 8, 1777, Lt. Col. Willett and Lt. Stockwell each left Fort Stanwix to get help carrying "a spear . . . eight feet in length . . ." (W. Willett, 1831, p. 60).

Gunflints

A Vein of prodigious fine black flint stone being discovered upon Mount Independence, the General desires the commanding officers of regiments will make enquiry if there are any old countrymen in any of their corps who understand hammering flints. Such person or persons found, to be sent to the General at Head Quarters. (Elmer, 1848, p. 41: Journal entry dated November 10, 1776.)

No record has been found of flint knappers stepping forth to ply their trade, and no gunflints recovered have been made from native chert in Revolutionary War contexts. The journal entry indicates that gunflints were in short supply in the American army.

Gunflints have been divided into five main groupings based on method and locale of manufacture (Witthoft, 1967, pp. 12–49). These are: Aboriginal (American Indian), Nordic, Dutch,

French and English. The Dutch gunflints also have been referred to in the literature as gunspalls. Morphologically, there was little difference in the method of manufacture of American Indian and Nordic gunflints, since both were bifacially chipped and square to rectangular in shape. The Dutch gunflints were struck individually from cores, and generally were plano-convex and D-shaped, with a prominent bulb of percussion on the dorsal surface. They were made in a variety of colors indicative of Riss glacial outwash material (Witthoft, 1967, pp. 25–26). French gunflints were generally of a honey-colored or blond translucent French flint, and were made from segments of long blades struck from a core. English gunflints were similarly made but more prismatic in shape and the flint graded in color from blond to black. Some of the lighter colored English specimens may have been made from imported French flint (Witthoft, 1967, p. 32).

A total of 3,826 gunflints were found at Fort Stanwix, 3,412 of these from a single deposit in Feature 69 (Levels I and II) in the east barracks. Of the total sample, 62.9 percent were Dutch and 37.1 percent French, with one English specimen found in a post-1781 context (Level I). It probably dated from the early 19th century.

Woodward (1960, pp. 29–39) has cited a number of standard sizes for gunflints including Pocket Pistol, Rifle, Musket, Long Dane, etc., for English gunflints, but we believe this was a late development and that prior to the 19th century there was no standardization into size categories. However, there was a wide range of sizes (especially French gunflints) and this needs to be further explored. More recently, Lyle Stone (1971) has proposed a formal classification based on such properties as manufacturing technique, shape, material and color. We applied this method to the Fort Stanwix sample, both as a means of describing that sample and to make comparison easier with the Fort Michilimackinac sample from northern Michigan.

The following terms are used to describe gunflints: The *bed* is the bottom surface; the *edge* is the striking surface at the front; the heel is the back of the gunflint opposite the edge; the *face* is the uppermost surface, usually parallel to the bed, and the *length* is the distance from heel to edge along the axis of the position of a gunflint in the jaws of a gun cock. Length measurements are recorded only for those specimens that do not appear

to have been used. Lyle Stone (1971, pp. 11–19) has established length-width ratios for his types which were tested with our samples.

Basically, Stone's formal analysis was accomplished by classifying the Fort Michilimackinac sample into three series, A, B, and C, based on manufacturing techniques. Series A, corresponding to what we call French gunflints, was subdivided into four types based on their longitudinal cross section. Series B and C, which we call Dutch, had only a single type each but Series C, Type 1, was subdivided into three varieties based on color. Specimens that could be classified by series, but not by type because they had been modified or broken, were placed into categories within the series.

We found no objection to the method as presented, but we encountered one difficulty in its application. Many fragmentary specimens could have been included in either Series B or Series C categories. This problem has been solved by converting Series B and C into types within the same series. At Fort Michilimackinac, Series B gunflints accounted for only .2 percent of the total sample, while at Fort Stanwix they were 10.0 percent of the total sample. Our larger sample shows the same color range as the Series C gunflints. This is in contrast to what Stone found with his much smaller sample (1971, p. 16), which were all of the darker variety (b). In this report we will refer to Series A as French, and Series B and C as Dutch, Types 1 and 2. Table 6 shows the breakdown of these types in the Dutch series by variety.

We feel that the transverse flake scar which distinguishes the Dutch Type 1 specimens from those of Dutch Type 2 is a by-product of the removal of a previous gunflint from the nodule, or core preparation. Therefore, it is likely that both types could have been produced from the same core and there would be no temporal difference. A few examples of Type 2 exhibit flake scars on the bed at the edge or on the side of the gunflint.

The same situation exists for the French gunflints. The flake scars that characterize the four types set up by Stone (1971, pp. 11–16) could have all been produced on a single core. In view of the mass production methods of the 19th century, it seems unlikely that many blades were considered so badly struck to be of no further use, although in some cases there is sufficient data to show that the finished product was later sorted by size or shape (Woodward, 1960, p. 32; C. Smith,

Table 6.

Unmodified Dutch gunflints separated on the basis of color (a, light gray; b, dark gray to black).

	Number	Percentage
Type 1		
Variety a	26	63.4
Variety b	15	36.6
Type 2		
Variety a	65	63.7
Variety b	37	36.3

1960, pp. 60–61). Although we feel that these types (not to be confused with the series) and varieties have little historical significance in terms of relative popularity, this is an unproven assumption, and they are retained for comparative purposes.

The following is a description of the types found and their frequencies on the site. A breakdown by area is shown in table 7.

French, Type 1. Three transverse flake scars form a beveled front and back, and a face parallel to the bed. The heel is generally rounded off with secondary chipping (fig. 44r). Three hundred and two specimens (one chalk heel and 277 burned) have the following dimensions: length, 21.5 to 28.0 mm., average, 24.4 mm.; width, 23.1 to 42.1 mm., average, 28.36 mm.; standard deviation, 4.74; thickness, 4.6 to 12.2 mm., average, 6.80 mm.

Stone (1971, p. 11) presents a regression formula, based on 18 specimens, for estimating length from the known width of used gunflints of this type. We applied his formula to our 15 unmodified French Type 1 gunflints and found that the results were not predictable. The Fort Stanwix specimens average 2.4 mm. longer than the formula would have made them, with individual variations from −1.0 mm. to +5.3 mm. Since length, the second dimension produced by this formula, is based solely on the width, no new information was generated from its application. While length may have been a more critical variable (Stone, 1971, p. 12), there simply are not enough unmodified specimens for meaningful comparisons. During the process of manufacture, there should have been a consistent length-thickness ratio, but this was obscured by secondary shipping on the heel in the finishing process. We attempted a scattergraph of the width-thickness ratio, and concluded that the two variables were unrelated in the final form.

Plotting the distribution of the widths alone shows two distinct size clusters, with a breaking point at 31 mm. There are 105 specimens below 31 mm. in width, and 22 specimens larger than 31 mm. where the width could be measured. Four of the latter were used with strike-a-lights; the smaller specimens were not used in this way. Since most of these specimens were burned and some partly destroyed, it is not possible to make a definitive statement that the larger specimens were intended for use with strike-a-lights. We feel, however, that they are too large to have served as gunflints and they do exhibit wear. If they were not repeatedly struck at the same point they would not exhibit the deep notching that we consider diagnostic of strike-a-light flints. Thus, we tentatively add a second trait, large size, to our definition of strike-a-light flints. We do not mean to imply that some individuals did not occasionally use small gunflints with strike-a-lights. At Fort Ligonier, 1758–1766, (Grimm, 1970, p. 89) there were 18 French gunflints over 31 mm. wide and 12 less than 31 mm. wide, which suggests that the size of French gunflints was decreasing through time although the range was the same for both sites.

French, Type 2. Two transverse flake scars form a beveled front and a face parallel to the bed. The heel is rounded off with secondary chipping (fig. 44t). Dimensions of 415 specimens (one chalk heel and 393 burned) are: length, 23.9 to 34.0 mm., average 26.4 mm.; width, 22.0 to 40.0 mm., average, 27.06 mm.; standard deviation, 3.63; thickness, 3.7 to 13.5 mm., average, 6.74 mm.

As with Type 1, Stone (1971, p. 13) presented a formula for estimating length from width. The Fort Stanwix specimens average 2.7 mm. longer than they should have, according to the formula. A breaking point also occurs in this type with 22 specimens wider than 31.0 mm. and 194 narrower than 31.0 mm. All three of the observed strike-a-lights are of the larger size.

French, Type 3. Two transverse flake scars form a beveled front and back with no face. Heel usually shows secondary chipping (fig. 44s). Dimensions of 79 specimens (one chalk heel and 75 burned) are: width, 22.0 to 39.1 mm., average, 27.50 mm.; standard deviation, 3.36; thickness, 4.2 to 11.0 mm.; average 6.97 mm. No lengths could be measured This type also could be broken into two width size classes at 31.0 mm., with three specimens in the larger class and 33 in the smaller. The only strike-a-light in this type is in the large size.

French, Type 4. A single broad flake scar forms a face parallel to the bed. The heel shows secondary chipping, although on a used specimen it was sometimes difficult to distinguish the heel from the edge. Dimensions of seven specimens are: width, 26.7 to 37.1 mm., average, 31.92 mm.; thickness, 5.7 to 8.5 mm., average, 7.10 mm. No lengths could be measured. There are too few specimens to make any statement about size classes.

French, Category 1. This category includes those specimens which were identifiable as French gunflints, but could not be typed due to breakage, modification or burning. There are 610 specimens in this group; 596 were burned and nine used with strike-a-lights.

Dutch, Type 1. A single bulb of percussion on top of the heel, with a transverse flake scar across the back of the heel on a bevel. There is some secondary chipping on the sides and occasionally on the edge and heel (fig. 44u). Dimensions of 379 specimens (two chalk heels and 338 burned) are: length, 22.0 to 40.0 mm., average 31.18 mm; width, 25.0 to 40.5 mm., average, 33.09 mm.; standard deviation, 3.13; thickness, 4.0 to 12.3 mm., average, 8.65 mm. Unlike the French specimens, these gunflints appear to be a homogeneous sample. Although there is a broad width spectrum, no breaking point could be defined. Seven gunflints were modified by use with strike-a-lights, but none could be measured. It is our impression that the strike-a-light flints have the same size range as the gunflints. The Fort Ligonier (Grimm, 1970, p. 90) sample had the same range and average width as the Fort Stanwix sample. Although most of these specimens were burned, a few were not, and these show color variations ranging from light gray to black. The significance of these variations will be discussed in the following type but the data is presented here for the record.

Variety a. Gray to brown in color. Dimensions of 26 specimens (one used as a strike-a-light) are: length, 25.0 to 36.8 mm., average, 32.52 mm.; width, 28.0 to 39.0 mm., average, 33.3 mm.; thickness, 5.9 to 11.4 mm., average, 9.27 mm.

Variety b. Dark gray to black in color. Dimensions of 15 specimens (two chalk heels and three used as strike-a-lights) are: length, 22.0 to 40.0 mm., average, 32.00 mm.; width, 25.0 to 38.9 mm., average, 33.83 mm.; thickness, 5.2 to 12.3 mm., average, 9.74 mm.

Dutch, Type 2. A single bulb of percussion on top of the heel with secondary chipping on the heel, and some secondary chipping on the sides and edge. A few exhibit a transverse flake scar on the bed (fig. 44v). Dimensions of 1,411 specimens (eight chalk heel and 1,254 burned) are: length, 21.0 to 38.3 mm., average, 30.48 mm.; width, 19.5 to 42.1 mm., average, 33.09 mm.; standard deviation, 3.39; thickness, 4.2 to 13.2 mm., average, 8.38. Some of these gunflints could be divided into two color varieties.

Variety a. Gray to brown in color. Dimensions of 65 specimens (one chalk heel and seven strike-a-lights) are: length, 24.3 to 34.6 mm., average 32.5 mm.; width, 26.9 to 42.1 mm.; average, 33.7 mm.; thickness, 5.8 to 12.0 mm., average, 8.8 mm.

Variety b. Dark gray to black in color. Dimensions of 37 specimens (six chalk heels and seven strike-a-lights) are: length, 25.4 to 36.8 mm., average, 31.9 mm.; width, 31.1 to 42.0 mm., average, 35.5 mm.; thickness, 6.2 to 12.0 mm., average, 9.8 mm. Lyle Stone (1972, pp. 47-49) has suggested that the black Dutch series gunflints (Types 1b and 2b) date prior to the American Revolution and were most prevalent in the 1745-1765 period. Although the sample from Fort Stanwix is small, it seems likely that the black gunflints continued in use later than at Fort Michilimackinac. In the dump on the east scarp (Level II) and in the sally port (Level II) which date post-1776, they constituted 39 percent of the sample (of 33 specimens).

Dutch, Category 1. This category includes those specimens which are identifiable as Dutch gunflints, but could not be typed due to modification or burning. There were 622 specimens in this category; 617 burned and two were used as strike-a-lights.

English. Three transverse flake scars form a beveled front and back and a face parallel to the bed. Small bulbs of percussion appear on each side of the face and there is some secondary chipping on the sides. Only one example was found; length, 24.1 mm.; width, 28.1 mm.; thickness, 7.9 mm. The specimen was found along a 19th-century retaining wall in an area heavily disturbed by tree roots (redout, Level I). It is probably post-1781 in time.

Discounting the large deposit of 3,412 gunflints in Feature 69, there were remarkably few gunflints found at Fort Stanwix, considering the span of time it was occupied. In the Feature 69 deposit, all the flints were burned and concentrated in the fill of one corner of the clay-lined cellar hole and the adjacent ground surface. Perhaps they represent a deliberate collection of discarded gunflints, since nearly all appear to have been used. An unresolved question is why anyone would bother to gather up worn-out gunflints in the first place.

A series of wood or clay-lined cellar holes was situated under the east and west barracks. Two of the wood-lined cellars (Features 56 and 63) were intruded by clay-lined cellars (Features 57 and 64) and we suspect that the wood-lined holes were pre-1776, while those that were clay-lined date from the Revolutionary War period. Although the presence of gunflints alone is not proof of this hypothesis, no French gunflints were found in the wood-lined cellars (23 found were Dutch) and, with the exception of the large deposit in Feature 69, there were 22 Dutch and 22 French specimens in the clay-lined cellars.

Although there is some frequency variation between units as shown on table 7, this variation was not statistically significant for the size of the samples. Even the known post-1776 deposits do not differ markedly from the rest of site.

Comparative data on gunflints are scant. It has been suggested elsewhere (Hanson, 1970, pp. 51–58; 1971b, p. 109) that the relative frequency of gunflints could be used as an indicator to the age of a site. Table 8 lists selected late 18th-century sites and the percentages of Dutch and French Series gunflints reported as a test of this hypothesis. There is no doubt that French gunflints were supplanting Dutch specimens in the last half of the 18th century, and that this change was gradually increasing in pace toward the end of the century. The Fort Leboeuf sample, while small, serves to point out that this process was subject to local variation due to factors we cannot control at the present time. Given the known shift in popularity of gunflint series it should be possible to develop a regression formula such as Binford (1962) has done for pipe stems or South (1972) for ceramics. The main problem is a lack of large documented samples. At the present time we feel that Dutch gunflints first appeared about 1650 (Witthoft, 1967) and remained in use until after 1780. French gunflints first appeared at North American sites about 1735 (Stone, 1971) and remained in use until about 1820 (Witthoft, 1967). English gunflints appeared after 1780 (Witthoft, 1967).

Table 7.

Distribution of gunflints. (Those found in the East Barracks include 2,145 Dutch and 1,267 French specimens from a single deposit.)

	Dutch		French		
	Number	Percent	Number	Percent	Total
Casemates					
North	38	62.3	23	37.7	61
West	3		2		5
Southwest	9		8		17
Southeast	24		2		26
East	29	65.9	15	34.1	44
Barracks					
East	2,174	62.9	1,284	37.1	3,458
West	34	54.8	28	45.2	62
Ditch	11		4		15
Ravelin	11		5		16
Sally Port	26	55.3	21	44.7	47
East Scarp	24	70.9	9	29.1	33
Elsewhere	11		9		20
Campbell					
Collection	18		3		21
Total	2,412	63.1	1,413	36.9	3,825

Table 8.

Comparison of sites by frequency percentage of gunflints.

	Dates	Dutch Percentage	French Percentage	Sample Size
Valley Forge, Pa.	1777	41.7	58.3	127
Fort Stanwix, N.Y.	1758-1781	62.9	37.1	3,825
Fort Ligonier, Pa.	1758-1766	82.2	17.8	275
Fort Leboeuf, Pa.	1755-1757	77.8	22.2	45
Fort Michilimackinac, Mich.	1745-1765	84.8	15.2	118
Fort Michilimackinac, Mich.	1715-1781	86.3	13.7	2,536
Fort Frederica, Ga.	1736-1748	87.5	12.5	56

The increase in French gunflint frequency (at the expense of Dutch gunflints) started accelerating between 1765 and 1770 so that "pure" Revolutionary War sites should have a relatively high percentage of French gunflints to Dutch (over 30 percent) and no English gunflints.

Gunflint Pads

Four lead gunflint pads were found in the guardhouse area (Level II), main gate area (two) (Level II) and on the east scarp (Level II) (fig. 45d). These are scraps of lead with a hole cut in the center and folded over the gunflints to hold them firmly in the jaws of a musket cock. The hole was cut to fit around the jaw screw.

Ordnance

Cannon Balls

Thirty-two solid iron cannon balls were excavated at Fort Stanwix (table 9). These were typed by weight. The only distinction that can be made between them is the presence of broad arrows on a few specimens. Mold markings appear to have no significance, although the variety suggests at least three sources of supply. These con-

sist of the presence or absence of a mold seam, a depression on one side away from the seam, or a depression surrounded by a depressed ring on one side away from the seam. Some balls show none of these markings. The only correlation is that all the depressions with a ring around them are present on balls with mold seams.

Type 3. 3-pounders (fig. 46a). These have diameters of 2.68 to 2.79 inches with an average of 2.75 inches.

Type 4. 4-pounders. These have diameters of 3.00 and 3.01 inches.

Type 6. 6-pounders (fig. 46b). These have diameters of 3.41 to 3.52 inches with an average of 3.47 inches.

Variety a. Plain, except for mold markings. Seven specimens were found. The largest from Feature 69 (Level II) is malformed, almost hemispherical in shape. It was not intended for bar shot and appears to be a miscast ball.

Variety b. Marked with a broad arrow. Four specimens were found. Three were in the southwest casemate (two in Level II and one in Feature 51) the fourth on the east scarp (Level II). The broad arrow is indicative of British ordnance, but there is no evidence whether these dated from the British occupation, were fired at the fort, or were captured stores.

Table 9.

Distribution of cannonballs, mortar bomb fragments, hand grenade and cannister shot.

	Cannonballs					16	Mortar Bomb Fragments		Hand Grenade	Canister Shot
	3	4	5	6	12		4.5	10		
Casemates										
North	1				1		26			14
West							1			1
Southwest				5			1			8
Southeast				1						2
East							12			7
Barracks										
East	5	1	1	2			67			403
West				1			4			20
Guardhouse							15			12
Parade Ground							22			2
Bombproofs										
Northeast	1			1			1			88
Northwest	1					1				3
Southwest	4						1			5
Bakehouse							4			3
Ditch	2		1		1		9	1		26
Ravelin										1
East Scarp		1		1			8			4
Sally Port							9			5
Campbell										
Collection							1		1	5
Totals	14	2	2	11	2	1	181	1	1	609

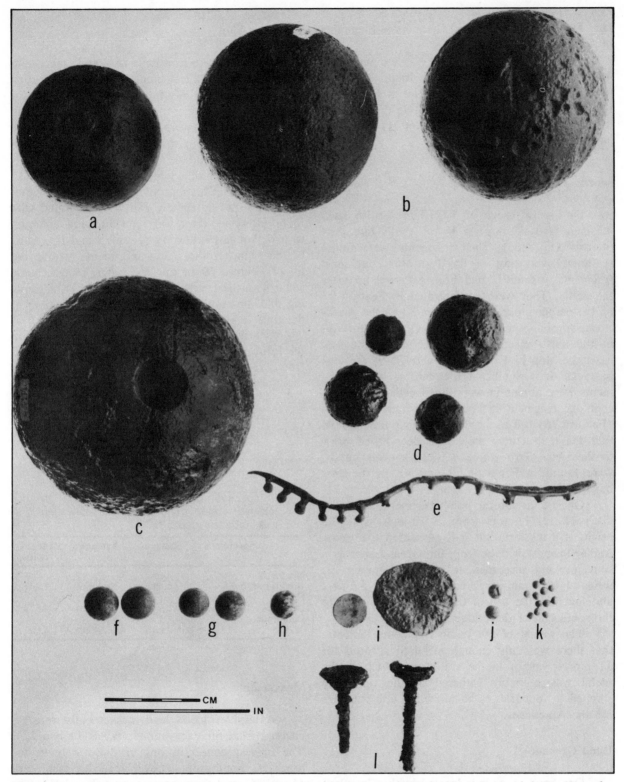

Figure 46. a, Type 3 cannonball from the southwest bombproof, Level II; **b,** Type 6 cannonballs from the northeast bombproof, Level II and the southwest casemate, Level II (note the broad arrow); **c,** 4.5-inch mortar shell from Feature 72, Level II; **d,** cannister shot from Feature 69, Levels II and III; **e.** lead sprue from the east casemate, Level I; **f,** .69 caliber musket balls from the north casemate, Level II; **g,** .63 caliber musket balls from the north casemate, Level II; **h,** .53 caliber musket ball with untrimmed sprue from the north casemate, Level II; **i,** cut and chewed musket balls from the north casemate, Levels III and II; **j,** buckshot from the east barracks, Level II; **k,** birdshot from the east barracks, Level II; **l,** cannon primers (?) from the sally port, Level II.

Type 12. 12-pounder. These have diameters of 4.38 and 4.43 inches.

Type 16. 16-pounder. This has a diameter of 4.56 inches. No records could be found of a cannon of this weight ever having been at Fort Stanwix. The ball was located just outside the entrance to the northwest bombproof (Level II) and may have been used as a doorstop.

Mortar Bombs

During the siege of 1777, the British used 4.5-inch "Royal" mortars to lob shells into Fort Stanwix (fig. 46c). Shell fragments were found scattered over most of the fort area, but most fragments apparently had been gathered up after the battle. They were concentrated in Feature 73 on the parade ground and Feature 58 by the guardhouse (probably temporary privies), in Feature 34 in the north casemate and Level II in the east casemate, and in Features 69 and 72 in the east barracks. It is significant that mortar bomb fragments were absent in wood-lined cellar holes, except one fragment in Feature 52, and the trench (Feature 76) before the ravelin. It is quite possible that these structures may have been filled prior to the siege. Two whole 4.5-inch mortar bombs were found in Features 69 and 72 in the east barracks.

One of the mortar bomb fragments from the ditch (Level I) was from a 10-inch shell. Its origin is a mystery, but it is suspected that some soldier brought it back from the Great Lakes as a souvenir and discarded it at Fort Stanwix. It weighs 1,491 grams (approximately 3 lbs., 4.6 oz.) and lay near the top of the counterscarp next to the south end of the bridge.

The weight of the bomb fragments indicates that there was only enough metal to account for 11 mortar bombs in the collection. Much of the metal was probably gathered at the time and shipped to foundries to be re-melted into weapons for the Americans.

Hand Grenade

One hand grenade is located in the Campbell collection, but its provenience is unknown. It is 3.75 inches in diameter. Another fragment reportedly found years ago on the site is in the Rome Historical Society collection.

Cannister Shot

Whether these iron balls (fig. 46d) were cannister or grape shot is moot, since the distinction was based largely on how they were fixed for loading into cannon: the former were loaded in cans and the latter were tied in a bag to a wooden sabot. References to the ammunition in the garrison referred to both.

One cluster of 45 balls from the passageway to the northeast bombproof (Level II) were either loose or in a bag since a can was not found with them. However, there were can remnants adhering to two shot in Feature 69 (Levels I and II). Most of the cannister shot (368 specimens) was in the fill of Feature 69 in the east barracks (the same cellar with the concentration of gunflints), suggesting that ammuntion was stored in the building at the time it burned.

Nearly all the shot shows casting marks in the form of seam lines and sprues. The size varied from area to area. In general, the shot fell into three sizes: 20 to 22 mm., 31.1 percent; 24 to 28 mm., 45.2 percent; and 37 to 40 mm., 6.1 percent. These sizes were not uniformly distributed (table 10).

Table 10.

Comparison of cannister shot sizes in selected areas. (The Campbell collection was not measured.)

	Specimens	Range	Average	Standard Deviation
Northeast Bombproof	88	20-32 mm.	22.4 mm.	2.737
East Barracks	387[1]	19-41 mm.	26.9 mm.	4.572
Remainder of site	113	20-40 mm.	24.9 mm.	4.857

[1] Sixteen specimens were too corroded to measure.

Musket Balls

A total of 1,008 lead musket balls were recovered from the excavations (tables 11 and 12). The highest concentrations of these were in the northeast bombproof (Level II), the east scarp (Level II) and the west casemate (Level II). The lowest concentrations were in the northwest bombproof, the ditch, and the headquarters area. Most of the fort had four to five balls per 100 square feet.

Table 11.

Distribution of musket balls by condition.

	Sprue Attached	Sprue Cut; Not Trimmed	Chewed	Mutilated	Fired	Miscast
Casemates						
North	15	21	5	7	2	2
West	1	1	2	2		
Southwest	2	3	7	3		1
Southeast				1		2
East	2	5	1	1		
Barracks						
East	5	16	5	5		2
West	5	9		7		
Guardhouse	2	1		7		2
Headquarters	1	1	1	1		
Parade Ground	1	2	1	3	2	1
Bombproofs						
Northeast	16	60	3	3		7
Northwest	3	1				2
Southwest	6	5		2		6
Ditch		2	1	3	1	1
Ravelin	1	4	2	8		
East Scarp	2	6	6	6	2	
Sally Port	1	8	6	5		
Campbell Collection	1			2		
Totals	64	145	40	66	7	26

Table 12.

Distribution of musket balls by caliber. (Ratios given are the number of specimens per 10 square feet of excavated area within the structure.)

	.47	.48	.50	.52	.53	.55	.56	.58	.59	.61	.63	.64	.66	.67	.69	.70	.75	?	Total	Ratio
Casemates																				
North		1	1			8	6	6	5	3	9	5	7	1	93	1		2	148	4.63
West	2						1	2		5	15	1			27			2	55	13.75
Southwest				1	1	1	3	1		2	5	2	1	1	30	1		5	54	5.40
Southeast				1				3			1				12			1	18	12.00
East						3	2	3			8	3	2	2	20			4	47	4.27
Barracks																				
East			2	1		4	4	3	2		9		1	1	19		1	4	51	3.62
West	2		3	3		4		1	1		4	3	4	3	25			6	59	4.65
Guardhouse	1		1			1		3			13	2	1	1	26			4	53	4.42
Headquarters									1		1			2	5			1	10	1.52
Parade Ground			1		2	1	1	2	1	1	4	1	1		17			2	34	3.77
Bombproofs																				
Northeast					1	3	9	5	18	6	27	1	8	5	26			3	112	20.36
Northwest							1	1					1	1				2	6	1.22
Southwest							6	3		4	4				13			8	38	6.91
Bakehouse															2				2	
Ditch			1			5	1	1		3	9		4		13	1		4	42	1.47
Ravelin			1		1	3				5	4			1	21			3	39	8.67
East Scarp						2	2	8			9	1	1	1	59			8	91	13.72
Sally Port	1		2	1		3	1	2	1		3	1	1	1	20			4	41	4.77
Campbell Collection					11						14				79		1	4	109	5.87
Total	6	1	5	4	12	26	67	23	39	36	139	20	32	20	507	3	2	67	1,008	5.15

Only seven balls appeared as if they had been fired and were flattened upon impact. Their distribution (table 7) suggests that they were fired from several locations, and the ones in the north casemate (Levels II and III) were probably souvenirs carried into the building. More balls had been cut or mutilated by chewing (fig. 46i) or were found with the sprue still untrimmed (fig. 46h). Joseph Moore (Simms, 1882, Vol. I, p. 590) remembered that two privates in 1776 who were whipped ". . . did not utter one word of complaint; but each taking a leaden bullet in his mouth, bit upon it as the punishment was inflicted." Two hundred and nine untrimmed balls were excavated, and, along with the lead waste encountered in various places, attested to the manfacture of musket balls in the fort. For details see entries under sprues and lead waste in this chapter.

Over half of the musket balls were .69 caliber, or 69 hundredths of an inch in diameter (fig. 46f). These could have been fired in a smoothbore .75 caliber weapon which was standard issue for both American and British Forces (Peterson, 1968, pp. 29–30). The smaller diameter ball was necessitated by the black powder used to fire the piece, which left a carbon deposit in the bore, and the paper cartridge used to seat the ball against the powder. All of the .66 to .72 caliber balls were probably used in .75 caliber weapons.

The next most frequent size found are .63 caliber balls (fig. 46g). These, with others ranging from .58 to .64 caliber, were probably made for imported French muskets of .69 caliber (Peterson, 1968, p. 37).

A final group of musket balls range from .47 to .56 caliber, dominated by the latter. These were probably used with American made rifles. To insure a tight fit in the rifled grooves of the bore, these balls were made with a smaller tolerance, and were wrapped in a greased patch rather than a paper cartridge. Some of these may have been made for pistols. The only pistol barrel in our collection is .63 caliber in size. At Fort Ligonier, 1758-1766 (Grimm, 1970, p. 109) the most common sizes were .69, .62 and .52 caliber. The first two sizes are comparable to the Fort Stanwix sample but apparently there is a shift from .52 caliber to .56 calibre during the period these forts were occupied.

Buckshot

There were 102 lead buckshot found in the excavation (table 13), (fig. 46j). These range in size from .25 to .44 caliber, and about a third still have sprues attached. No attempt was made to compute a mean since it is evident from the data that the buckshot cluster at .25, .31, .34 and .40 calibers.

Birdshot

There were 198 lead birdshot found on the site (table 13) (fig. 46k). These range in size from .06 to .21 caliber, and most are sub-spherical in shape. The sizes cluster at .135 to .165 calibers. Some were molded, others probably were made in a shot tower, and a few were cut from a small diameter lead wire. These were uncommonly numerous on the parade ground, largely due to a single concentration in a small area near its center.

Table 13.

Distribution of buckshot and birdshot. (Ratios given are the number of specimens per 10 square feet of excavated area within the structure.)

	Buckshot	Ratio	Birdshot	Ratio
Casemates				
North	10	.31	8	.25
West	6	1.50	2	.50
Southwest	10	1.00	9	.90
East	2	.18		
Barracks				
East	21	1.49	48	3.40
West	3	.24	1	.08
Guardhouse	15	1.33	3	.25
Parade Ground	2	.22	99	11.00
Bombproofs				
Northeast	10	1.82		
Northwest	1	.20		
Ditch	2	.07	3	.10
Ravelin	2	.44		
East Scarp	5	.75		
Sally Port	9	1.04		
Campbell				
Collection	4	.22	25	1.35
Totals	102	.52	198	1.01

Sprues and Lead Waste

Sprue fragments, untrimmed musket balls and lead waste comprise abundant evidence of the manufacture of musket balls, buckshot and birdshot at the fort (table 14). This industry appeared to have been concentrated in the north and southwest casemates, and the southwest bombproof. The high concentration of lead waste in the barracks probably represents storage, since it was not accompanied by sprues or untrimmed balls.

Individual sprues indicate molds for 1, 2, 5, 6, 9 and 15 balls (fig. 46e). The spacing of the sprues, however, is too close for balls larger than buckshot in size, and most made balls of birdshot size only. On "gang" molds the largest ball size possible was .56 caliber, and most are in the .20 caliber range. Inasmuch as larger balls were found with cut but untrimmed sprues, the question of where the sprues went remains. Probably, because there would have been much waste, they were remelted. While possible, it is unlikely that all large balls were made with single-shot molds.

Table 14.

Distribution of sprues and lead waste.

	Sprues	Lead Waste	Lead Waste in Grams
Casemates			
North	11	56	827
West		3	51
Southwest	8	21	265
East		5	106
Barracks			
East	3	136	1,481
West		172	1,820
Guardhouse	4	4	37
Parade Ground		3	29
Bombproofs			
Northeast		3	26
Northwest	2	13	178
Southwest	2	49	206
Ditch	1	4	74
Ravelin		7	171
East Scarp	1	11	91
Sally Port	1	15	211
Total	33	502	5,573

Cannon Primers

One specimen was found in Feature 51 in the southwest casemate, one in the east casemate (Level II), six in Feature 69 (Level II) in the east barracks, one in the south ditch (Level XI) and three in the sally port (Level II). They consist of a hollow iron tube 5 mm. in diameter attached to a concave iron funnel 22 to 25 mm. in diameter (fig. 461). They were identified from a comparable specimen at Fort Ligonier (Grimm, 1970, pp. 74–76) for which the identification was uncertain. Three of our specimens have nail holes in the funnel part with the nails driven from the outside as if to attach the object to the end of a pole. This makes the identification even less certain. Nine of these were associated with post-1776 deposits.

Match Case

A brass grenadier's match case was found in the northwest corner of the west casemate (Level II) (fig. 47). This is a perforated cylinder with reinforcing bands around the top and bottom.

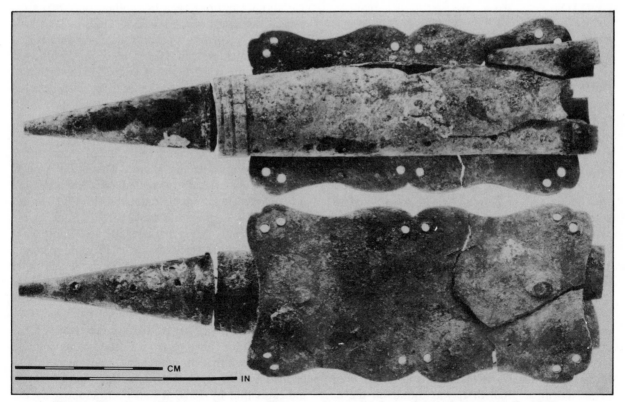

Figure 47. Grenadier's match case, observe and reverse, from the west casemate, Level II.

There is a perforated cone in one end. The whole case is 7 inches long and 1 inch in diameter. It was held by two rivets to a brass plate 4.2 by 2.1 inches in size which was sewn to a belt. It was designed to carry a slow match for igniting incendiaries, such as grenades. The slow match and pull ring were not found. A similar specimen is illustrated by Darling (1970, p. 1). It was probably a relic of the British occupation.

Clothing and Ornamentation

Cloth

Nine fragments of cloth were found in pre-1781 contexts at the site. They had been preserved by charring or contact with metal. All were a simple over one and under one weave with course thread. Where it could be discerned, the thread had a Z-twist. All could be classed as coarse cloth. A piece from Feature 51 retained a hem-stitched seam. The other specimens came from the southwest casemate (Level II and Feature 48), the north casemate (Level IV), the west casemate (Levels II and III), the northwest bombproof (Level II) and the west barracks (Feature 60, Level II).

Braid

Five fragments of braid were found. One, from the north casemate (Level I), consists of three tassels joined together. The tassels, formed from loops of heavy Z-twisted two-ply thread, were preserved by contact with a Type A-1 lead button.

Two strips of silver braid were recovered, one on the east scarp (Level II) and one in the sally port (Level II). The first specimen was backed with cloth with a Z-twist twined weave and was stitched to the garment by a single thread down the center (fig. 48a). It is 9 mm. wide and over 18 cm. long, and was cut or broken on both ends. The other specimen was woven over two-ply warp threads in an over-and-under technique to produce a twisted rope pattern (fig. 48b). It is 8.5 mm. wide and over 5 cm. long, and was broken at both ends. A brass specimen 7 mm. wide and over 2.7 cm. long, was found in Feature 57 (Level IV). It has a Z-twist twined weave method of manufacture. The fifth piece is of brass, and is too poorly preserved to be studied. It was found on the east scarp (Level II).

Buttons

Buttons were a common find, particularly in the barracks and casemate areas (table 15). Some specimens could be identified by their markings as post-1775 in vintage. A total of 558 buttons were recovered, and in order to handle this large group, they were divided into types based on the method of manufacture and the materials used. It is not possible to classify an additional 55 specimens because they are too fragmentary. The method of analysis follows L. Stone (1971) but the types are our own. References will be made to Stanley South's typology (1964, pp. 113–134) since this is a standard work on the subject. We have not followed this typology because it does not meet our descriptive needs. This typology does not incorporate all of South's types, because some were not found in the pre-1781 component at Fort Stanwix. We have added new types found at Fort Stanwix.

Basically, the buttons at Fort Stanwix fall into two size ranges: 11 to 20 mm. and 18 to 25 mm. in diameter. Some types are generally larger than others which accounts for the overlap. However, the number of specimens within these ranges is so high that we can state with confidence that, despite variations from one type to another, only two sizes served the needs of the soldiers. The smaller specimens were probably used on waistcoats and in lieu of knee buckles; the larger ones on regimental coats and the waist band of pants. Diameters were measured from edge to edge and the thickness includes the length of the shank.

Series A—One-piece cast buttons
Type 1. White metal with a mold seam on the back running over the shank. The seam around the edge was usually trimmed off (South's Type 11). Dimensions: small: diameter, 15 to 20 mm., average, 17.3 mm.; thickness, 8 to 12 mm., average, 10.7 mm.; large: diameter, 22 to 28 mm., average, 23.2 mm.; thickness, 9 to 13 mm., average, 11.0 mm. There are several varieties of this type, distinguished by their lettering or decoration. This type appears to be far more common at Fort Stanwix than at Fort Ligonier (Grimm, 1970, pp. 63–66). L. Stone (1970, p. 162) gives dates of *ca.* 1745-1780 for this type from Fort Michilimackinac and suggests that it may have been primarily a civilian button style. The data from Fort Stanwix indicates that by 1776 it had been adopted by the American military.

Table 15.

Distribution of button types. (The column headed with a question mark in Series D represents specimens not identifiable as to type; ratios given are the number of specimens per 10 square feet of excavated area within the structure.)

Series	A				B			C	D							E		F	G			H	I	J		Totals	Ratio
Type	1	2	4	6	1	2	3	1	1	2	3	4	5	6	?	1	2	1	2	3	4	1	1	1	1		
Casemates																											
North	26	1			5	22	7	3	2	6	2				4	11			3			2				94	2.94
West	1		1			4	2	3	4	1						4			1							21	5.25
Southwest	4		1		3	6	3	5	2	7	1	1			2	9			1					1		46	4.60
Southeast	1					1	1					1			1											5	3.33
East	19					2	5	5	2	1	2				1	5			2			1				45	4.09
Barracks																											
East	10	1			5	1	1	3	1		2				6	5			2			1				38	2.69
West	8				13	1	7	2	1	2	1	1			4	9			2			1	1	1		54	4.25
Guardhouse	6					2		5	2			2	2		2	3					2					26	2.16
Headquarters							1	1	1							1							1			5	.61
Parade Ground	2					2			1							4										9	1.11
Bombproofs																											
Northeast	1					1		1	1							1	1									6	1.09
Northwest							1									1	1									3	.61
Southwest																1										1	.18
Bakehouse															2			1								3	
Ditch	1				1	1	6	1		1					4	9			3	1						28	.97
Ravelin	6					5	1	2		2									2			1				19	4.22
East Scarp	9		1	1	7	16	6	1	1		2	1			2	2			1			1	1	1		53	7.91
Sally Port	35		1	1	2	2	6		2	2	1				4	9			3							68	7.91
Burial	9																									9	
Campbell Coll.	4				4	1	1	3	2						1	8						2				26	1.41
Totals	142	1	6	1	45	67	51	2	30	16	29	15	2	3	27	82	2	1	20	2	2	9	1	1	2	559	2.86

Variety a. Plain with no markings. Dimensions of 73 specimens (fig. 48c): small: diameter, 15 to 20 mm., average, 17.2 mm.; thickness, 8 to 12 mm., average, 10.4 mm.; large: diameter, 22 to 26 mm., average, 23.0 mm.; thickness, 9 to 13 mm., average, 11.4 mm. Nine of the large specimens, all 23 mm. in diameter, came from a single burial. They were located on the upper part of the body, but disturbances made determination of their original position impossible. The heaviest concentrations of this variety were in the north casemate and Level II in the sally port, 16 and 13 specimens respectively.

Variety b. Face cast with intertwined "USA" and rope border. Dimensions of 11 specimens (fig. 48d): diameter, 19 to 24 mm., average, 21.6 mm.; thickness, 8 to 11 mm., average 9.8 mm. This variety was a common Revolutionary War button (Calver & Bolton, 1950, p. 83) worn by a number of different American units. There were four in the sally port (Level II); one on the east scarp (Level II); one in Feature 68; one in Feature 69 (Level III); one in the north casemate (Level I); one in the east casemate (Level III); one in the ravelin (Level II) and one in the guardhouse area (Level II).

Variety c. Face cast with a separated "NY" The back has a raised area below the shank. Dimensions of four specimens (fig. 48e); diameter, 17 to 18 mm., average, 17.5 mm.; thickness, 11 to 12 mm., average, 11.7 mm. This was a button of one or more of the New York regiments during the Revolution. Two were found in the sally port (Level II), one in the southwest casemate (Level I) and one in the north casemate (Level III).

Variety d. Face cast with a connected "NY" Two specimens (fig. 48f) were found. One is 18 mm. in diameter and the other 11 mm. thick. This too was a button associated with one or more of the New York regiments during the Revolution. One came from the sally port (Level II) and one from the east casemate (Level II). A similar specimen was found at Fort Constitution (Calver and Bolton, 1950, p. 91).

Variety e. Face cast with "N. York," "3^d B^t". The back exhibits a raised area below the shank. Dimensions of four specimens (fig. 48g): diameter, 24 mm.; thickness, 11 to 12 mm. One specimen was in the north casemate (Level I), two in the east casemate (Level II) and one in Level II in the sally port. This variety belonged to the Third New York Regiment of the Continen-

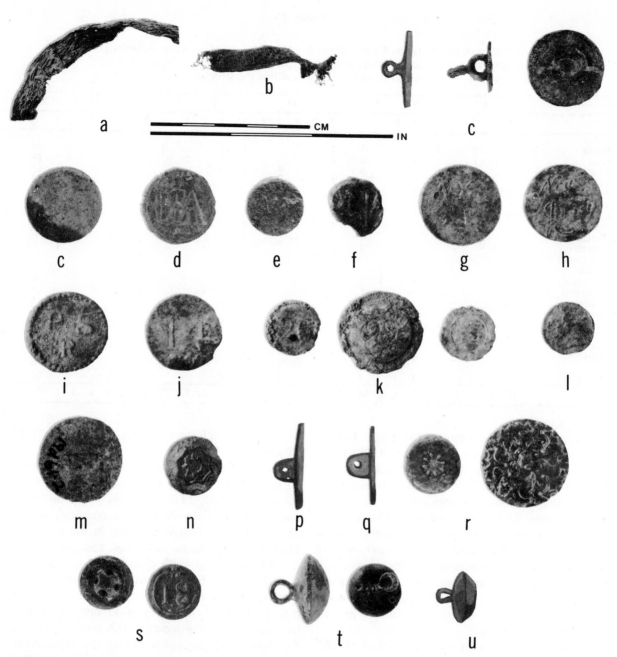

Figure 48. a-b, braid from the east scarp, Level II and the sally port, Level II; buttons: **c,** Type A1a from the north casemate, Level II, the sally port, Level II and the northeast bombproof, Level II; **d,** Type A1b from the sally port, Level II; **e,** Type A1c from the north casemate, Level III; **f,** Type A1d from the east casemate, Level II; **g,** Type A1e from the east casemate, Level II; **h,** Type A1f from the east scarp, Level II; **i,** Type A1g from the guardhouse area, Level II; **j,** Type A1i from the sally port, Level II; **k,** Type A1j from the east casemate, Level II, the ravelin Level II and the sally port Level II; **l,** Type A1l from the sally port, Level II; **m,** Type A1o from the sally port, Level II; **n,** Type A1z from the north casemate, Level II; **p,** Type A2 from the east scarp, Level II; **q,** Type A3a from the southwest casemate, Level II; **r,** Type A3z from the north casemate, Level I and the sally port, Level II; **s,** Type A4 from the sally port, Level II (reverse and obverse); **t,** Type B1a from Feature 72, Level II and the north casemate, Level III; **u,** Type B2 reconstructed from specimens on the east scarp, Level II.

tal Line. The regiment was sometimes referred to on muster lists as the 3rd New York Battalion. It was stationed at Fort Stanwix from April, 1777, to December, 1778, (Luzader, 1969, pp. 64–162).

Variety f. Face cast with "New Jersey" in script. One specimen (fig. 48h) has a diameter of 23 mm. and a thickness of 12 mm. This button was in Level II on the east scarp. It was a New Jersey regimental button of the Revolutionary period; the 3rd New Jersey Regiment was at Fort Stanwix from July to October, 1776, (Luzader, 1969, pp. 56–61). Another similar specimen (but not from the same mold) was found at Fort Ticonderoga (Calver and Bolton, 1950, p. 91).

Variety g. Face cast with "PS", and "R" and beaded edge. Three specimens (fig. 48i) are 24 mm. in diameter. No thickness measurements were possible. One was found in the north casemate (Level I), one in the guardhouse area (Level II) and one in Level II in the sally port. The button was probably worn by troops of the Pennsylvania State Regiment organized in April, 1777. It became the 13th Regiment of the Pennsylvania Line in October, 1777, and was incorporated into the 2nd Regiment of the Pennsylvania Line in July, 1778, (Lefferts, 1926, p. 52). No records could be found of this unit having been at Fort Stanwix. Another specimen was found in a grave near Philadelphia (Calver and Bolton, 1950, p. 140).

Variety h. Cast with "IX" on face. One specimen is too fragmentary to measure. Found in the east casemate (Level II), it probably belonged to the 9th Massachusetts Regiment of the Continental Line, elements of which were at Fort Stanwix in August, 1777, (Luzader, 1969, p. 106).

Variety i. Cast with an Arabic numeral on face. Nine specimens (fig. 48j) have the following dimensions: diameter, all 22 mm. except one, 17 mm., which has the numeral "8" on it; thickness, 10 to 11 mm.

One of these buttons was in the north casemate (Level II), two in the east casemate (Level II), one on the east scarp (Level II) and five in Level II in the sally port. They exhibit the numerals "7" (two), "8" (two), "9" (one), "12" (two) and "14" (two). These were probably worn by American militia units.

Variety j. Cast with Arabic numerals and other designs on face. Three specimens (fig. 48k) have diameters of 17 mm., 25 mm. and 17 mm. No thickness measurement is possible. These were British regimental buttons of the 26th, 29th and

53rd regiments of Foot, respectively. The 26th button has the number "26" in the center with a rope border. The 26th Regiment served in New Jersey in 1767, (Darling, 1970, p. 56). Part of the 26th was captured at Fort St. John's, N.Y., in November, 1775 (Dupuy and Dupuy, 1963, pp. 88–70) and the regiment later served out of New York City until December, 1779. This button was probably grafted onto a New York uniform at St. John's or Montreal. It was found in the east casemate (Level II). Others like this were found at a British camp in New York City (Calver and Bolton, 1950, p. 115). The 29th button exhibits the number "29" in the center with a broad arrow border. This regiment arrived at Boston in 1768 (Lefferts, 1926, p. 172), serving primarily in Canada. Two companies were with Burgoyne at Saratoga (Bird, 1963, p. 280) where they were captured. It was found in the ravelin (Level II). Similar specimens have been found on Carleton Island (Calver and Bolton, 1950, p. 57) and at Fort Erie (Calver and Bolton, 1950, p. 118). The 53rd Regiment button has a "53" on a depressed ribbed center. This regiment arrived at Quebec in 1776, and served with Burgoyne as a rear guard at Fort Ticonderoga (Bird, 1963, p. 94). It was found in the sally port (Level II). While none of these regi-

Table 16.

Distribution of sleeve links and clasps.

Series	Sleeve Links										Clasps			
	A			B			C	D	E	F	1		2	3
Types	1			2			1	1	1	1	1		2	3
Varieties	a	b	c	a	b	c					a	b		
Casemates														
North	2				2								2	
West		1						1						
Southwest			2										1	
East			1	1				1		1				1
Barracks														
East							1							
West	1					2		1						
Guardhouse							1							
Ditch	1								1				2	
Ravelin										1				
East Scarp			2								1			
Sally Port			3										2	
Burials			4											
Campbell Collection	1							1				1		
Variety totals	5	1	11	1	2	2					1	1		
Type totals	17			4			5				2		7	1
Series totals	21			5			2	3	1	1	10			

ments were at Fort Stanwix, all had stores captured by the Americans between 1775 and 1777.

Variety k. Face cast from a coin mold. Dimensions of four specimens: 28 by 11 mm., 23 by 11 mm., 27 by ? mm., and 18 by 10 mm. The first of these was made from a George II halfpenny mold. The second was from a Spanish coin dated 1767 and the last two were from Spanish coins with illegible dates. They were found in the north casemate (Level II), the east casemate (Level II), the east scarp (Level II) and the sally port (Level II).

Variety l. Cast with horse and rider on its face. Three specimens (fig. 48l) have the following dimensions: diameter, 24 mm., 16 mm. and 16 mm.; thickness, 8 mm. for the smaller size. These buttons exhibit horse and rider in "curvet" position. Two were found in the sally port (Level II) and one in the guardhouse area (Level II).

Variety m. Back cast with initials "PN" flanking the shank. Diameter of one specimen: 17 mm. The shank is broken off. Buttons with these initials were found at Fort Ligonier, 1758-1766 (Grimm, 1970, p. 63), but they were probably comparable to our Type B–2. This suggests a pre-Revolutionary context for this specimen which was found in the north casemate (Level I).

Variety n. Silver plated. One specimen found in the sally port (Level II) has a diameter of 17 mm. and a thickness of 11 mm.

Variety o. Face cast with urn and wreath border. One specimen (fig. 48m.) has a diameter of 25 mm. and a thickness of 12.5 mm. It came from Level II in the sally port.

Variety z. Face cast with geometric or symmetrical designs. Dimensions of 21 specimens (fig. 48n): small: diameter, 15 to 19 mm., average, 17.3 mm.; thickness, 8 to 12 mm., average, 10.1 mm.; large: diameter, 22 to 25 mm., average, 23.3 mm.; thickness, 10 to 13 mm., average, 11.0 mm. These specimens were found in the north casemate (Levels I and II), the east casemate (Level II), the southeast casemate (Level II), the east barracks (Feature 52, Level III), the west barracks (Feature 57, Level II), the ravelin (Feature 76) and the sally port (Level II).

Type 2. White metal with a hole drilled through a solid cast shank on the back, otherwise like Type 1 (fig. 48p). This plain button has a diameter of 23 mm. and a thickness of 8 mm.

Type 3. Brass with a hole drilled through a solid cast shank on the back.

Variety a. Plain face. Dimensions of two specimens (fig. 48q): diameter, 19 and 20 mm.; thickness 6 and 9 mm. They were found in the southwest casemate (Level I) and west casemate (Level II).

Variety z. Decorated face with symmetrical designs. Diameters of four specimens (fig. 48r): 16 mm., 17 mm., 19 mm., and 26 mm.; thicknesses: 6 mm., 6 mm., 8 mm. and 9 mm. No two designs are alike. One, from the north casemate (Level I) with a snowflake motif has a concave face. An identical specimen was found at Valley Forge in the Weeden Brigade area (personal observation). Another, from the east scarp (Level II), has holes punched through it as part of the design. A similar specimen was found at Carleton Island (personal observation).

Type 4. Brass specimen with two transverse holes crossing through a solid cast shank (fig. 48s). This specimen has a diameter of 17 mm. and a thickness of 6 mm. Cast on the front is the number "18" in a broken circle. This was probably a button of the British 18th Regiment of Foot which arrived at Boston in October 1774, and the officers, at least, returned to England in July 1776, (Lefferts, 1926, p. 171). Darling (1970, p. 56) listed this regiment as having arrived in Philadelphia in 1767. The button was found in Level II in the sally port

Series B—Two-piece buttons with a brazed or flux-jointed seam and a separate shank.

Type 1. Brass specimen with a brass wire shank, a brazed seam and two vent holes.

Variety a. Plain face. Dimensions of 44 specimens (fig. 48t): small: diameter, 16 to 17 mm.; thickness, 14 mm.; large; diameter, 20 to 24 mm., average, 21.2 mm.; thickness, 14 to 17 mm, average, 15.5 mm. Eleven of these were in Feature 60 (Levels II and III) in the west barracks and seven were on the east scarp (Level II). Others were scattered about the fort.

Variety b. Silver plated. One specimen from the north casemate (Level III), is 22 mm. in diameter.

Type 2. White metal with an iron wire shank and two vent holes (South's Type 12?, Grimm's Type 1?; fig. 48u). Dimensions: small: diameter, 15 to 17 mm., average, 16.3 mm.: large: diameter, 19 to 32 mm., average, 21.3 mm. All shanks were broken off. A concentration of these buttons was found in the east end of the north casemate (Level I) and the east scarp (Level II). South's Type 12 was defined as a solid button, but apparently he had only one badly preserved specimen to describe (South, 1964, p. 119). A few of our buttons were so badly corroded as to appear solid, but the presence of vent holes and a few well-preserved specimens leads us to conclude that all were hollow. Grimm (1970, pp. 62-63) noted one-piece hollow pewter buttons with two holes and iron shanks as the most common type at Fort Ligonier, 1758-1766. These were probably two-piece buttons since it would be difficult to cast a hollow pewter button and imbed an iron shank, and the only function of the vent holes would be to allow gases to escape while the two halves were joined together. They were the third most popular type at Fort Stanwix, and the most common at Fort Ligonier which suggests that they are pre-1776 in time, or British military buttons. L. Stone (1970, p. 171) also believes that they are British, and notes that they occur in a post-1769-1781 context at Fort Michilimackinac. It should be noted that only one possible specimen came from the civilian context of Brunswick Town, North Carolina, 1726-1776 (South, 1964, p. 119).

Type 3. Brass with a brass wire shank (South's Type 6; fig. 49a). Dimensions: small: diameter, 14 to 18 mm., average, 16.2 mm.; thickness, 11 to 14 mm., average, 12.1 mm.; large: diameter, 19 to 24 mm., average, 21.4 mm.; thickness, 13 mm. One specimen from the east scarp (Level II) has a leather thong through the shank and another from Feature 73 has an iron shank. Symmetrical designs are on about 25 percent of the faces, but the faces of many buttons of this type are broken off. These were not separated from the plain specimens since we could get no accurate count.

Series C—Two-piece cast button, flux-joined with a drilled shank.

Type 1. Brass (South's, Type 1; fig. 49b). Diameters: 19 mm. and 29 mm. No thickness measurement was possible because the faces were broken off.

Series D—Two-piece button with brass face and crimped edge; separate shank on some types.

Type 1. Four-hole bone back (South's Type 3; fig. 49c). Dimensions: small: diameter, 15 to 18 mm., average, 15.9 mm.; thickness, 3 to 5 mm., average, 4.0 mm.; large: diameter, 19 to 26 mm., average, 22.2 mm.; thickness, 5 mm. Most were

complete enough to subdivide on the basis of decorative motifs.

Variety a. Plain. Nineteen specimens were found.

Variety b. Gilded. Four specimens were found. One of these, from the north casemate (Level II), has heavy thread through the holes forming an "X" on the back. Another, from Feature 48, was gilded over an embossed basketweave pattern. The others came from Feature 52 (Level IV) and Feature 76.

Variety c. Silver plated. Two specimens were found. One, from the west casemate (Level II), was plated over an embossed basket-weave pattern. The other was from the northeast bombproof passageway (Level II).

Variety z. Various symmetrical embossed designs. Five specimens (fig. 49c) were found. The most common patterns were a basket-weave motif and a lattice motif.

Type 2. Specimens with a four-hole wooden back (South Type 3; fig. 49d, e). Dimensions: small diameter, 15 mm., 16 mm., 16 mm. and 17 mm.; large: diameter, 21 mm., 21 mm., 21 mm. and 22 mm.; warping of the wood prevented thickness measurements. Most were complete enough to subdivide on the basis of decoration.

Variety a. Plain. Six specimens were found.

Variety b. Gilded. One from the north casemate (Level I) was gilded over a symmetrical embossed design of six leaves and scallops (fig. 49e).

Variety z. Various symmetrical embossed designs. Eight specimens (fig. 49d) were found.

Type 3. Specimens with a bone back, a central hole and a brass wire shank (South Type 4; fig. 49f). Dimensions: small: diameter, 14 to 16 mm., average, 14.8 mm.; thickness, 10 mm.; large: diameter, 18 to 24 mm., average, 21.1 mm.; thickness, 11 to 13 mm. One specimen from the west casemate (Level II) was gilded, and a few have embossed designs.

Type 4. Stamped brass back with a central hole and a brass wire shank (fig. 49g). Dimensions: small: diameter, 15 to 16 mm., average 15.9 mm.; thickness, 9 mm.; large: diameter, 21 to 28 mm., average, 24.0 mm. No thickness was measurable. Most specimens have an embossed wild rose motif surrounded by vines or ferns. One back (the largest specimen) from Feature 69 (Level III) exhibits the initials "I F" flanking the hole.

Type 5. Brass back with a brass wire shank soldered to it. Face covers only the edge of the

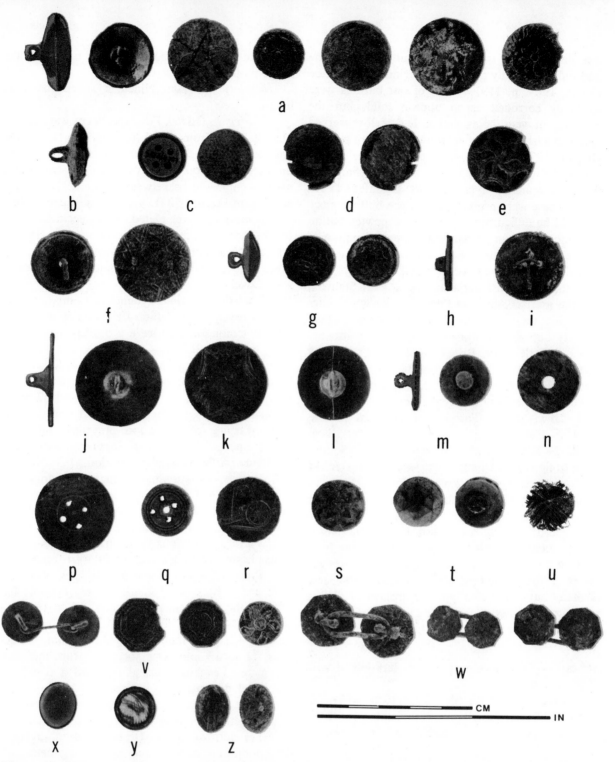

Figure 49. Buttons: **a,** Type B3 reconstructed from a specimen on the east scarp, Level II, the southwest casemate, Level II, the guardhouse area, Level II (2), the bridge area, Level X, the sally port, Level II and the north casemate, Level I; **b,** Type C1 from the northeast bombproof, Level II; **c,** Type D1z from the guardhouse area, Level II and Feature 48; **d,** Type D2z from the north casemate, Level I (reverse and obverse); **e,** Type D2b from the north casemate, Level I; **f,** Type D3 from Feature 48 and the north casemate, Level II; **g,** Type D4 reconstructed and from the south ditch, Level II and the north ditch, Level I; **h,** Type D5 from the southwest casemate, Level I; **i,** Type D6 from Feature 18; **j,** Type E1a from the south ditch, Level I; **k,** Type E1z from the southwest bombproof, Level III; **l,** Type E2 from the east scarp, Level II; **m,** Type F1 from the west casemate, Level II; **n,** Type F2 from the north casemate, Level II; **p,** Type F3 from Feature 57, Level IV; **q,** Type F4 from the east scarp, Level III; **r,** Type G1b from the guardhouse area, Level I; **s,** Type H1 from Feature 69, Level II; **t,** Type I1 from Feature 56, Level II (obverse and reverse); **u,** Type J1 from the surface. Sleeve links; **v,** Type A1 from the north casemate, Levels II and I, Feature 50, and the east casemate, Level I; **w,** Type B1 from Feature 3, Level III, the bridge area, Level XI and Feature 56, Level II; **x,** Type C1 from the ravelin, Level II; **y,** Type D1 from the east casemate, Level I; **z,** Type E1 from the west casemate, Level II.

button (South Type 16; fig. 49h). One has a diameter of 18 mm. No thickness was measurable. It exhibits an eight-pointed star motif and was found in the southwest casemate (Level I).

Type 6. Brass back with two crossed brass wires soldered to it (fig. 49i). Diameters: 16 mm., 22 mm. and 22 mm., and thicknesses of ?, 7 mm. and 8 mm. All were plain.

Category 1. Faces only, with the backs missing. These may have been Types 1, 2, 3, 4, or 6. Dimensions: small: diameter, 15 to 18 mm., average, 16.4 mm.; large: diameter, 23 to 34 mm., average, 25.7 mm. Most of these have symmetrical embossed designs and two from the southwest casemate (Level I) and the sally port (Level II) are gilded.

Series E—Cast one-piece buttons with a separate shank.

Type 1. Brass with a spun back and a brass wire shank imbedded in a casting spur (South's Type 7; fig. 49j, k). Dimensions: small: diameter, 13 to 19 mm., average 17.2 mm.; thickness, 6 to 12 mm., average, 9.0 mm.; large: diameter, 22 to 29 mm., average, 25.1 mm.; thickness, 6 to 13 mm.; average, 10.3 mm. Coarse cloth was found adhering to two of these buttons, but this appeared to be a fortuitous association. The shanks were usually broken off. Several varieties could be discerned.

Variety a. Plain. Sixty-seven specimens (fig. 49j) were found.

Variety b. Gilded. Three specimens were found. They came from the north casemate (Level I), the west ditch (backfill) and Feature 69 (Level I). These may all be post-1781, but this is unlikely.

Variety c. Silver plated face. Six specimens were found. One came from the south ditch (Level XV), one from the north casemate (Level I) and four from the sally port (Level II). One of the latter was engraved with a central flower motif, and a scalloped border.

Variety z. Engraved symmetrical designs. Six specimens (fig. 49k) were found.

Type 2. Brass with a visible mold seam and a brass wire shank imbedded in the back (South's Type 8; fig. 49l). Diameter: 24 mm. and 28 mm., thicknesses: 10 mm. and 11 mm. One specimen from the northwest bastion (Level I) is plain and the other from the east scarp (Level II) has a flower motif on its face.

Series F—Cut bone or shell buttons drilled for suspension.

Type 1. Bone with a single transverse hole through a node on the back (South's Type 14; fig. 49m). One specimen, 16 mm. in diameter and 5 mm. thick, was found in the west casemate (Level II).

Type 2. Bone with a single drilled hole (South Type 15; fig. 49n). Dimensions: small: diameter, 9 to 17 mm., average, 13.6 mm.; thickness, 1 to 3 mm., average, 2.1 mm.; large: diameter, 19 to 23 mm., average, 21.4 mm.; thickness, 2 to 3 mm., average, 2.4 mm. They were scattered about the site but a small concentration of partially finished buttons, the cow ribs from which they were cut, and an iron bit for cutting them, were found in Level II in the sally port (fig. 76l).

Type 3. Bone drilled with four holes (South's Type 20; fig. 49p). Diameters: 17 mm. and 25 mm., thicknesses: 3 mm. and 2 mm., respectively. This and the following type have been dated *ca.* 1800-1865 by South (1964, p. 121) but both specimens had an indisputable pre-1781 provenience. They came from the south ditch (Level XI) and Feature 57 (Level IV).

Type 4. Bone drilled with five holes (South's Type 19; fig. 49q). Diameter, 17 mm., thickness, 3 mm. They came from the east scarp (Level II) and the ravelin (Level II).

Series G—One-piece stamped with the shank soldered on.

Type 1. Hand stamped (South Type 9).

Variety a. Plain. Diameters of two specimens: 21 mm. and 24 mm. The latter has a thickness of 6 mm.

Variety b. Depicts a cannon pointing right with a "Grand Union" flag mounted on the trail. Diameters of six specimens (fig. 49r): 21 to 22 mm. All shanks were broken off. These were American artillery buttons of the Revolutionary period (Calver and Bolton, 1950, p. 85). Companies of Colonel Lamb's Artillery Regiment were stationed at the fort from 1777 to 1781 (M. Willett, 1777-78; Lauber, 1932). Two were found in the north casemate (Level II), one in Feature 56 (Level II), one in the sally port (Level I), one in the guardhouse area (Level I) and two in the Campbell collection.

Series H—Three-piece button with a drilled back or with a separate shank.

The face was of two pieces with the outer one pierced to expose the inner one.

Type 1. Bone back drilled with four holes (South's Type 5; fig. 49s). Diameter, 17 mm., thickness, 4 mm. It came from Feature 69 (Level II).

Series I—Cast, faceted glass button with a shank imbedded in it. May have had a brass back.

Type 1. Brass shank (South's Type 13; fig. 49t). Diameter, 15 mm., thickness, 11 mm. It was found in Feature 56 (Level II).

Series J—A wire-wrapped button.

Type 1. Wood back drilled with four holes and wrapped with brass wire in a cross-wise fashion (fig. 49u). Preservation was too poor to permit measurements. One came from Feature 48 and the other from the surface.

Sleeve Links

Thirty-three sleeve links, or fragments, were recovered from the fort. The number and distribution are shown on table 16, broken down by type and variety. Diameter and thickness were measured like the buttons.

Series A—One-piece cast with integral shank.

Type 1. Brass with a drilled brass shank coupled with a brass wire (fig. 49v). Dimensions: diameter, 13 to 17 mm., average, 14.8 mm.; thickness 5 to 9 mm., average, 5.7 mm.

Variety a. Plain. Five specimens were found. One was octagonal.

Variety b. Bust of a man flanked by the initials "PR." One specimen was found in the west casemate (Level II).

Variety c. Various symmetrical designs. Eleven specimens were found. Five are octagonal.

Type 2. White metal with a white metal or iron wire coupling. Diameters, 15 mm., 16 mm., 17 mm. and 14 mm. by 16 mm. The thickness of the second specimen is 6 mm. One has a plain face, two have symmetrical designs and one from the east casemate (Level II) appears to have been made from a coin mold (George I). One is oval in shape.

Series B—One-piece cast with a separate shank.

Type 1. Brass (fig. 49w). Dimensions: diameter, 11 to 16 mm.; average, 13.2 mm.; thickness, 4 to 6 mm.; average, 5.0 mm.

Variety a. Plain. One specimen was found.

Variety b. Stamped symmetrical design. Two octagonal specimens were found.

Variety c. Cast symmetrical designs. Two octagonal specimens were found.

Series C—Cast with a separate shank and a glass setting.

Type 1. Brass (fig. 49x). Dimensions: diameter, 13 mm. by 16 mm. and 12 mm. by 14 mm.; thickness, ? and 7 mm. Both are oval in shape. One has a purple faceted setting and the other is an opaque light blue. Two pressed glass settings, one blue and one amber, were found in the north casemate (Levels III and II) and a pressed clear glass setting was found in the southwest casemate (Level I). These may have come from sleeve links.

Series D—Cast with a drilled integral shank and a paste setting.

Type 1. Brass (fig. 49y). Dimensions: diameter, 12 mm., 12 mm. and 13 mm.; thickness, 7 mm., 8 mm. and 8 mm. One has a purple-and-white setting and the other two a blue-and-white setting.

Series E—Two-piece, cast with brazed seam, separate shank, and two vent holes in the back.

Type 1. Brass (fig. 49z). Diameter: 15 mm. by 11 mm.; thickness: 9 mm. It is oval and gilded.

Series F—Three-piece, brass, shell and glass composite (South Type 34).

No measurements were possible, as the shank was broken off and the shell worn down around the edge. The shank and backing were cast as one piece with the shell as a collar below the glass setting. This was found in Level I and may be post-1781.

Clasps

Type 1. Two-piece clasps (table 16) with studs and hook or eye on each piece (stock clasps).

Variety a. Plain cast brass with three studs (fig. 50a). A piece of one specimen was found with a length of 30 mm., a width of 50 mm. and a thickness of 1 mm.

Variety b. Engraved cast brass with three studs. This has a length of 29 mm., width of 48 mm. and thickness of 1 mm. Only the hook half of one specimen was found by Campbell. A similar clasp was found at Fort Montgomery (Jack Mead, personal communication).

Type 2. Two-piece sheet brass clasps with hooks or holes for attachment to cloth (haversack or stock clasps); (fig. 50b, c). Dimensions: length, 31 to 33 mm.; width, 38 to 40 mm.; thickness .5 mm. These specimens have a row of six to eight holes along the back edge which allowed them to be sewn to cloth. One complete set from the north casemate (Level II) still retained the thread (fig. 50b). There was either a wide hook at the other end, or three rectangular holes in the center; the hook of one fits into the hole of the other. One specimen from the east scarp (Level II) which formerly had a hook, had been broken longitudinally and was converted by piercing with three crude holes (fig. 50c).

Type 3. Cut cast brass nailed to wood (function unknown). This has a length of 26 mm., width of 28 mm. and thickness of 2 mm. It has a single nail hole and was a reworked specimen, having been cut and hammered from a piece of cast brass.

Buckles

A large assortment of buckles were found on the site, most of which were made for shoes (table 17). The following classification is tenuous in part because many buckles could have served several specific functions, although they were divided on the basis of form. There is an easily discernible relationship between form and function for some, such as shoe and stock buckles, but some of the smaller specimens could have been used on haversacks, belts, or small harnesses. All buckles are of a copper alloy unless otherwise noted. In terms of types found, frequency of occurrence and size of specimens, the Fort Stanwix sample closely resembles the sample from Fort Ligonier, 1758-1766. (Grimm, 1970). There was apparently no great change in styles between 1758-1766 and 1766-1781 except for an increase in the popularity of Type 1f shoe buckles.

Type 1. Single frame with pin post and two-part fork, and toothed loop for double straps (shoe buckles).

Variety a. Large plain rectangular buckles with sharply rounded corners and a high arch (fig. 50d). Dimensions: length, 57 to 58 mm.; width, 44 to 45 mm.; thickness, 3.5 to 4.0 mm. These are heavy buckles and probably military issue.

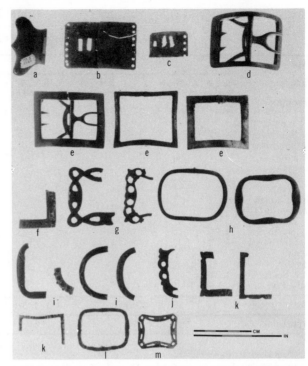

Figure 50. **a,** stock buckle (Type 1a clasp) from the east casemate, Level II; **b-c,** Type 2 clasps from the north casemate, Level II and the east scarp, Level II; shoe buckles: **d,** Type 1a from the north casemate, Level II; **e,** Type 1b from the north casemate, Level I, the bridge area, Level X and the ravelin, Level II; **f,** Type 1c from the north casemate, Level II; **g,** Type 1d from the southwest casemate, Level II and the sally port, Level II; **h,** Type 1e from Feature 72, Level II and Feature 51; **i,** Type 1f from the east casemate, Level I, the east scarp, Level II and the east casemate, Levels II and I; **j,** Type 1g from Feature 48; **k,** Type 1h from the ravelin, Level II, the north casemate, Level I and the east scarp, Level II; **l,** Type 1i from the north casemate, Level III; **m,** Type 1j from the north casemate, Level IV.

None were found at forts Ligonier (Grimm, 1970, pp. 56–58) or Michilimackinac (Lyle Stone, 1970). One fragment from the southwest bomb-proof (Level I) is silver plated and somewhat larger and thinner than the others.

Variety b. Large plain rectangular buckles with angled corners (fig. 50e). Dimensions: length, 47 to 58 mm., average, 51.3 mm.; width, 43 to 52 mm., average 46.5 mm.; thickness, 1.5 to 3.0 mm., average, 2.5 mm. These were probably military issue. Peterson (1968, p. 230) illustrates one from the *Philadelphia,* which was sunk in Lake Champlain in 1775. Two were made of iron. This was Grimm's Type 1 (1970, p. 56) at Fort

Table 17.

Distribution of buckles.

Type	1										2				3				4	5		6	7					8	9	10
Variety	a	b	c	d	e	f	g	h	i	j	a	b	c	d	e	a	b	c	d	a	b		a	b	c	d	e	a	b	a	b
Casemates																															
North	3	11	3	3	5	7		2			1	1			1		1	3		2	2		1	2	1		4		1	1	
West			2						1											1											
Southwest		2		2	2	3	1				3									2	1										
Southeast	1			1	2	2								1			2	1		1	2	1					1				1
East	1			1	2	4									1		2	1		1	2	1					1				
Barracks																															
East	1				2	3					1		1							1							1				
West	2			2	1	2	6									2	1	2		2	2			2			1	1			
Guardhouse		1			2	1	3													2											
Bombproofs																															
Northeast																				1				1							
Northwest	1											1																			
Southwest	1	1																													
Ditch			4	1		1	4	1			1		1	1						2										1	
Ravelin			3	2		1	4													1										1	
East Scarp	1	4			1	1	1	1	1		2									3					1		1				
Sally Port		6	1	2	4	3	1			1				1		1	1	4		1				1	1	1				1
Variety totals	9	34	11	12	23	40	4	1	3	2	9	1	1	3	2	1	4	11	1	18	1		5	1	2	9	2	2	1		
Type totals	139										16				17		8		19		1		19					3	1	2	225

Ligonier where it was also the most common type of shoe buckle. Three of ours are stamped "TURNER" and another "S. WILLSON" on the tongues. Two tongues with the latter mark on it were found at Fort Ligonier (Grimm, 1970, p. 62). Our example came from Feature 75 on the east scarp and the three "Turner" buckles came from the north casemate (Level I).

Variety c. Large relief molded rectangular buckles with angular corners (fig. 50f). Dimensions: length, 51 mm.; width, 38 to 44 mm., average, 40.3 mm.; thickness, 1.5 to 3.0 mm., average, 2.1 mm. These were probably civilian buckles. One from the southeast bastion (Level II) was silver plated. This was Grimm's Type 5 (1970, p. 58).

Variety d. Large relief molded rectangular buckles with excised areas and angular corners (fig. 50g) (Grimm's Type 3). Dimensions: length, 58 mm.; width, 46 to 50 mm.; thickness, 1.5 to 2.5 mm., average, 1.8 mm. These were probably civilian buckles.

Variety e. Large plain rectanguloid buckles with rounded corners (fig. 50h) (Grimm's Type 2). Dimensions: length, 54 to 58 mm.; width, 41 to 52 mm., average, 45.8 mm.; thickness, 2 to 3 mm., average, 2.6 mm. Peterson (1968, p. 230) refers to this type as a British military pattern. Two are made of iron and one of pewter.

Variety f. Large relief molded rectanguloid buckles with rounded corners (fig. 50i) (Grimm's Type 6). Dimensions: length, 63 to 67 mm.; width, 44 to 53 mm., average, 47.9 mm.; thickness, 1.5 to 3.0 mm., average, 2.3 mm. This was the most common variety, which argues against its having been civilian, but probably indicates the use of civilian buckles by the military. Very few of these (five) were found at Fort Ligonier (Grimm, 1970, p. 50). One from the east scarp (Level II) is silver plated.

Variety g. Large relief molded rectanguloid buckles with excised areas and rounded corners (fig. 50j) (Grimm's Type 3). Dimensions: length, unknown; width, 55 mm.; thickness, 2 mm. These were undoubtedly civilian buckles.

Variety h. Small relief molded rectangular buckles with angled corners (fig. 50k). This specimen is 38 mm. long and 2 mm. thick. It was probably worn on a woman's shoe because of its small size.

Variety i. Small relief molded rectanguloid buckles with rounded corners (fig. 50l). Dimensions: length, 39 to 43 mm.; width, 33 to 36 mm.; thickness, 2.0 to 2.5 mm. These were probably women's shoe buckles.

Variety j. Small relief molded rectangular buckles with excised areas and rounded corners (fig. 50m). No measurements were possible except thickness: 1.5 to 2.0 mm. These were probably from women's shoes.

Type 2. Single frame with pin post and two part fork and anchor. These buckles were nearly square (knee buckles) and had steel pins.

Variety a. Plain rectangular buckle with angled corners (fig. 51a). Dimensions: length, 24 to 30 mm., average, 27.9 mm.; width, 25 to 33 mm., average, 28.9 mm.; thickness, 1.5 to 3.0 mm., average, 1.9 mm. These were probably military issue and greatly resemble Type 1b shoe buckles.

Variety b. Relief molded rectangular buckle with angular corners (fig. 51b). This is 25 mm. long, 23 mm. wide and 2 mm. thick.

Variety c. Plain rectangular buckle with rounded corners (fig. 51d). This was 20 mm. long, 20 mm. wide and 2 mm. thick. This is probably a spur buckle.

Variety d. Relief molded rectangular buckle with rounded corners (fig. 51c). Dimensions: length, 33 mm.; width, 27 to 32 mm.; thickness, 1 to 2 mm.

Variety e. Relief molded rectangular buckle with excised areas and rounded corners. Dimensions: 33 mm. long, 30 mm. wide and 1.5 mm. thick.

Type 3. Single frame with pin post and a one piece fork and anchor (function uncertain). These were wider than they were long, and all movable parts were made of steel.

Variety a. Plain rectangular with angular corners (fig. 51e). This was 28 mm. long, 32 mm. wide and 3 mm. thick.

Variety b. Plain rectangular with rounded corners. These were about 33 mm. wide and 2 mm. thick. All specimens were fragmentary and one was made of pewter.

Variety c. Relief molded rectangular with rounded corners (fig. 51f). Length, 27 to 28 mm.; width, 28 to 42 mm., average, 34.4 mm.; thickness, 1 to 2 mm. Two specimens were made of pewter.

Variety d. Relief molded oval (fig. 51g). This was 30 mm. long, 38 mm. wide and 1.5 mm. thick and had a recessed pin terminal which Grimm (1970, p. 62) considered to date *ca.* 1775-1795. This specimen came from Feature 57 (Level IV) in the west barracks and cannot, therefore, date later than May, 1781. As it was the only one with this style of terminal found it was probably quite late, and a beginning date for the style of *ca.* 1775 would be acceptable.

Type 4. Single frame plain buckle with pin

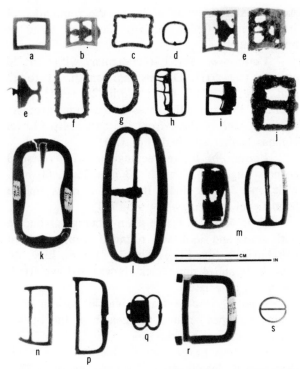

Figure 51. **a,** Type 2a knee buckle from the north casemate, Level II; **b,** Type 2b knee buckle from the north casemate, Level IV; **c,** Type 2d knee buckle from the sally port, Level III; **d,** Type 2c spur buckle from the north ditch, Level I; **e,** Type 3a buckles from the bridge area, Level XI, the east scarp, Level II and the north casemate, Level II; **f,** Type 3c buckle from the east casemate, Level I; **g,** Type 3d buckle from Feature 57, Level IV; **h,** Type 4 stock buckle from the southwest casemate, Level II; **i,** Type 5a belt buckle from the east scarp, Level II; **j,** Type 5b harness buckle from the east casemate, Level I; **k,** Type 6 sword belt buckle from the north casemate, Level II; **l,** Type 7a baldrick buckle from the north casemate, Level III; **m,** Type 7d belt buckles from Feature 3, Level I and the sally port, Level II; **n,** Type 7e sling buckle from the sally port, Level II; **p,** Type 8a buckle from the north casemate, Level I; **q,** Type 8b buckle from the north casemate, Level IV; **r,** Type 9 harness buckle from the southeast casemate, Level I; **s,** Type 10 decorative silver buckle from the sally port, Level II.

post, two-part fork and hook and rounded corners. Width greater than the length (stock buckle) (fig. 51h). See also: *Clasps.* Dimensions: length, 26 to 27 mm.; width, 39 to 44 mm.; thickness, 1.5 to 2.5 mm. One of these, from the east casemate (Level I) was marked "A BAHLER" on the hook part.

Type 5. Single frame with tongue looped over one side of the frame (belt or harness). Two small specimens were made of brass, the remainder of iron. Grimm (1970, p. 56) identified these as harness buckles.

Variety a. Small rectangular with angled corners (fig. 51i). Dimensions: length, 21 to 42 mm., average, 31.2 mm.; width, 24 to 45 mm., average, 33.9 mm.; thickness 2 to 5 mm., average, 4.2 mm. One of these from the east scarp (Level II) has leather attached (fig. 51i).

Variety b. Large rectangular with rounded corners (fig. 51j). This is 33 mm. long, 60 mm. wide and 5 mm. thick. It was a harness buckle from Level I and may be post-1781.

Type 6. Single frame plain rectangular buckle with studs and hook and rounded corners (sword belt buckle) (fig. 51k). This is 86 mm. long, 46 mm. wide and 4 mm. thick. It was in Level II of the north casemate.

Type 7. Double frame buckle with a steel tongue wrapped around the center of the buckle (baldric and belt buckles).

Variety a. Large plain double oval (fig. 51l). Dimensions: length, 46 to 51 mm., average, 48.3 mm.; width 7.4 to 10.7 cm., average, 8.5 cm.; thickness, 2.0 to 2.5 mm. One of these, from Feature 60 (Level III), has leather associated with it; a British broad arrow is cut into the leather. It appears to have been a bayonet frog but is too fragmentary to reconstruct.

Variety b. Small plain double oval. This is 38 mm. long, approximately 40 mm. wide and 2 mm. thick.

Variety c. Small plain rectangular with angled corners. These are 28 mm. wide and 2 mm. thick. Only fragmentary specimens were found. One from the northeast bombproof still has leather around the center post.

Variety d. Small plain rectangular buckles with rounded corners. Dimensions: length, 32 to 37 mm., average, 34.0 mm.; width, 43 to 63 mm., average, 51.3 mm.; thickness, 2 to 3 mm. One of these from Feature 3 (backfill) has leather around the center post (fig. 51m).

Variety e. Small plain D-shaped buckles (sling buckles) (fig. 51n). These are 47 mm. wide and 2 mm. thick. Both specimens are fragmentary.

Type 8. Double frame with steel tongue wrapped around one side of the frame which was notched (function unknown).

Variety a. Large plain rectangular buckles with rounded corners (fig. 51p). These are 61 mm.

wide and 2 mm. thick. Both specimens are fragmentary.

Variety b. Small plain double oval buckles with a folded copper strap around the center post (garter?) (fig. 51q). This is 26 mm. long, 28 mm. wide and 1.5 mm. thick. The strap is 19 mm. long.

Type 9. Single frame, large plain U-shaped buckle with raised center post and rounded corners. Steel tongue wrapped around center post (harness buckle) (fig. 51r). This is 50 mm. long, 56 mm. wide and 4.5 mm. thick.

Type 10. Single frame, small round buckles with tongue wrapped around one side of the frame which was notched (ornamental) (fig. 51s). These have a diameter of 21 mm. and are .5 mm. thick. Both examples are silver and were probably made for the Indian trade.

Eyelets

These are all brass wire clothing fasteners (fig. 52a). They probably served a variety of clothing. Table 18 shows their distribution. Dimensions: length, 8 to 21 mm., average, 15.0 mm.; width, 7 to 19 mm., average, 11.7 mm.

Bracelet

A stamped and engraved copper strip was found in the sally port (Level II) (fig. 52b). It is 82+ mm. long and 18 mm. wide and has been broken off at one end. Two engraved lines running 2.5 mm. inside each edge appear to have been part of the original decoration. This had been modified by the addition of notches on both edges, two engraved stick figures with triangular bodies, and four clusters of designs stamped with a small octagonal tool and a punch. It was flat when found but appeared to have been bent at one time, and was probably a bracelet.

Ring

One brass finger ring with an octagonal bezel 11.5 by 9 mm. was found on the east scarp (Level II). The bezel was engraved "PI" with a rocker-stamped border. This type has been referred to as a "Jesuit ring" (Noël Hume, 1970, p. 266), distributed among the Indians as marks of conversion. The initials have been found on other rings and Cleland (1972, p. 206) suggests that these initials

Table 18.

Distribution of eyelets, pendants, tinkling cones and beads.

	Eyelets	Pendants						Tinkling Cones	Beads										
Types		1			2	3	4	1	1				2	3		4		5	
Varieties		a	b	c					a	b	c	d		a	b	a	b	a	b
Casemates																			
North		1						1	1	49		93	116				1		1
West	1			1				1											
Southwest								3	1	1			10	1					
East	1							1			1		1						
Barracks																			
East								1	7				16			2			
West					1														
Guardhouse							1	1					1						
Headquarters	1																		
Ditch			1						2			2		3					
Ravelin									2										
East Scarp	3								1	1			1						
Sally Port	1					1		3	2						1				
Campbell Coll.																		1	
Variety totals		1	1	1					16	51	1	95		4	1	2	1	1	1
Type totals	7	3			1	1	1	11	163				145	5		3		2	

represent stylistic drift from an "IHS" design (*Isus Hominis Salvator*) dating pre-1700.

Pendants

Several types of pendants were found on the site. See table 18 for their distribution.

Type 1. Disc.

Variety a. Plain lead (fig. 52c). This has a diameter of 35 mm. and is 3 mm. thick. It was probably hammered from a musket ball and perforated near one edge.

Variety b. Engraved lead. This has a diameter of 43 mm. and is 2 mm. thick. It was probably made from a musket ball and was perforated near one edge. On one side it is engraved with a Masonic emblem of an arch, an altar and an open eye. It may have been a post-1781 artifact since it came from Level X of the south ditch.

Variety c. Plain copper. This has a diameter of 28 mm. and is 2 mm. thick. It was probably a worn coin perforated near one edge.

Type 2. Lead cross. This is 58 mm. long, 50 mm. wide and 12 mm. thick. It was made in a crude wooden mold with a hole molded at one end (fig. 52d).

Type 3. Silver teardrop shape. This is 15 mm. long and 5 mm. in diameter. It is beaten silver with base, side and loop soldered together. It was probably an Indian trade item (fig. 52e) and was found in Level III of the sally port.

Type 4. Amorphous stone. This is 22 mm. long, 21 mm. wide and 4 mm. thick. This small piece of siltstone was ground and notched with a hole drilled in one corner (fig. 52f). It was probably Indian made, dating from a pre-fort occupation of the site, although found in Level II in the guardhouse area.

Tinkling Cones

These were all made from scraps of brass bent to form a hollow cone (fig. 52g). They were attached to the fringes of clothing. One still has a leather thong in it. See Table 18 for their distribution. All but one from the north casemate were in definite pre-1781 context. They are 12 to 40 mm. long, averaging 20.7 mm.; comparable to specimens found at Fort Michilimackinac (Stone, 1970, p. 373).

Earrings

Two tin-plated brass earrings were found (fig. 52h), one in Feature 52 (Level IV) in the east barracks and one in the sally port (Level III). Both are wire loops .5 mm. thick and 10 to 10.5 mm. in diameter. One is broken but the other is divided at one point with thickened ends.

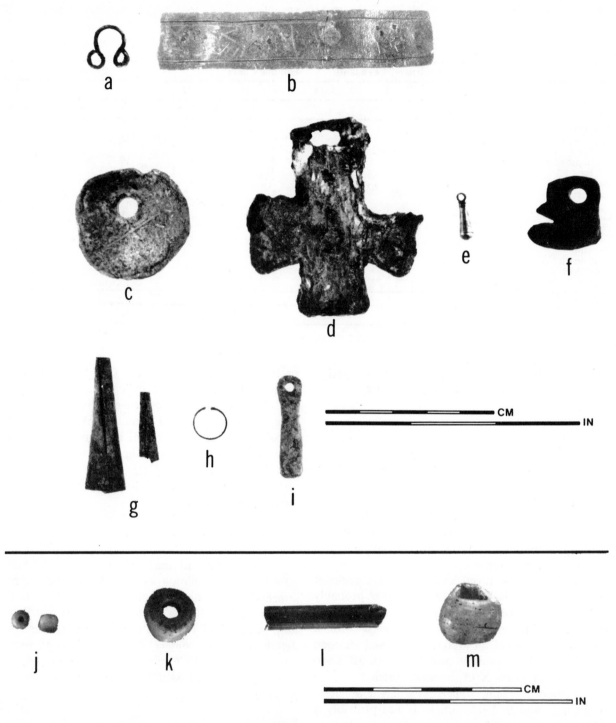

Figure 52. a, brass eyelet from the sally port, Level II; **b,** copper bracelet with engraved figures from the sally port, Level II; **c-d,** lead pendants from the north casemate, Level II and the west barracks, Level II; **e,** silver pendant from the sally port, Level III; **f,** stone pendant from the southwest bombproof, Level II; **g,** brass tinkling cones from the sally port, Level II and the west casemate, Level II; **h,** silver plated brass earring from Feature 52, Level IV; **i,** lead net sinker from the northeast bombproof, Level I; **j,** Type 2 beads from Feature 69, Level III; **k,** Type 3a bead from the bridge area, Level XI; **l,** Type 4b bead from the north casemate, Level I; **m,** Type 5a bead from the guardhouse area, Level II.

Beads

A total of 318 beads were recovered from the site (table 18). Only three, one bone, one ceramic and one plastic, were not manufactured from glass. Fourteen of the beads were definitely from post-1781 contexts, and another 15 were types manufactured over the past 200 years and were found in questionable context. These are not described below. The bead inventory was unvaried compared to those of historic period Indian habitation sites in this area. The beads exhibited only one surface color and were rather drab and monotonous. The beads were of types that had a long time range so they were of no use in separating the British from the American occupations of the fort.

Type 1. Simple, drawn, doughnut bead. This was the most abundant type found. They range in diameter from 2.0 to 4.0 mm. and have been called embroidery beads, versus seed beads that measure under 2.0 mm. in diameter (Hsu, 1969, p. 41). These are equivalent to Stone's seed beads, Class I, Series A, Type I (L. Stone, 1970, p. 350).

Variety a. Opaque white. These have a diameter of 2.0 to 4.0 mm. with 90 percent between 3.0 and 3.5 mm. The exterior is smooth and has a luster.

Variety b. Opaque turquoise. These have a diameter of 3.0 to 4.0 mm. with 90 percent between 3.0 and 3.5 mm. A majority of the turquoise beads have eroded or pitted exterior surfaces.

Variety c. Opaque grey-blue. One bead of this variety is 3.5 mm. in diameter. It has a smooth exterior surface.

Variety d. Translucent turquoise. These have a diameter of 3.0 to 4.0 mm. with 90 percent between 3.0 and 3.5 mm. The exterior surface is pitted and eroded.

Type 2. Compound, drawn, doughnut bead. This is identical to Type 1 except for the number of constituent parts (fig. 52j). The beads are white over white but the inside layer of glass does not have the same luster as the outer layer. These are equivalent to Stone's seed beads Class I, Series B, Type I (L. Stone, 1970, p. 353).

Type 3. Compound, drawn, tube bead.

Variety a. Clear over opaque white (fig. 52k). These have a diameter of 9.0 to 11.0 mm. and a length of 6.0 to 9.0 mm. A transparent glass layer over an opaque white glass gave this type a pearl-like appearance. This is equivalent to Stone's necklace bead Class I, Series B, Type III (L. Stone 1970, p. 307).

Variety b. Opaque red over translucent green (Cornaline d'Aleppo). This has a diameter of 3.5 mm. and a length of 16.0 mm. This was recovered during the excavations of 1965, but no provenience data was given for it. It was cut from a longer tube and the ends have been fire polished. This is equivalent to Stone's seed bead Class I, Series B, Type III (L. Stone, 1970, p. 354).

Type 4. Simple, drawn tube bead. These are equivalent to Stone's necklace bead, Class I, Series A, Type VI (L. Stone, 1970, p. 301).

Variety a. Blue, translucent. These are 2.5 to 3.0 mm. long and 4.0 to 5.0 mm. in diameter. They were cut from longer tubes and heat tumbled to smooth the broken edges.

Variety b. Black, opaque (fig. 52l). This has a diameter of 5.9 mm. and is 22 mm. long. This section was snapped off a longer tube and the ends are jagged and irregular.

Type 5. Simple, mandrel wound bead. These are equivalent to Stone's necklace beads, Class II, Series A, Type VIII, Variety A (L. Stone, 1970, p. 325).

Variety a. This has a diameter of 10.5 mm. and a length of 10.0 mm. The molten glass strand from which this bead was constructed was very thick, so the contact lines are quite distinct (fig. 52m).

Variety b. Clear, painted. This has a diameter of 7.5 mm. The exterior surface was painted to imitate a pearl. The beads found at Fort Ligonier were essentially the same as at Fort Stanwix (Grimm, 1970, pp. 49-50), except for a few wound beads at Fort Ligonier that were different colors. Neither fort had complex, multi-colored beads. It seems rather unusual that more beads and bead types were not found at Fort Stanwix considering the trade activities in and around the fort. There were accounts of Indian scouts, messengers and families staying for various spans of time. In 1775, it was reported that:

. . . the people who live on the ground are one John Roof, Thomas Mayers, William Cloyne, Bartholemew Brodhock—John Steers and Stephanus Delyrod a Frenchman—who trades there for Major Fonda—the fort is all in ruins and the barracks by an accident last fall was burnt to the ground, nothing now remains but a room which the officers used to mess in, now occupied by the Frenchman mentioned above . . . (Duncan, 1969).

During the siege, Col. Willet stripped the Indian camps of bag and baggage, and in 1779 troops passed through the fort before and after destroying the Indian villages to the southwest. Two major treaty signings and many minor meetings were held with the Indians, and Indians are known to have visited the fort many times. Despite this, trade items, in general, were not found. See also: Buckles, Type 10; Bracelet; Ring; Pendants, Type 3; and Tinkling Cones.

Tools

Many tools were used to erect fortified positions; the most common were picks, shovels, spades, axes and billhooks. Picks, shovels and spades were needed to dig ditches and form earthworks. Axes and billhooks were used to clear trails and to cut wood and brush for revetting the earthworks.

In 1776, General Philip Schuyler requested intrenching tools for his various field commands, but was told that there were very few and that he should buy and borrow suitable tools from local inhabitants (Geo. Washington to Schuyler 6/13/76, Washington Papers, 1932). In December 1776, he ordered Henry Glen to:

Apply to Mr. Rensselaer for what iron he may have in store, and employ the blacksmiths at Schenectady and in its vicinity, in making axes, spades, shovels and pick-axes, for which they will be allowed the same price as those at Albany. The iron for the shovels, and the steel for the axes, is not yet arrived. You will desire Mr. Rennselaer to forward you as much of each as will suffice for 1600 each . . . (Schuyler, 1880, p. 49).

Capt. De La Marquese, the French engineer at Fort Stanwix, reported making helves for axes, pickaxes and spades and other implements shortly after he arrived in 1777, but he did not inventory the number of tools. When the English troops retreated from Fort Stanwix on August 23, 1777, leaving behind much of their equipment, the American troops listed 100 picks, 50 billhooks, 80 falling (sic.) axes and 106 spades as part of the captured stores (Scott, 1927, facing p. 289). An inventory of engineer's stores taken on July 1, 1778, listed 238 picks, 90 billhooks, 170 axes and 150 spades (Clinton, 1900, #1554).

Spades and Shovels

Four types of spades and one type of shovel were found at the fort. The spades were rectangular with flat edges and flanged at the top for pushing with the foot. The shovels had slightly curved blades with pointed tips and no flanges. Our spades did not fit well into Peterson's typology (Peterson, 1968, pp. 181-182).

Type 1. Rectanguar with straight sides and square corners (fig. 53b). The socket for the handle attachment is primarily above the blade so that only an inch or less of the bottom of the handle rests against the back of the blade. A rivet through the socket and the wood handle kept the handle from slipping or turning. The top ¼ inch of the blade is bent forward to form the flange. The thickness of the blade is approximately 5/32 inch at the top and gradually tapers down to 3/32 inch at the bottom. The two spades of this type were found in the fill of the ditch (Levels XI, XIII) near the bridge area. One is 6½ inches wide and 8 inches long and the other measures 6 inches wide and 8¼ inches long. The sockets of both are broken.

Type 2. Rectangular with slightly tapering sides and square corners (fig. 53c). The socket for the handle is more a part of the blade, rather than added on at the top. Approximately 3 inches of the handle rested against the back of the blade. A rivet kept the handle in place. The thickness and the flange are the same as Type 1. Two specimens of this type were found; one in Feature 57 (Level IV) in the west barracks measures 6½ inches wide at the top, 5½ inches at the bottom and 9¼ inches long and the other, from Feature 69 (Level II) in the east barracks, was 7 inches wide at the top, 5¾ inches at the bottom and 9¼ inches long.

Type 3. Metal spade with a wood core (fig. 53a). A wooden paddle and handle were carved from one piece of wood, fitting inside the blade of the metal spade. The back of the blade is one piece of metal and another piece of metal is welded on beginning about halfway up the front. The top of the front piece was bent backward and the back piece forward over the top of the wood paddle to form the top of the spade. Each part of the blade has a 4-inch shank at the top to secure the handle with rivets plus two or more rivets through the blade and paddle. Four specimens were found, one near the bridge (Level XIII), one in the sally port (Level II) and two in the middle of the southwest casemate (Levels I, II). They are quite uniform in size, measuring 6 to

Figure 53. a, Type 3 spade from the bridge area, Level XIII; **b,** Type 1 spade from the bridge area, Level XI; **c,** Type 2 spade from Feature 69, Level II; **d,** Type 4 spade from the southwest casemate. Level II; **e,** shovel from the southwest casemate, Level I.

6½ inches in width at the bottom, 6¼ to 7 inches in width at the top and 11½ to 12 inches in length.

Type 4. Wooden spade with a metal casing around the edge (fig. 53d). The casing is 2 to 4 inches long and 7 to 10 inches wide with two side flanges up to 9 inches long for attachment to a wood paddle. There is a V-shaped groove on the inside edges of the casing to seat the wood paddle. According to Noël Hume (1970, p. 275) nails driven through the flange and wood secured the two parts. The flanges of the casings in our collection are fragmentary but no evidence of nails or nail holes were observed. Eight specimens, five from the southwest casemate (Level II), one each from the east and west barracks (Level II) and one outside the ravelin (Feature 76) were found. None of the specimens are complete and no wooden portions survived.

The 18th cenury was a transitional period in the developmental sequence of spades. Noël Hume (1970, pp. 274-275) suggests that Type 4 spades were common before the 17th century, but were gradually being replaced by Types 1, 2 and 3 during the 18th century and by the beginning of the 19th century had been replaced completely. Type 3 was probably a transitional type between Type 4 and Types 1 and 2. The fact that half our spades are Type 4 suggests that they retained their popularity in this region or enjoyed a revival due to the scarcity of iron during the American Revolution.

Shovels

One shovel blade was found in the southwest casemate (Level I) 80 percent intact, and fragments of two others came from the southwest casemate (Level I) and the south ditch (Level XIII). The blade was approximately 12 inches long, 10 inches wide at the top and the sides rounded gradually to a point (fig. 53e). The socket extended approximately 3 inches above the blade and protruded about 5 inches into the blade. A rivet through the socket and handle acted as a fastener. A nearly identical specimen was found at Fort Ligonier, 1758-1766 (Grimm, 1970, p. 144).

Picks

Two types of picks were found during the excavations. Type 1 is large and heavy while Type 2 is smaller and for light duty work. No handles were found.

Type 1. Large. These measure 21 to 22 inches from tip to tip along the top of the pick. The lengths of the blades and points were 9 to 9¼ inches. The differences in the total length are due to the size and shape of the oval eyes. The top of the cheeks varied from flat to slightly rounded, while the bottoms formed an ear approximately 1 inch wide.

Variety a. Two piece construction (fig. 54b). The blade, point and cheeks of the eye are two halves welded together. Two of these were found, one at the botom of the scarp in the north ditch (Level XI) and one in the ravelin (Level II). The specimen in the ravelin has a heart stamped on the underside of the blade. Two axes, one from near Ft. Ticonderoga (Peterson, 1968, p. 184 and 1972 personal communication) have similar marks but no information about the mark has been found.

Variety b. Three piece construction. The blade of the three-piece pick was separate; it was welded to the two pieces that formed the point and the cheeks. This was found in the north casemate (Level II).

Type 2. Small (fig. 54a). These are 4 to 5 inches shorter and only two-thirds the weight of the larger type. The points and blades are 1 to 2 inches shorter than those of Type 1. The blades are only 1½ inches wide, or less, all of two piece construction. The top of the cheek is slightly rounded while the bottom protrudes to a rounded ear. One was found in the north casemate (Level I) and the other in the east casemate (Level II). The right cheek of an undeterminable type was found in the north ditch (Level X).

Axes

The axe was an important tool in the construction, maintenance and everyday living in the fort. They were made in many different sizes and shapes; some for general purpose cutting and others for specific tasks. A great number of names, based upon size, shape, purpose, and/or area of origin have been used to classify axes.

Three terms were used in the inventories of axes at the fort dated August 23, 1777: "80 falling [sic.] axes were captured from the English," (Scott, 1927, facing p. 289) and July 1, 1778: 170 "narrow" axes and 16 "broadaxes" were part

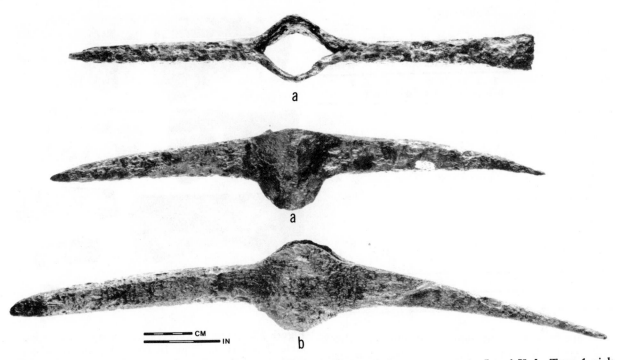

Figure 54. a, Type 2 picks from the north casemate, Level I and the east casemate, Level II; **b,** Type 1 pick from the north ditch, Level XI.

of the engineer's stores, (Clinton, 1900, #1554). The felling axes and narrow axes were undoubtedly one and the same. A large number of axes would have been used by the Americans during the reconstruction of the fort and just prior to the siege. While finishing construction, parties of axmen were sent along Wood Creek to obstruct that waterway with trees and bushes. The British were using axes to clear the obstructions in Wood Creek and the military road between Fort Oswego and Fort Stanwix.

A wide variety of terms have been applied to the parts of an axe; some are fanciful, some are manufacturer's terms, and some are traditional. A few terms seem to be widely accepted, but even knowledgeable writers have differences of opinion as to their meaning. For this reason, we include the following definitions:

Blade—The wedge-shaped portion of the tool.
Butt—The back part of the eye. When the butt is rounded it is considered unpolled, and when it is squared it is polled. Also referred to as the head.

Cheeks—The metal on the sides of the eye.
Ear—The metal projection below and sometimes above the cheek to give added strength to the handle. Also called a beard or eye lip.
Edge—The cutting edge of the tool. Also referred to as the bit and occasionally made of steel. Specimens from Fort Stanwix seldom had a steel edge.
Eye—The hole for hafting onto the handle or helve.

Measurements of the axes were made as follows: the maximum length was taken from the butt to the edge; blade length from the front of the eye to the edge; edge width was the length of the cutting surface, butt width was the length of the butt; butt thickness was measured from the back of the eye to the back of the butt. The distribution of the axe forms is shown in table 19.

Type 1. European-style axe with the butt at an angle to the edge. The cheeks are flat on top and the bottom tapers upward from the butt toward the blade. The butt is rounded and the edge is convex. Usually, the blade measures well over one-half the total length of the tool. All of the Type 1

Table 19.

Distribution of axes and wedges.

	1a	1b	2	3a	3b	4a	4b	4c	4d	5	6a	6b	7	Wedges
Casemates														
North		1	1			2				1	1			
Southwest	1	1		1							1			1
East					1									
West								1						1
Barracks														
East				2		2		1						2
West										1		1		1
Parade Ground										2				
Bombproof														
Northwest						1								
Ravelin				1	1					1				
East Scarp	1	1	1										1	
Sally Port							1	1	1					1
Surface		1												
Variety totals	2	4		4	2	5	1	3	1		2	1		
Type totals	6		2	6		10				5	3		1	6

(The columns headed 1–7 are Axes; the final column is Wedges. Types 1, 3, 4 and 6 are divided into varieties a, b, c, d.)

Figure 55. Axes: **a,** Type 1a from the southwest casemate, Level II; **b,** Type 1b from the southwest casemate, Level II; **c,** Type 2 from the east scarp, Level II; **d,** Type 4b from the sally port, Level II; **e,** Type 4c from the sally port, Level II; **f,** Type 5 from the north casemate, Level IV; **g,** Type 6a from the north casemate, Level II; **h,** Type 7 "pipe tomahawk" from the east scarp, Level II.

axes are broken in the same pace with one cheek and part of the butt missing. They also show signs of having been hammered on the butt, perhaps being used as wedges.

Variety a. Top of the axe flat from butt to edge, but the bottom of the blade flared from the front of the eye to the edge (fig. 55a). Two specimens were found, one 80 percent complete and the other consisting only of the right cheek. The measurable specimen is 7 inches long, the blade 4¾ inches long, the edge 4¼ inches wide and the butt 3¼ inches wide. It is of two-piece construction, welded along the blade and in the midline of the butt. The right cheek is missing, probably broken off when someone hammered on the butt attempting to use the axe as a wedge. From the size of the fragmentary specimen, it appears to have been very similar in size and shape.

Variety b. Blade flared both on the top and bottom (fig. 55b). It is of one-piece construction with the weld in front of the eye. Three measurable axes and one cheek fragment are representative of this variety. They are 7½ to 8 inches long; the blade 4½ to 5½ inches long; the edge 3¾ to 4¾ inches wide and the butt 3 to 3⅛ inches wide. One cheek and part or all of the butt are missing on all of these specimens.

Type 2. An intermediate form between the European form and American form of axes (fig. 55c). The butt and edge are parallel and the top is flat but the blade is still more than one half the total length. The butt is squared and there is

an ear on the bottom of the cheek. Two specimens belong in this category. They meure 9¼ inches and 7¼ inches long; they have 6¼-inch and 4½-inch blades, 4-inch and 3¾-inch wide edges, 2¼-inch and 2⅞-inch wide butts, and ½-inch thick polls. The larger one has sharp lower ears and the smaller one has rounded lower ears. Although the butts are polled, the center of gravity is still in front of the eye.

Type 3. Very similar to Type 2 but the butt has a much more distinct poll. There are no complete specimens of this type, only the butt and one cheek remaining from any single axe. The butt and bit were probably parallel.

Variety a. Flat top and lower ear. Four specimens make up this variety; the butt width ranges from 2 to 2⅝ inches and the poll thickness from 5/16 to ½inch.

Variety b. Ears on the top and bottom of the cheek near the back of the eye. The blade flares outward from the cheek on both the top and bottom. The two specimens of this variety fall into the same measurement range as Type 3a axes.

Type 4. American style axe. The blade is one half the total length of the tool and the center of gravity is near the eye. The top is flat and there are ears on the bottoms of the cheeks.

Variety a. A two-piece axe. the blade, cheeks and butt fashioned from one piece of metal. Another heavy piece of metal was welded onto the butt to square off the poll and counterbalance the weight of the blade. Five complete specimens make up this variety. Dimensions: length, 6¾ to 7½ inches; blade length, 3½ to 4 inches; edge width, 3¾ to 4 inches; butt width, 2¾ to 3⅛ inches; and poll thickness, ⅞ to 1 inch.

Variety b. A three-piece axe with a steel bit (fig. 55d). This is identical to Type 4a, except for a steel wedge that was welded to the front of the blade to form a harder and longer lasting cutting edge. The one axe in this variety is 7 inches long and has a 3⅝-inch-long blade, 4⅛-inch-wide edge, 3½-inch-wide butt and 1-inch thick poll.

Variety c. Three-piece construction with separate polls (fig. 55e). The two sides of the blade each have a cheek with the poll welded between the ends of the cheeks. Two specimens are in this variety. Dimensions: length, 6¾ and 7¼ inches; blade length, 3½ inches; edge width, 3⅞ and 3¾ inches; butt width 3⅛ and 3 inches; poll thickness, 1 and 1⅛ inches. The longer axe has the initials "EB" under an axe stamped on the left side of the blade.

Variety d. Unknown number of pieces (at least two). This variety has ears on the top and bottom of the cheeks and the top and bottom of the blade flares outward. Only the butt and cheek remain. The butt measures 2¼ inches wide and the poll ⅞ inch thick.

Type 5. Small, one-piece belt axe similar in shape to Type 1 (fig. 55f).

The top is flat, the bottom of the blade flares to the edge, the eye is circular and the butt is rounded. Three complete specimens and two cheek fragments are in this type. Dimensions: length, 5 to 5½ inches; blade length, 3 to 4⅛ inches; edge width, 2¼ to 2⅝ inches; and butt width, 1½ to 1⅝ inches. The incomplete ones are of comparable size.

Type 6. Small, one-piece belt axe similar in shape to Type 3. The eye is wedge-shaped and the butt is squared.

Variety a. These exhibit a flat top while the bottom of the blade flares to the edge (fig. 55g).

Two specimens have the following dimensions: length, 4 and 4⅛ inches; blade length 2 and 2⅛ inches; edge width, 1½ and 2 inches; butt width, 1½ and 1⅜ inches; poll thickness, ⅜ and ½ inch.

Variety b. Blade flares on top and bottom toward the edge. One specimen has cheeks with small upper and lower ears. It is 5 inches long with a 3¼-inch-long blade, 3½-inch-wide edge, 1¼-inch-wide butt and ⅜-inch-thick poll.

Type 7. A "pipe tomahawk" of two, possibly three-piece construction (fig. 55h). The steel blade is one piece but corrosion at the juncture of the eye and bowl prevented us from determining how these were attached. The draw hole in the eye of the axe was drilled at least partially from the eye side before the eye was formed. The top and bottom of the blade flare to the edge, and the rim of the bowl is approximately twice the diameter of the bottom of the bowl. The specimen is 5⅛ inches long with a blade 2⅞ inches long, bit 2½ inches wide, and pipe 1½ inches long with a ¾ inch inside rim diameter. It was in Level II of the east scarp.

From the inventory lists, apparently there was no distinction between "types" that performed the same general function. Broad axes were listed, but none were found during excavations. This may have been due to the relative few on hand, i.e., 16 in July 1778 (Clinton, 1900, #1554). Also, a broadaxe was a specialized tool that required some training before any degree of proficiency was reached. The master carpenter probably had direct control over these tools and kept close track of them because they were scarce. All of the belt axes were probably personal property; none were mentioned on any of the inventories.

The American style axe (Type 4) supposedly was developed by 1750 (Mercer, 1960, p. 7) while Hodgkinson (1965) gives a date of 1775. It was a well established type in the American colonies by the time of the Revolution (Mercer, 1960, p. 4). No examples of this type were found at Fort Ligonier, 1758-1766, (Grimm, 1970, p. 47) while at Fort Stanwix 10 out of 24 felling axes were American style. It would seem then, that Hodgkinson's date is best supported by the data. Hodgkinson (1965) dates Types 2 and 3 from about 1750, but none of these were found at Fort Ligonier. The presence of Types 1 and 2 axes on the east scarp (Level II) indicates that the European style axe had not been completely abandoned by 1776. There were not enough documented sources to attribute particular types of axes exclusively to one army or the other during the American Revolution. Probably both had certain difficulties in supplying the troops in the field, so all captured equipment would have been incorporated into the captor's stores. The British were using Tories and Canadians as militia (Luzader, 1969, p. 96) and these men were probably very familiar with the American style axe.

Wedges

The Officers who Command Fatigue parties, who are daily employ'd in Cutting Wood for the use of this Garrison, will divide their men in three parties, The First to Cutt. The Second to Splitt, and the Last to pile all the Wood which has been cutt. Lieut Stockwell will Order as many Wedges made, as said parties stand in need of so as to enable them to Comply with said Orders . . . (M. Willett 12/4/77)

Splitting the logs into usable proportions was a formidable task that required considerable effort and skill with an axe. A wedge and hammer could have been handled with a minimum of instruction and would have been less fatiguing to the worker. Either the fatigue parties were small, Stockwell's wedges were made of wood, or the above-mentioned order was not fully carried out because only six iron wedges were listed on the two 1778 inventories. A good deal of wood was needed just for daily cooking, baking and heating. This did not include wood needed for construction, shingles and rails for fences which had to be split, and rough splicing of joints which could best be done with wedges.

Wedges could be made from metal, wood, or a combination of a metal bit and wood top. Only iron wedges were recovered during the excavation, and none appear ever to have had a wood top. All their heads had been pounded with a metal tool. Some are badly splayed and one shows signs of having split and been repaired by welding another wedge in the crack. No wooden mallets or beatles were found, nor were any metal ferrules from them identified.

Six wedges, four relatively complete and two broken in half, came from separate locations scattered around the fort (table 19). They were approximately 7 inches long and 2⅜ to 1½ inches wide (fig. 56e). All but one are beveled on both edges and the exception is beveled on one edge at the bit. The heads are rectangular and relatively

flat while all the faces and edges are straight and smooth.

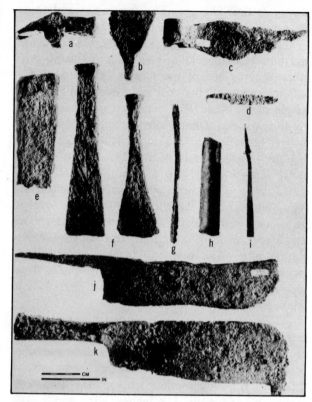

Figure 56.   a, claw hammer from Feature 51; **b,** Category 1 hammer from the east scarp, Level II; **c,** frow from Feature 76; **d,** Type 5 file from the parade ground, Level I; **e,** wedge from Feature 56, Level III; **f,** chisels (one marked with a broad arrow) from the southwest casemate, Level II and the bridge area, Level X; **g-h,** augers from Feature 57, Level II and the southwest casemate, Level II; **i,** screwdriver from the southwest casemate, Level II; **j,** cleaver from the west barracks, Level I; **k,** billhook or facine knife from the guardhouse area, Level II.

Frow

Another tool for splitting wood was the frow. Only one was found, in front of the ravelin (Feature 76) (fig. 56c). A frow was used when greater cutting control or uniformity of product was desired. Its use was also faster than, and did not expend as much energy for the same results as, a wedge or axe. The blade is only partially preserved; it measures 5¾ inches long, 2 inches in maximum width and is approximately ⅛ inch thick. It is of one-piece construction. The eye is 1⅛ inches in diameter and 1¼ inches deep.

Billhook

The billhook, also called a facine knife (Peterson, 1968, p. 185), was used to clear brush and small trees from fortifications and trials, and to trim saplings for use in making facines (bundles of sticks used in revetting fortifications). They were employed much like modern machetes are used today. Fifty were captured from the English forces in 1777 (Scott, 1927, facing p. 289) and 90 were on the inventory in 1778 (Clinton, 1900, #1554). This specimen is shaped much like a cleaver with a hooked end on the cutting edge (fig. 56k). It was found between the southwest casemate and the west barracks (Level II) and has a cutting edge 8 inches long, and a hook 1 inch long at its widest part. The back of the blade is flat, the same as a knife blade. A one-piece conical socket handle, $4\frac{1}{2}$ inches long, could have been used without hafting it onto a wooden shaft.

Cleaver

The garrison was periodically supplied with cattle which were slaughtered at the fort (see Appendix B). A single butchering tool, an iron cleaver, was found in the west barracks. The blade is $8\frac{1}{2}$ inches long, $2\frac{1}{2}$ inches wide and $\frac{1}{4}$ inch thick. The tip is rounded and the top is flat (fig. 56j). A pointed, tapered tang 4 inches long is $\frac{3}{4}$ inch wide at its juncture with the top of the blade.

Hammers

Claw. The claw hammer has been in existence as long as the nail. The tool was used by both carpenters and farriers. Until the cheap wire nail changed the pattern of fastening in carpentry, farriers used the claw hammer even more than carpenters (Mercer, 1960, p. 264). One wrought iron specimen was found in Feature 51 in the southwest casemate. The head is 4 inches long with probably $\frac{1}{2}$ inch of the claw missing (fig. 56a). The poll is $1\frac{1}{2}$ inches long and almost 1 inch in diameter. The claw was formed by splitting the metal. A U-shaped metal strap was welded inside the eye so that the top of the eye was capped. The arms of the "U" protruded $\frac{1}{2}$ inch below the bottom of the eye to reinforce the handle.

Peen. One half of a wrought iron light hammer, similar to an upholsterer's hammer, was found in the north casemate (Level I). The poll is $1\frac{7}{8}$ inches long, $\frac{3}{4}$ inch in diameter near the eye, tapering to a $\frac{1}{4}$ inch diameter at the peen. The top, bottom and outside surfaces of the eye are flat. The other end of this tool is missing.

Sledge. One-third of what appears to have been a sledge hammer was found in the bridge area (Level X). The polls are octagonally shaped, each side $1\frac{1}{2}$ inches wide, and $2\frac{1}{2}$ inches long. The cheek is $1\frac{1}{2}$ inches wide, $1\frac{1}{2}$ inches long, and 1 inch thick. One peen has been broken off and the remaining one has a concave surface.

Category 1. Two unknown metal tools, both broken and missing the same parts, were found in the sally port (Level II) and in the southeast casemate (Level II). They were classified under hammers because the remaining portion most likely was used as a hammer (fig. 56b). The one from the sally port is smaller, better preserved and shows better workmanship. Its functional parts are distinct and well formed. The poll measures $1\frac{1}{4}$ inches long, $\frac{5}{8}$ by $\frac{3}{8}$ inches at the eye, and $\frac{3}{8}$ inch square at the peen. The cheeks are $2\frac{1}{2}$ inches wide with two metal rivets holding the head and handle together. The eye is only $\frac{1}{2}$ inch wide and at least 3 inches long. The handle was probably elliptical in shape. Since the eye was so wide, the missing portion may have been a large hammering surface or a cutting edge. The specimen from the southeast casemate has a poll $1\frac{3}{8}$ inches long, $\frac{3}{8}$ by $1\frac{1}{8}$ inches at the eye, and $\frac{3}{8}$ by $\frac{5}{8}$ inches at the peen. The cheeks are $2\frac{3}{8}$ inches wide and also have two rivets for attachment to the handle. The eye is $\frac{5}{8}$ inch wide and approximately 3 inches long. There are similarities between these artifacts and shingling hatchets or lath hatchets. However, both of these types of hatchets would have had a flat top and been of heavier construction.

Files

Files have traditionally been divided into two classes: metalworking and woodworking. Within these two classes, there were a large number of specialized forms for various craftsmen. Eighteenth century files were made by cutting grooves into the face of a blank bar with a cold chisel. The spacing of the grooves was judged by eye (Mercer, 1960, p. 293). Files could be singly cut with parallel grooves or doubly cut with crosshatched grooves. The inventories from the fort did not specifically mention files. However, they listed one carpenter's chest of tools and one set of blacksmith's tools which probably contained files. Several types of saws were listed and these had to be continually sharpened if they were put to much use. An inventory of sundry stores sent from Boston to Springfield, Bennington and Albany in January of 1777, had a large number of files listed (Gates Papers, Reel XI). Some of these were probably sent on to Fort Stanwix.

Metalworking Files. Used for sharpening, honing and smoothing. The grooves are relatively shallow but well-defined. All are made of steel.

Type 1. Elongated diamond cross section with two knife edges. The one specimen from Feature 69 (Level II) in the east barracks is incomplete; most of the tang and one-third to one-half of the blade survive. It has a flat tapering tang, round heel and straight edges. It is a single cut file with approximately 20 grooves to the inch. The ridge along the face of the blade is slightly off center and the blade is 1¼ inches wide.

Type 2. Rectangular cross section. The heel is square, the tang tapering to a point and the blade tapering slightly from the heel to a square or rounded tip. It is a single cut file with grooves on the faces and edges. Two specimens are in the collection. A complete file was found in the east barracks (Level I) and one blade was in the southeast casemate (Level III). The complete file is 9¾ inches long, ¾ inch wide, tapering to ⅝ inch, 3/16 inch thick and has a 7¾ inch long working surface with approximately 40 grooves to the inch. The other is 1 inch wide, ¼ inch thick and has approximately 32 grooves to the inch.

Type 3. Triangular cross section with tapered tang and blade. These were probably used primarily for sharpening saws. The three faces are equal in width ranging from ¼ to ⅞ inch. None of the specimens are complete but they probably ranged in length from 7 to 10 inches.

Variety a. Single cut files with 50 to 60 grooves to the inch. One came from the north casemate (Level I) two from the west ditch (Level I) and one from the east casemate (Level II).

Variety b. Double cut files with 40 to 60 grooves to the inch. Two came from the north casemate (Levels I, II) two from the passageway of the northeast bombproof (Level II) and one from Feature 64 (Level III) in the west barracks.

Category 1. Three badly deteriorated specimens were in a tool kit found in Feature 60 (Level II) of the west barracks.

Type 4. Piano-convex cross section. One incomplete specimen from the southwest casemate (Level III) measured ½ inch in width, tapering to a point, and 3/16 inch thick. The flat face was double cut and the convex face was single cut. It was too badly corroded to obtain a reasonable estimate on the number of grooves. Two more were found in Feature 60 and are described under tool kit.

Type 5. Knife file (Mercer, 1960, pp. 295–296). This has the same shape as a chef's knife, except for a uniform thickness (fig. 56d). The tang is a continuation of the upper half of the blade and is approximately one-half as long as the blade. Two specimens, one from the west ditch (Level I) and one on the parade ground near the headquarters (Level I) were complete. They had 2⅜ and 2½-inch-long blades, 1¼-inch-long tangs, ½ and 9/16-inch widths and were ⅛ inch thick. All of the grooves had been obliterated. This type of file was definitely used for sharpening saws.

Woodworking files. These are generally coarse with deep cut grooves. They are not rasps because the cutting surface was made by cutting grooves into the face of the metal rather than punching points out from the back of the cutting surface.

Type 1. Rectangular in cross section. The sides taper slightly to a square tip and the tangs on both specimens are missing. They have double cut faces and single cut edges, with approximately 16 grooves to the inch. They are 1 1/16 and 1⅛ inches wide, 3/16 inches thick and approximately 9 inches long. One was found in the north casemate (Level I) and the other in the east casemate (Level I).

Whetstones

Two natural sandstone cobbles were found in the west end of the north casemate (Level II) which had been used as whetstones. Dimensions: length, 13.9 and 14.0 cm.; width, 31 and 47 mm.; and thickness, 31 and 38 mm. A fragment of a shaped slab of fine-grained sandstone, 49 mm. wide and 10 mm. thick was found in the west casemate (Level II).

Saw Blade

Saws appeared on all the inventory lists that have been found for the American occupation of the fort. They were categorized into three types: crosscut, whip and hand. Presumably, hand saw was a miscellaneous category for all small saws. One small fragment of a steel saw blade was recovered from the sally port (Level II). The blade is 7/8 inch wide and less than 1/16 inch thick. The teeth are short and number 10 to the inch.

Saw Dog

One small saw dog was found in Feature 76. The wedge-shaped tangs are 1½ inches long and spaced 4½ inches apart. This was used to hold a log in position while it was being trimmed and shaped.

Punch

A metal punch from the southwest casemate (Level I) was recovered. It is a heavy, stout tool that could have been used on either soft or hard material, but the head does not show heavy hammer marks. This tool was not on any of the inventory lists but neither were many other tools that artificers used. The punch was 5½ inches long; 3⅜ inches of the upper part of the stem is round and ⅝ inch in diameter. The lower part is square, tapering uniformly on all four sides to a sharp point.

Augers and Gimlets

Although there were no specific mention of the use of augers, the carpenters probably used them quite often since all the structures and furniture were constructed of wood. Pegging pieces of wood together was a common 18th-century method of joining. One fairly complete auger from Feature 57 (Level II), two possible shanks of augers from the northeast bombproof (Level I) and the east casemate (Level II), one auger bit from the southwest casemate (Level II) and one gimlet from the sally port (Level II) were recovered during excavations. The complete auger measures 7⅛ inches long with a 5-inch-long shank, and a bit 2⅛ inches long and ½ inch in diameter. The bit has two parts, a short screw tip and a spoon-shaped cylinder that cut out the wood clockwise (fig. 56g). The shank is ¼ inch square and flattened out on two sides to a point to fit into a rectangular chuck.

The two shank fragments are 5 and 6 inches long respectively. The shorter one has a ¼-inch-square shank with a round end, and the other has a ¼-inch-diameter shank with a square tapered end like a modern auger (fig. 56h). The bit fragment is missing the shank and the upper part of the bit. It is a nose auger (Mercer, 1960, p. 185), that is, all the cutting occurred at the tip by the knife-shaped cutting edge that is almost perpendicular to the length of the bit. There is no screw tip, so a hole was started for this auger and pressure was applied via the handle in order to cut the hole. The bit is a half cylinder and had to be continually withdrawn from the hole to discharge the shavings. This bit cut a hole 1 inch in diameter with a flat bottom. The bit cut in a clockwise turn.

A gimlet is a small diameter bit for drilling wood. Ten "Gimbletts" were listed on the April 1778, engineers' inventory (Clinton, 1900, 1554), while all other references to "Gimblets" were under artillery stores. Gimlets could have been used like vent picks for cannon as well as for boring holes in wood. There were other uses as well.

A Regimental Court Martial to sit . . . for the tryal of John Honeywell . . . on suspicion of aiding William McCord to draw Rum belonging to the Publick without Leave, and Supplying him with a Gimblet for that purpose . . . (M. Willett 1/18/78).

Only one gimlet fragment was found. The bit is missing but the shank is 4⅛ inches long, round at the end and square towards the bit.

Button Bit

A total of 20 bone buttons (see Buttons, Type F-2), 33 bone blanks and three button bits were found. All of the blanks except three came from the sally port area (Level II). One complete bit, 1 inch in diameter, was found in the sally port (Level II) (fig. 76l). One with the cutting edge missing, about ¾ inch in diameter, was found in the north casemate (Level I) and the shank of a third was found in the bridge area (Level II). Several of the cuts in the used blanks could be matched with the larger bit found with them. This type of bit dates back to Roman sites of the First Century A.D. (Mercer, 1960, pp. 195–198).

The bit consists of three pointed cutting surfaces on a flat blade; one in the center and two at the edges, the area between the center and the edges arched and never cutting deeply into the bone. Most of the buttons have circular striations on both faces which indicates cutting from both sides of the blank. The bit is 3⅛ inches long, the end of the tang 5/16 inch wide and the sides flaring out to 1 inch at the tip. It is uniformly ⅛ inch thick and has flat faces and squared edges. The three points are all of different lengths; the center point being the longest, 1/16 and ¼ inch longer than the other points. The center point is beveled on three surfaces to come to a sharp tip, while the outer points are beveled on the inside and outside surfaces to form a knife edge. The bit was turned clockwise when cutting out the button; it could be turned by hand without a handle but it was probably fitted with a wooden handle with a rectangular socket that fit over the end of the bit. There was a hole in the shank for securing the handle.

The second bit was incomplete and the cutting surface had rusted away. It has a tang 2 inches long and ¼ inch square, a shaft 3/16 inch in diameter and 1¼ inches long and a flat blade ⅛ inch thick and about ¾ inch wide. This bit would have required a handle or a brace. The shank of the third was shaped the same as the complete bit but no measurements could be taken.

Chisels

Two chisels were found in the excavation, one in the bridge area of the ditch (Level X) and the other in the southwest casemate (Level II) (fig. 56f). They may have been part of the blacksmith's kit or perhaps a brickmason's kit. They were different from wedges in that there was a distinct handle for the worker to grasp and the blade flared out from the handle to the bit. The chisel from the casemate is heavy and massive. It is 8½ inches long, with a 2-inch-wide bit. The handle was 1 by 1¼ inches wide and 4 inches long and the head and bit are splayed. There was a broad arrow stamped into one face. The other chisel was 7⅛ inches long with a 2¼-inch-wide bit and has a round handle ¾ inch in diameter and 3¾ inches long. The head is slightly splayed from hammering.

Screwdriver

Although screws were not common fastening devices during the late 18th century, one screwdriver was found in the southwest casemate (Level

II) (fig. 56i). The blade is 4⅛ inches long, ¼ inch square at the guard and flattened out to ⅜ by ⅛ inch at the tip. The tang is ¼ inch square at the guard, 1⅜ inches long and tapered to a point. The guard is ½ inch square and ⅛ inch thick. This tool does not have a well-defined head distinct from the shank; the tip is merely blunted.

Tool Kit

Pieces of five assorted files, one punch, an iron bar and a nail, all wrapped together in a piece of coarse cloth and bound with twine, were found in Feature 60 (Level II). Three of the files are triangular (Type 3) and the other two are plano-convex (Type 4). One triangular file is ¼ inch on a side; the others are smaller but too fragmentary to measure. Grooves were barely distinguishable but no count could be made. One plano-convex file was broken, but both halves were put into the kit. It is 10¼ inches long, 1 inch wide and ¼ inch thick. The pointed tang is flat on the top and bottom and the blade is widest about 2 inches in front of the tang, tapering to a square tip ¼ inch wide. All the grooves on the flat surface were obliterated. The top was double cut, but not enough remained to obtain a count. The fifth file is the tip half of another plano-convex file. It is smaller than the other and has a pointed tip. It is ¾ inch wide and was double cut on both faces; the grooves were too badly deteriorated to count. The punch is only 3 inches long and ¼ inch in diameter at the head, and ⅛ inch in diameter at the point. The metal bar may have been the middle section of a handle or a tang. It is rectangular in cross section, ¼ inch wide at one end and 3/16 inch wide at the other. The wrought iron nail is corroded and incomplete.

There was such a mixture of items that this kit could not be easily identifiable with any particular craft. All the files appear to have been used for metalworking. This kit probably belonged to some sort of a "smith."

Sheaves

Parts of at least two iron sheaves were found in Feature 69 (Level II) in the east barracks. Rope, three poles and some sheaves are all that were needed to make a gin for lifting cannon tubes onto their carriages, or hoisting barrels and bales of supplies. The cellars of the barracks were probably used to store supplies, much of which were packed, shipped and stored in barrels that weighed up to 200 lbs. apiece (Leonard, 1780). The sheaves were approximately 3¾ inches in diameter and 1 inch wide at the rim. The center of the sheave rim was recessed ½ inch to hold a rope. It was impossible to tell how the sheaves were mounted or whether they were part of a block.

Net Sinkers

Three lead net sinkers were found ranging from 30.5 mm. to 35.5 mm. in length with a hole at one end (fig. 52i). These were found in Feature 76, on the east scarp (Level II) and in the northeast bombproof (Level I). Occasional fish bones in the fill indicated that fish were a part of the soldiers' diet (Appendix B) and the absence of fishhooks coupled with these net sinkers suggests that fishing was not an individual enterprise but was an organized group activity. Netting usually requires cooperation between several individuals.

Transportation Objects

Overland travel on the frontier was principally by foot, although wealthy gentlemen and ranking officers used horses when they could. Horses and oxen were used primarily as draft animals to pull wagons and sleighs although we have no direct references to oxen at the fort.

The quantity of camp equipage, clothing, blankets and stores which Colonel Willett found in the two camps, rendered it necessary to hasten a messenger to the fort and have the wagons sent, seven of which were stored in the fort with the horses. (W. Willett, 1831, p. 195).

. . . horselers and Slaymen . . . First returning Slays to Albany . . . All the Slays . . . are to be detained two days to draw wood . . . (M. Willett, 12/31/77 and 1/3/78)

Horseshoes

Fourteen whole and fragmentary horseshoes (table 20) were found scattered around the site. A farrier must have been shoeing horses for so many of them to have been found here.

Type 1. Flat surfaces with no calkings. The nail holes are rectangular in shape with no consistent pattern of spacing within the type.

Table 20.

Distribution of horseshoes and oxshoes.

| Type | Horseshoes | | | | | | | Oxshoes | |
| | 1 | | | 2 | | 3 | 4 | 1 | 2 |
Variety	a	b	c	a	b	a	b		a	b
Casemates										
North	1	1		1¹						
East				1						
Barracks, West	1¹				1¹					
Parade Ground								1¹		
Bombproof,										
Southwest				1						
Ditch				1		1			1 1	1
Ravelin					1¹		1¹			1
East Scarp			1			1¹				
Sally Port		1¹								
Variety Total	2	2	1	4	2	1	1		1 1	
Type Total		5			6		2		2	2

¹ Complete specimens

Variety a. U-shaped with parallel branches (fig. 57a). The ground surface was convex and the foot surface (Noël Hume, 1970, p. 237) was flat. The branches taper slightly toward the heel but otherwise the shoes are of even width throughout. The complete shoe is 4 inches long and 4⅜ inches wide. These were made from straps ¾ inch wide and 5/16 inch thick. Seven holes, three on each branch and one in the toe were cut into the complete shoe. The other shoe has three holes on the branch.

Variety b. U-shaped with converging branches and fullered. The complete shoe has a flat foot surface and convex ground surface while the fragmentary shoe has two flat surfaces. They measure 3¾ inches and 4½ inches in width; the complete specimen is 5 inches wide. The metal strips from which they were made measure 1⅛ by ¼ inches for the larger and ⅝ by ¼ inch for the smaller. The larger shoe has three closely spaced rectangular holes on each branch. The smaller one has two holes and only a very narrow and shallow fuller.

Variety c. U-shaped with diverging heels. A fragment of one shoe was found. The metal strip is ¾ inch wide while the thickness varies from 1/16 inch on the outside edge to ⅛ inch on the inside and increased to ⅜ inch at the heel.

Type 2. Branches with calkins.

Variety a. U-shaped with converging branches and fullered (fig. 57b). The calkins vary in size and shape. Small ones are the width of the shoe, ⅛ to ¼ inch and projected ¼ inch from the ground surface. Large ones are ¼ to ½ inch wide and project ⅜ inch. Each branch has three or four nail holes, flat foot surfaces and convex ground

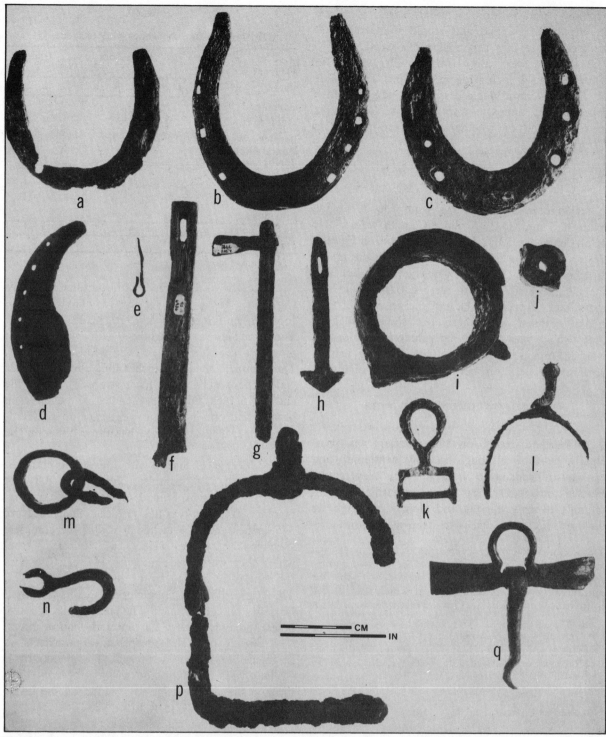

Figure 57. a, Type 1a horseshoe from the west barracks, Level I; **b,** Type 2a horseshoe from the north casemate, Level IV; **c,** Type 3b horseshoe from the east scarp, Level II; **d,** Type 2 oxshoe from the bridge area, Level XI; **e,** cotter pin from Feature 51; **f,** Type 1b linch pin from the bridge area, Level XI; **g,** Type 1a linch pin from the ravelin, Level II; **h,** Type 2 linch pin from the bakehouse, Level II; **i,** wheel hub from Feature 51; **j,** wheel hub from the sally port, Level III; **k,** harness fastening from the north casemate, Level I; **l,** spur from the east scarp, Level I; **m,** harness fastening (?) from the northeast bombproof, Level II; **n,** harness fastening (?) from the sally port, Level II; **p,** stirrup from Feature 56, Level III; **q,** snaffle bit part from the north casemate, Level I.

surfaces. The one complete specimen is $4\frac{3}{4}$ inches long and 5 inches wide; the metal strip from which it was formed is $\frac{3}{4}$ inch wide and $\frac{1}{4}$ inch thick.

Variety b. U-shaped with converging branches. The calkins on both specimens are approximately $\frac{3}{8}$ inch long and project $\frac{1}{8}$ inch. They are $5\frac{1}{4}$ and $5\frac{1}{2}$ inches long and $4\frac{3}{4}$ inches wide. The larger specimen was made from a strip 1 inch wide and $\frac{3}{16}$ inch thick and has three holes in one branch and four in the other. The other is $\frac{3}{4}$ inch wide and $\frac{3}{16}$ inch thick and has two holes in one branch and three in the other. They have flat foot and convex ground surfaces.

Type 3. Branches with calkins and cleated toes.

Variety a. U-shaped with parallel branches. This was the heaviest shoe found. The metal is 1 inch wide at the toe, tapered to $\frac{5}{8}$ inch at the calkin and is $\frac{1}{4}$ inch thick. The toe cleat is $1\frac{1}{2}$ inches wide, the same width as the shoe and $\frac{1}{4}$ inch high. At least two nail holes were found approximately $1\frac{1}{2}$ and $2\frac{1}{2}$ inches from the point of the toe. It is $4\frac{1}{2}$ inches long and probably more than 5 inches wide.

Variety b. U-shaped with parallel branches and welded cleat (fig. 57c). The toe is $1\frac{1}{4}$ inches wide and the width narrows to $\frac{1}{2}$ inch at the calkins. Three nail holes were made in each branch. A 1 by $\frac{1}{2}$ by $\frac{1}{4}$ inch iron cleat was welded on the front ground surface. Both surfaces are flat. The shoe is $4\frac{3}{4}$ inches long and $4\frac{3}{4}$ inches wide.

Type 4. Branches with calkins and clipped toe. This specimen is badly worn and misshapen. The point of the toe is bent up to form the clip and the calkins are indistinct knobs at the ends of the branches. One branch has two nail holes and was fullered, the other has four nail holes and was not fullered. The shoe is 5 inches long and $4\frac{1}{8}$ inches wide. The metal is $\frac{3}{4}$ inch wide and $\frac{1}{8}$ inch thick. Both surfaces are flat.

Oxshoes

An ox's hoof is split, so two shoes for each hoof are needed. Since oxshoes serve the same functions as horseshoes, they have many features in common and the terminology is the same. Since the shoes are not symmetrical, left and right side of the hoof is easily identifiable. Four complete shoes were found (table 20). The toes are the narrowest part and the branch widens out to the maximum width at the heel.

Type 1. Cleated toe and branches with calkins.

Variety a. Without fullering. One right side shoe was found. It is 4 inches long, $\frac{1}{8}$ inch thick and $\frac{1}{2}$ to $1\frac{3}{4}$ inches wide. The cleat and calkin project $\frac{1}{8}$ inch below the shoe and both surfaces are flat. Five nail holes were bored along the branch.

Variety b. With fullering. One left side shoe was found. It is 4 inches long, $\frac{1}{8}$ inch thick and $\frac{1}{2}$ to $1\frac{3}{8}$ inches wide. The cleat and the calkin are $\frac{1}{8}$ inch high. Three nail holes were bored in the branch.

Type 2. Flat surface with fullered branches. Two specimens, both right side, were found (fig. 57d). The one from the east ditch (Level II) is considerably larger than the one from the ravelin (Level II). The former may date post-1781. They measure $5\frac{1}{8}$ inches and 4 inches long, $1\frac{3}{4}$ inches and $1\frac{3}{8}$ inches maximum width and $\frac{1}{4}$ inch thick. The larger one has five nail holes and a shallow narrow fuller while the smaller one has four nail holes and a wide deep fuller.

Stirrups

Two iron stirrups were found. One, found by Campbell, has a divided foot bar and an opening at the top for the harness. The other, from Feature 56 (Level III) in the west barracks has a foot bar divided into four rods and an iron loop welded (?) to the top (fig. 57p). It is $6\frac{1}{2}$ inches high including the loop and $5\frac{1}{2}$ inches wide.

Spurs

Two iron spur fragments were found, a wrought one by Campbell and a cast one (fig. 57l) on the east scarp (Level I). The latter has a rowl mounted horizontally. It is 4 inches long and 3 inches across, cast with a scale motif. The one Campbell found is fragmentary but the rowl was mounted vertically.

Bits

Two parts of an iron snaffle bit were found in the north casemate (Level I) (fig. 57q). It is approximately 9 inches long with $4\frac{1}{2}$ inch cheek pieces on either side. It might date post-1781. However, identical specimens were found at Fort Ligonier, 1758-1766 (Grimm, 1970, p. 51).

Harness Fastenings

Two iron frames with a loop at one end and a post riveted across the other (fig. 57k) were interpreted as harness parts. Both showed wear in the loop and a notch in one end of the rivet similar to a screw. They came from the north casemate (Level I) and the east casemate (Level II). Another possible fragment with an iron ring in the loop was fund in the northeast bombproof (Level II) (fig. 57m). A hook with a T-shaped tip and a worn-through eye (fig. 57n) was found in the sally port (Level II). See also: Buckles, Type 5.

Wheel Parts

The metal parts, hubs, reinforcing bands and fasteners have survived, but no wooden parts identifiable as wheel spokes or felly sections were found.

Wheel Hubs. Two wheel hubs, one large and one small, were found (fig. 57i, j). The large specimen found in Feature 51 in the southwest casemate was made from an iron strap wrapped around a round mandrel with the ends bent outward and welded together. This ridge, approximately $\frac{1}{2}$ inch high and one nipple $\frac{3}{8}$ inch in diameter and $\frac{1}{2}$ inch high kept the wooden part of the hub from slipping. It is $2\frac{1}{4}$ inches wide and $\frac{5}{8}$ inch thick with an axle bore of $2\frac{3}{4}$ inches in diameter. The small hub, found in the sally port (Level III) may have been for a wheelbarrow or small cart. It is cast steel $1\frac{1}{8}$ inches in diameter, $1\frac{1}{2}$ inches wide and $\frac{1}{4}$ to $\frac{3}{8}$ inch thick. The bore tapers from $\frac{5}{8}$ to $\frac{1}{2}$ inch in diameter. There were two $\frac{1}{4}$-inch high wedge-shaped protuberances directly opposed to each other on the exterior.

Flange. A wrought iron circular disc, concave on one side and convex on the other, was found in the sally port (Level II). It is 3 inches in diameter and $\frac{1}{2}$ inch thick; the concavity is $\frac{1}{2}$ inch deep. A hole bored in the middle is 1 inch in diameter and the wall is $\frac{3}{4}$ inch thick. This may have been part of the pivot assembly of the front axle on a wagon.

Reinforcing Band. A metal band approximately $4\frac{1}{2}$ inches in diameter was found in Feature 56 (Level III). It is $1\frac{1}{4}$ inches wide and $\frac{1}{2}$ inch thick. When found, it was broken and too deteriorated to clean. Remnants of one nail driven from the exterior were still visible in the only hole found. See: Ferrules.

Cotter Keys and Pins. These two items served the same function, keeping pins and washers locked in place. Four keys were found (see: Linch Pin, Type 1a for distribution). They are shaped in an isosceles triangle, approximately 3 inches long, $\frac{3}{4}$ inch wide at the base and $\frac{1}{8}$ inch thick. They were inserted into the slot of the pin and bent 180 degrees to prevent them from slipping out. Cotter pins have not changed in form in the last two hundred years (fig. 57e). Two were found in Feature 51 (Level II), one in Feature 69 (Level II), one in the north casemate (Level III), one in the sally port (Level II) and one in the ravelin (Level II). Two were made from nail rods and the other four from flat metal strips. They vary in length from $1\frac{3}{4}$ to 2 inches long.

Linch Pin. Linch pins were inserted through holes at the end of axles to lock wheels on. They varied in length depending upon the diameter of the axle and hub.

Type 1. A slot at one end for a cotter key and the other end split so the prongs could be divided once the pin was set in place.

Variety a. Made from round steel rods with a slightly tapering point on the slotted end (fig. 57g). Four specimens, one from the guardhouse area (Level II), one from the ravelin (Level II) and two from the Campbell collection were found. All are broken off where the rod splits; the exact lengths are unknown. They measure $\frac{1}{2}$ inch in diameter, approximately $8\frac{3}{4}$ inches from tip to beginning of prongs and 8 inches from key to prong. The slots are $\frac{3}{8}$ to $\frac{1}{2}$ inch from the tip, $\frac{3}{8}$ to $\frac{1}{2}$ inch long and $\frac{1}{8}$ inch wide. All four pins still retained their keys.

Variety b. Made from a rectangular iron bar $\frac{5}{8}$ by $\frac{3}{4}$ inch (fig. 57f). It was found in the ditch (Level II). The prongs are broken off and the key was not attached. It measures 6 inches from the end to the beginning of the prongs and $5\frac{3}{4}$ inches from slot to prongs. The slot is $\frac{3}{8}$ inch from the end and measures $\frac{3}{4}$ inch long and $\frac{1}{4}$ inch wide.

Type 2. Shaped like an arrow so the expanded "arrow head" replaced split prongs (fig. 57h). One specimen was found in the bakehouse (Level II).

It measures 4¾ inches long and the shaft is ½ inch square. The maximum width of the triangular head is is 1¼ inches and the slot is ½ inch from the end. The slot measures ½ inch long and 3/16 inch wide. The key was missing.

Containers

Dishes

Ceramics have proven a valuable archeological tool for assigning dates to sites and interpreting the economic level of the occupants. Since the dates for Fort Stanwix are known, the taxonomic system set up here is geared to a description of the ceramics and an interpretation of the vessel forms represented in the collection. The basic breakdown into series is based on the paste of the vessels, which is a product of the types of clays used in making the vessels and the temperature at which they were fired. There are three series: porcelain, stoneware and earthenware. These are further divided into types based on color and treatment of the paste (coarseness), and the kind of glaze applied to the surface. A final division was made on the basis of surface decoration. It should be kept in mind that all these types were essentially contemporaneous in that they were in use between 1758 and 1781, and that the introduction of a new type did not necessarily mean that earlier types ceased to be made or used.

An effort was made to identify and count the minimum number of vessels in each type. This was accomplished by sorting all the sherds by their attributes (of which rim form and decoration were the most important) into separate clusters until no further matchups were possible. At this point we discovered the cross-mends between the north casemate and the east scarp (Level II) and sally port (Level II). A vessel might, therefore, be represented by from one to any number of potsherds. This provided us with an entirely different perspective to the ceramic inventory, and allowed us to develop some hypotheses regarding the economic status of various buildings' occupants. At the same time, it was noted that certain ceramic types were quite restricted as to their vessel forms, at least for the period and locality under study. Table 21 lists the sherd counts for the various units of the fort and tables 22 and 23 list the minimum vessel counts based on the sorting of the sherds.

Stanley South (1972) has developed a formula for dating pottery samples by averaging the sum of the product of the median dates for ceramic types (of their known time range) and the number of potsherds found for each type. We applied his formula to our total sherd sample from the site. We omitted porcelain and Type 1 earthenware because their known time range is too long to give meaningful median dates. The site has a median date of 1770.0 ± 11.5 years. For the potsherds (2705 sherds) we obtained a mean date of 1772.7 ± 14.3 years, with one standard deviation. Using the same method with the minimum vessel count (365 vessels) we arrived at a mean date of 1767.9 ± 12.9 years. Both of these mean dates are well within tolerable limits for the site (+2.7 years and −2.1 years off respectively). We conclude that the formula is applicable to the Upper Mohawk Valley and yields accurate results. It would appear that minimal vessel counts yield more accurate (not necessarily better) dates, but this is an illusion created by using absolute numbers. A more accurate way of looking at these figures would be to say that Fort Stanwix was occupied from 1758 to 1781, while the potsherds indicate an occupation from 1758 to 1787, and the minimum vessel count indicates an occupation from 1755 to 1781. On the east scarp (Level II) and in the sally port (Level II) were large deposits which can be dated from 1776 to 1781. Dates derived from the potsherds in the deposits were 1755 to 1782 and by minimum vessel count, 1755 to 1783. This substantiates what we had already suspected, that these deposits included a lot of pre-1776 material in their fill. For comparison we applied the South technique to Fort Ligonier, 1758-1766 (Grimm, 1970, pp. 159–166) and obtained dates of 1756-1767 for the pottery sample (1761.8 ± 5.47 years).

No marked specimens of pre-1781 vintage were found at Fort Stanwix. Consequently, the identification of specimens rests largely upon a body of comparative data built up over the years and by documented specimens in various collections. Some names, such as creamware, are applied so generally that we use them in the discussion in preference to "refined buffware coated with a clear lead glaze." Other names, like Queensware, were trade names that have no utility in an archeological report. Josiah Wedgwood used Queensware to refer to his high quality creamware, but since we lack any marked pieces it is impos-

Table 21.
Distribution of pottery types.

	N	W	Casemates SW	SE	E	Barracks E	Barracks W	Guard-house	Head-quarters	Parade Ground
Porcelain										
Type 1										
Variety a	31		19	11	7	41	19	18	1	
b	106	3	97	17	27	78	50	24	6	6
c	3			2		1	3	1		
d	1		15	3	1	4	9	6	2	2
						1				
Type 2										
Stoneware										
Type 1										
Variety a	185	12	237	9	61	84	89	133	17	27
b	53	8	41	7	20	15	30	28	6	8
c	3					1	1			
d	10		24	1	1	2	4	7		
e										
Type 2										
Variety a	1							1		1
b						12	52			
Type 3										
Earthenware										
Type 1										
Variety a	82	11	72	29	25	35	56	56	7	6
b	83	15	55	26	19	44	68	34	1	8
c										
d	13	2	9	2	3	7	2	7		
e	1	2	3	4				2		1
Type 2										
Variety a	194	5	104	11	64	40	140	181	3	30
b	1						1			
c	3					1				
d					3		5			
e	22	3	3	1	2	2	4	5		
f	7			2				1	1	
g							4			
h										
i										
Type 3	5		2		10	3	3			
Type 4	15			1	4	5	1		1	
Type 5										
Variety a	2		7				4	24		
b						1				
c	1		6	1	1		2	1		
d										
Type 6										
Variety a	4		21	4	7	2	14	19	4	1
b	8			1						
c	4					1		1		1
d					6					
e	5			2	12	12	5			
f						6	1			
g	9					4				
Type 7	3		4		3	1	2	10		
Totals	855	61	719	134	276	403	569	559	49	91

sible to be certain that any of our creamware was made by Wedgewood.

Dimensions of vessels were taken whenever possible. Because most vessels were fragmentary it was necessary to measure the component parts and give composite dimensions expressed as the size ranges of the component parts. The measured components were rim diameters, foot-rings or basal diameters, and heights. Vessels referred to as "complete" were represented by sherds large enough to allow us to make the three basic measurements. All measurements were taken in the English system since this was the way they generally had been measured in the literature (Noël

	Bombproofs			Bake-house	Ditch	Ravelin	East Scarp	Sally Port	Total Varieties	Total Types	Total Series
	NE	NW	SW								
Porcelain											
Type 1											
Variety a	1	1		1	2	3	15	13	183		
b	4	6	1	2	19	12	52	60	570		
c									10		
d					3		6	11	63	826	
										1	827
Type 2											
Stoneware											
Type 1											
Variety a	12	6	5	8	76	50	85	117	1,213		
b	5	1		1	19	21	36	24	323		
c	1								6		
d	2				3	1		3	58		
e					1				1	1,601	
Type 2											
Variety a						1	1		5		
b					4			1	69	74	
Type 3					1		1			2	1,677
Earthenware											
Type 1											
Variety a	12	6	2	6	63	56	98	76	698		
b	5	9	4	7	42	45	81	71	617		
c							13		13		
d	1			1	8	15	13	5	88		
e					3				16	1,432	
Type 2											
Variety a	6	21	3	5	36	11	59	60	973		
b					2		2	5	11		
c						1		1	6		
d						6		4	18		
e	4	4		1	28	1	8	11	99		
f				2			2	1	16		
g								1	1		
h									4		
i					1				1	1,129	
Type 3					2					25	
Type 4	2	1			6	1	2	2		41	
Type 5											
Variety a					1			1	39		
b							1	1	3		
c	1				5	9	8		36		
d							2		2	80	
Type 6		2		2	7		1	7	95		
Variety a					1			2	12		
b					4		1		12		
c									6		
d					8	3	5	5	57		
e								1	8		
f						3			16	206	
g											
Type 7				2	2					27	2,940
Totals	56	57	16	38	347	239	492	483			5,444

Hume, 1970), and to the nearest half inch to minimize the inaccuracies of projecting rim curves from small fragments, and because shrinkage during firing required potters to compensate by making vessels larger than desired. Variations in the paste of a vessel or the heat of the kiln would affect the size of the final product. On some porcelains this shrinkage might be as high as 11 percent of the original size. (Pascale, n.d., p. 63).

Porcelain

Type 1. Hard paste Oriental. Chinese porcelain was made from a combination of kaolin and

Table 22.

Distribution of pottery vessel forms by type.

	Plates	Saucers	Cups	Tea-pots	Sugar Bowls	Pit-chers	Tank-ards	Handled Cups	Bowls
Porcelain									
Type 1									
Variety a		2	1						3
b	8	36	33	3					18
c		3	1						
d	3	8	3						5
Type 2		1							
Stoneware									
Type 1									
Variety a	58	38	31		4		7		22
b		35	28		1		1		7
c		2							
d		9	7						3
e				1					
Type 2									
Variety a							?		
b							1		
Type 3				1	1				
Earthenware									
Type 1									
Variety a	1								5
b	10.	3	2						34
c									1
d	1	1							6
e									4
Type 2									
Variety a	16	12	16	8		1	17		11
b		2	1						3
c		1							
d		1							1
e	1	1	1	12			4		3
f		1		1					
g									
h									
i						1			
Type 3									3
Type 4		3		10	1				1
Type 5									
Variety a									
b									
c									
d								8	5
Type 6									
Variety a									3
b									1
c									1
d							1		
e									1
f									1
g									
Type 7								1	3
Totals	98	159	124	36	7	2	31	9	145

petuntse fired at a temperature of about 1400 degrees centigrade. Most Chinese porcelain was manufactured in Ching-tê-Chên, China, and shipped from the port of Nanking (Pascale, n.d., p. 255). No clearly identifiable Japanese ceramics were found. Out of deference to the possibility, we refer to these sherds as Oriental rather than Chinese.

The bulk of the sherds were decorated in underglaze blue, a few were painted in red around the lip and some were painted in red and gold over an underglaze blue, or in several overglaze colors.

Variety a. Undecorated. Most of the sherds in this variety probably came from undecorated portions of decorated vessels. A minimum of only

	Punch Bowls	Pans	Platters	Drug Jars	Jars	Jugs	Total Varieties	Total Types	Total Series
Porcelain									
Type 1									
Variety a							6		
b							98		
c							4		
d							19	127	
Type 2								1	128
Stoneware									
Type 1									
Variety a	1			1			162		
b							72		
c							2		
d							19		
e							1	256	
Type 2									
Variety a									
b					1	1	3	3	
Type 3								2	261
Earthenware									
Type 1									
Variety a				9			15		
b	1			7			57		
c							1		
d	1			1			10		
e							4	87	
Type 2									
Variety a							81		
b							6		
c							1		
d							2		
e							22		
f							2		
g									
h								115	
i							1	3	
Type 3								3	
Type 4								15	
Type 5									
Variety a			7				7		
b			1				1		
c							13		
d			1				1	22	
Type 6									
Variety a		23	2				28		
b		2					3		
c		6	1				8		
d							1		
e		13			1	1	16		
f							1		
g		2					2	59	
Type 7		1		1		1		7	308
Totals	3	47	12	19	2	3			697

six vessels were counted, two saucers, one cup and three bowls. One bowl has a foot-ring 2 inches in diameter.

Variety b. Decorated in underglaze blue paint (fig. 58a-c, e, h). There were a minimum of 98 vessels in this variety, eight plates, 36 saucers, 33 cups, three teapots and 18 bowls. Decoration was confined to the upper surfaces of plates and saucers, the exterior of cups and teapots and the interiors and exteriors of bowls. In most cases, the designs on the body are landscape scenes, and the rims are decorated with a ribbon of geometric motif. While the ribbon designs on the rims are often found on many vessels, the landscape de-

Table 23.

Distribution of pottery vessel forms by area. (Ratios given are the number of specimens per 10 square feet of excavated area within the structure.)

	Plates	Saucers	Cups	Tea-pots	Sugar Bowls	Pit-chers	Tank-ards	Handled Cups	Bowls
Casemates									
North	18	31	30	5			8		30
West	1	2	3	1					2
Southwest	12	15	18	4			2	1	17
Southeast	3	8	6	1				1	4
East	5	6	5	2			2	1	6
Barracks									
East	6	11	5	3	1		1		11
West	7	17	15	5	1		5	1	10
Guardhouse	5	10	6	1	1		2		10
Headquarters	3	2	1	1			1		2
Parade Ground	2	3	3		1				4
Bombproof									
Northeast	2	7	3	1			1	1	4
Northwest	2	2	1	2					1
Southwest	1	2						1	2
Bakehouse	3	3	1						
Ditch	5	15	9	5	1	1	3	1	11
Ravelin	4	6	3	1			1		7
East Scarp	10	9	7	3	2		3	1	12
Sally Port	9	10	8	1		1	2	1	12
Totals	98	159	124	36	7	2	31	9	145

	Punch Bowls	Pans	Plat-ters	Drug Jars	Jars	Jugs	Total	Ratio
Casemates								
North	1	4	2	5			134	4.19
West				1			10	2.50
Southwest		5	1	1			76	7.60
Southeast	1	3		1			28	18.67
East		3		1			31	2.82
Barracks								
East		5	1	3		1	48	3.40
West		7	3		1		72	5.67
Guardhouse		4	1			1	41	3.42
Headquarters							10	1.54
Parade Ground		2					15	1.67
Bombproof								
Northeast							19	3.45
Northwest							8	1.63
Southwest							6	1.09
Bakehouse		2					9	
Ditch		9	2	2			64	2.24
Ravelin		1				1	24	5.33
East Scarp	1		2	3	1		54	8.06
Sally Port		2		2			48	5.58
Totals	3	47	12	19	2	3	697	3.56

signs are not repeated. Most of the decoration was done in light blue with well-defined lines, but a few specimens (fig. 58e) exhibit a darker smudged blue decoration typically found on early 19th-century "Canton" Chinese export porcelain (Noël Hume, 1970, pp. 262-263). These specimens are, however, clearly associated with pre-1781 deposits and the designs are not the "Canton" motifs.

One saucer, from the southwest casemate (Level II), measures 5½ inches in diameter and 1 inch high with a 3-inch foot-ring and has a dark brown glaze on the exterior down to the foot ring (fig. 58b). Noël Hume, (1970, pp. 259-260) suggests that this type of glaze was popular ca. 1740-

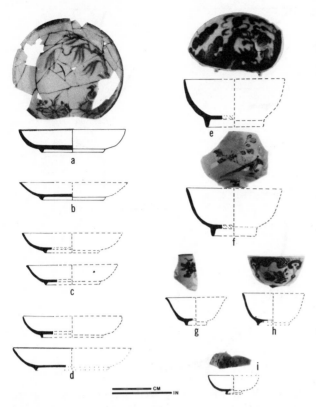

Figure 58. **a,** Oriental blue painted porcelain saucer from the southwest casemate, Level II; **b,** Oriental blue painted porcelain saucer with brown exterior from Feature 56, Level II; **c,** Oriental blue painted porcelain saucers from the guardhouse area, Level II and Feature 69, Level II; **d,** Oriental polychrome painted porcelain saucers from the north casemate, Level I and the southwest casemate, Level II; **e,** Oriental blue painted bowl from the southwest casemate, Level II; **f,** Oriental polychrome painted bowl from the sally port, Level II; **g,** Oriental polychrome painted cup from Feature 57, Level III; **h,** Oriental blue painted cup from the sally port, Level II; **i,** polychrome painted white saltglazed cup from Feature 52, Level III. All polychrome painted vessels are painted overglaze except for the basic design which is in underglaze blue.

1780. This specimen dates between 1758 and 1781. One plate has a rim diameter of 6½ inches while four others have foot-ring diameters of 4 to 5 inches. Rim diameters of saucers range from 4 to 5½ inches and four measurable specimens are 1 inch high. The relationship of rim diameter to foot-ring diameter for these four specimens was 5½ inches to 3 inches, 5 inches to 3 inches, 4½ inches to 3 inches and 5 inches to 2½ inches. Cups have rim diameters of 3 to 3½ inches, a foot-ring diameter of 1½ inch and one was 2 inches high.

Bowls are 4 to 6 inches in diameter at the rim, 2 to 3 inches diameter at the foot-ring and one specimen was 2 inches high. This had a rim to foot-ring relationship of 5 inches to 2½ inches. Miller and Stone (1970, p. 88) have suggested that there is a proportional relationship between the rim diameter and foot-ring diameter of oriental porcelain punch bowls on the order of 2:1. Since archeological specimens are rarely intact, it occurs to us that it might be worthwhile to check the dimensions of other vessel forms by type to see if some useful information would result. This will be explored further in the summary to this section.

Variety c. Decorated with overglaze red paint. Only a minimum of four vessels were found, three saucers and one cup. These vessels are generally thinner than the other varieties and decoration is confined to a narrow area below the lip on the interior of the vessel. This variety continued to be used into the second quarter of the 19th century, having been found in Feature 8, a privy, dating no earlier than 1840 (Hanson, 1974, p. 35). No complete specimens were found. One saucer has a 5-inch diameter while another has a 3-inch foot-ring diameter. The cup has a 3-inch diameter.

Variety d. Decorated with overglaze red, black, white, green and/or gold (fig. 58d, f, g). There were at least 19 of these vessels, three plates, eight saucers, three cups and five bowls. Two of the saucers also have underglaze blue decoration. Two complete saucers have rim diameters of 5 and 6 inches and foot-rings of 3 and 3½ inches in diameter, respectively. Both are 1 inch high. A complete cup is 3 inches wide at the rim, 1½ inches wide at the foot-ring and 1½ inches high. A bowl is 4½ inches wide at the rim with a 2 inch foot-ring and is 2½ inches high. Another specimen has a 2½-inch foot ring.

Stoneware

English ceramic production of the mid-18th century was dominated by the manufacture of a thin, white, salt-glazed stoneware. By the late 1730's slip-casting and press-molding in alabaster and plaster-of-paris molds enabled the manufacture of plates and other vessels in a variety of intricate relief patterns (Mountford, 1971, pp. 29-34). The salt glazing left a surface that can best be described in appearance as like that of an orange peel. This and the relief decoration, made these vessels hard to clean despite their durability and they were later replaced in popularity by refined earthenware (Godden, 1966, XV). No examples of white slipped over gray paste specimens (Noël Hume, 1970, pp. 114-115) were found on the site.

Type 1. White salt glazed.

Variety a. Undecorated, except for relief molding (figs. 59, 60). There were at least 162 vessels of this variety, 58 plates, 38 saucers, 31 cups, four sugar bowls, seven tankards, one punch bowl, 22 small bowls and one drug jar. Slip-casting and press-molding came into vogue in the 1730's and from 1740 to the 1770's were in common use to produce plates with elaborately molded rims (Noël Hume, 1970, pp. 115-118). A number of rim patterns were introduced. Those found at Fort Stanwix are:

Diaper Pattern. Twenty-four plates have alternating panels of basketry, dot and lattice or basketry, star and lattice designs (fig. 60a). These have 9- to 9½-inch rims and one of the latter, from the southwest casemate (Level II) has a 4½-inch base and is 1 inch high.

Gadrooned. Twelve plates have a simple gadrooned or "bead and reel" design along the rim edge (fig. 60b). These are 9½ to 10 inches in diameter with 6-inch basal diameters and are 1 inch high.

Barley. Seven plates have panels of small ovals separated by ribbing (fig. 60d). One plate, from the east scarp (Level II) is 9½ inches in diameter with a 5-inch base and is 1½ inches high.

Queens. Two plates from the sally port (one from Level II and one from Level III) have a ribbed edge and plain panels separated by ribbing. One is 9 inches in diameter with a 6-inch base and is 1 inch high. The other has a rim diameter of 8 inches.

Barley and Wavy Lines. One 10-inch plate from the east scarp (Level II) has alternating panels of small ovals or nested wavy lines separated by ribbing (fig. 60e).

Feather-edge. One 10-inch plate from the sally port (Level II) has a feather edge design.

King of Prussia. One plate celebrating England's alliance with Prussia during the Seven Years War (fig. 60c) (Noël Hume, 1970, pp. 115-117) was found in the guardhouse area (Level II) and cannot be dated

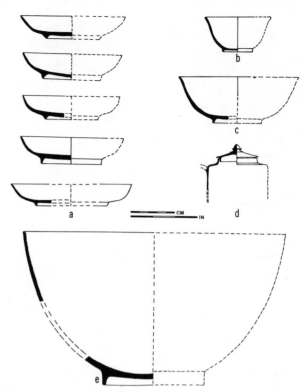

Figure 59. a, white salt-glazed saucers from Feature 56, Level II, Feature 63, Level II, the sally port, Level II, Feature 76 and Feature 3, Level III; **b,** white salt-glazed cup from the east scarp, Level II; **c,** white salt-glazed bowl from the southeast casemate, Level II; **d,** white salt-glazed sugar bowl or creamer from Feature 57, Level III; **e,** white salt-glazed punch bowl from the north casemate, Level II.

more closely than 1758-1781. It has a 9-inch diameter with a 6-inch base and is 1 inch high.

An additional five plates have undecorated rims (fig. 60f). These range in diameter from 9 to 10 inches with 6-inch bases and are ½ to 1 inch high. There are five complete saucers (fig. (59a); four with 4½-inch rim diameters, 2½-inch-foot-rings and 1 inch heights. The other is 5 inches in diameter with a 3-inch foot-ring and is 1 inch high. Other fragments have 4-inch rim diameters or 2-inch foot-rings. One cup has a 3-inch rim diameter with a 1½-inch foot-ring and is 1½ inches high (fig. 59b). Other fragments have a 4-inch rim diameter or foot-rings 1 to 2 inches in diameter. The identification of four sugar bowls as such is tenuous, but there seems little likelihood they could be anything else. One has a relief molded pattern similar to the diaper pattern on plates. It might have been a creamer. One plain specimen has a 1½-inch rim diameter (fig. 59d). Tankard frag-

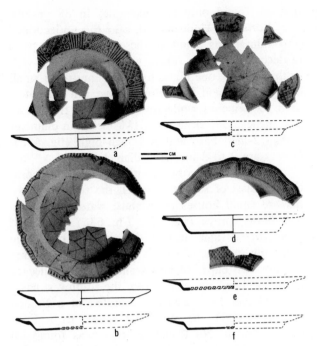

Figure 60. White salt-glazed stoneware plates: **a,** Diaper pattern from the southwest casemate, Level II; **b,** Gadrooned pattern from the southwest casemate, Levels II and I; **c,** "Success to the King of Prussia" pattern from the guardhouse area, Level II; **d,** Barley pattern from Feature 75; **e,** Barley and Wavy Lines pattern from the bridge area, Level XI; **f,** plain plate from the southwest casemate, Level II.

ments have 3- to 4-inch rim diameters or 3- to 3½-inch bases. One punch bowl has a 12-inch rim diameter and a 5-inch foot-ring. It stood approximately 6½ inches high (fig. 59e). Other bowls range in diameter from 4½ inches to 9 inches with foot-rings 2 to 3½ inches in diameter (fig. 59c). A drug jar fragment could not be measured.

Variety b. Decorated with incised lines filled with cobalt blue (fig. 61b, e). There were a minimum of 72 vessels of this variety, commonly known as "scratch blue," 35 saucers, 28 cups, one sugar bowl, one tankard and seven small bowls. Decoration is confined to the exteriors of the cups, tankard and bowls, except for parallel scalloped lines which sometimes occur around the interior rims of cups. Saucers are decorated on the interior and sometimes have a rouletted band of chevrons around the bottom. Saucers range in diameter from 4 to 5 inches with 2- to 3-inch foot-rings and are 1 inch high. Cups are 2½ to 3 inches in diameter with 1- to 1½-inch foot-rings and 1½ inches high. One sugar bowl lid from Feature 52 (Level

IV) has a diameter of 1½ inches and a tankard fragment has a rim diameter of 2 inches. Bowls range from 4 to 5 inches in diameter and one foot-ring 2½ inches in diameter was found.

Variety c. Decorated with red paint. At least two saucers have red lines painted on their interior rims. One vessel is 5 inches in diameter with a 2½-inch foot-ring and is 1 inch high. The other is 4 inches in diameter.

Variety d. Decorated with polychrome paint (fig. 61a). A minimum of ten saucers, seven cups and three small bowls have floral motifs painted in overglaze enamels. Colors include black, red, yellow, blue and green. One saucer is 5 inches in diameter with a 2½-inch foot-ring and is 1 inch high. Another is 2½ inches in diameter with a 1-inch foot-ring and is 1 inch high. This specimen, from Feature 56 (Level IV), was originally thought to be English porcelain but taking into account the style of decoration and the fact that it appears to have been refired (by the burning of the barracks?) led us to change its designation even though the paste compares well with English soft paste porcelain sherds from Fort Michilimackinac loaned to us by Lyle Stone. Other fragments have 4½-inch rim diameters or were 3 inches across at the foot-ring. Cups are 3 inches in diameter and 1½ inches high with 1½-inch foot-rings. One bowl is 5 inches in diameter. None are decorated in a "Fazackerly" style (see Type 1d earthenware below).

Variety e. Covered with copper-tinted lead glaze. A single teapot lid fragment was found.

Type 2. Gray salt-glazed. These vessels are slightly thicker than the white salt-glazed and wheel thrown.

Variety a. With stamped designs filled with cobalt blue. There are only five sherds of this variety, all too small to identify by vessel shape, although thinness suggests tankards or chamber pots. These were probably made in the German district of Westerwald. Noël Hume (1970, p. 280) discusses the problems of identifying the source of this material. As this pottery was out of fashion by 1775 (South, 1972, p. 85), it was not surprising that so few sherds were found.

Variety b. Undecorated or with cobalt blue paint. A tankard, a jug and a jar were identified. These vessels are thicker than Variety a and may have been made in North America. They are indistinguishable from vessels common in the 19th century. Identification rests solely on their being found in pre-1781 contexts. It is possible that a few sherds of this variety were included with the post-1781 sherds where context was in doubt. The tankard is 3 inches across at the rim and the jug has a 1-inch opening. The jar is 4 inches in diameter at the base.

Type 3. Red stoneware with no glaze. A teapot lid fragment 3 inches in diameter and a fragment of a sugar bowl, both with sprigged decoration, were found. This has commonly been called "Elers" ware which is a misnomer since it was made by other potters besides the Elers brothers (Noël Hume (1970, pp. 120-121).

Earthenwares

Earthenwares are made from low grade clays and fired at a relatively low temperature compared to stoneware and porcelain. Distinctions could be made on the basis of whether the paste was refined or coarse (with granules of grit and sand), whether the body was fired to a red or buff color and the kind of glaze applied to the surface. Given these variables, there was almost an infinite variety of wares produced and the typology must, of necessity, be rather arbitrary.

Type 1. Tin-glazed refined buffware. A few of these sherds have pinkish colored bodies but are included here for convenience, since they are otherwise indistinguishable in glaze and decoration. Tin-glazed earthenware was the first attempt to imitate Oriental porcelain and is actually lead-glazed with a tin oxide (Noël Hume, 1970, p. 106). John Cotter (personal communication) suggests that the origin lies in the Iranian tile-making industry of the first millenium B.C. It was being produced under the name "Majolica" in Spain and Italy after the 14th century and was derived from 8th century Moorish pottery (Pascale, n.d., p. 153). By the 16th century, potters from Faenza, Italy, began production in France under the name "Faience" (Pascale, n.d., p. 157) and in Holland and England where it was called "Delftware," a name that did not become popular until the 18th century (Noël Hume, 1970, p. 106). Most tin-glazed earthenwares were decorated with blue designs in imitation of the popular Chinese porcelain. It reached its zenith of popularity early in the 18th century and by mid-century was being replaced by white salt-glazed wares. Ivor Noël Hume's observation (1970, p. 111) that delftware cups should be rare after 1750, is born out by the fact

that we found only two examples in 88 vessels.

Variety a. Undecorated. Like the undecorated porcelain sherds, many of these are probably parts of decorated vessels. There were at least 15 vessels of this variety; one plate, five bowls and nine small drug or ointment jars. Bowls have rim diameters of 5 to 8 inches while foot-rings vary from 2 to $3\frac{1}{2}$ inches. One drug jar is $1\frac{1}{2}$ inches in diameter with a 2-inch base and is 1 inch high (fig. 62e). Others are 2 to 3 inches in diameter.

Variety b. Decorated with blue paint. Decoration consists of scenes in which the recurring motifs are small houses on islands, water and boats and floral sprays (fig. 62c, f-h, 63a). Bands of geometric designs around the rim are rare. The minimum number of vessels is 56; 10 plates, three saucers, two cups, 34 bowls and seven apothecary jars. One bowl rim sherd from the southwest casemate (Level I) is clearly decorated in a French style (fig. 62d); the remainder appear to be English or Dutch. No Rouen Faience was found on the site. One plate is 9 inches in diameter and 1 inch high with a $4\frac{1}{2}$ inch foot-ring while another is 7 inches in diameter and 1 inch high wth a $4\frac{1}{2}$ inch foot-ring. Other rims are 7 to 9 inches in diameter while a foot-ring is 5 inches across. These plates are slightly smaller than comparable specimens at Fort Michilimackinac (L. Stone 1970, p. 439). Two saucer fragments have a $4\frac{1}{2}$-inch rim and a $3\frac{1}{2}$-inch foot-ring, respectively. A cup is 3 inches in diameter. One punch bowl, from the southeast casemate (Level II) is 11 inches in diameter. Other bowls are 5 to 9 inches in diameter with $2\frac{1}{2}$- to 4-inch foot-rings. Two complete specimens are 5 inches in diameter and 2 inches high with a $2\frac{1}{2}$-inch foot-rings, while another is 6 inches in diameter and 3 inches high with a 3-inch foot-ring. Apothecary jars are 4 to 6 inches in diameter with 3- to 6-inch bases decorated with horizontal blue bands.

Variety c. Decorated with black paint. A single bowl from the east scarp (Level II) has flowers outlined on the exterior in fine black overglaze painted lines while in the bottom is the slogan, "Success to Co[ngress]," or "Co[mmerce]." It is too fragmentary to measure the height, but the foot-ring is 3 inches across and the rim diameter is approximately 9 inches.

Variety d. Decorated with red, black, blue, green and/or yellow paint. The common motif is brightly colored floral sprays. There are at least 10 vessels, one plate, one saucer, two punch bowls,

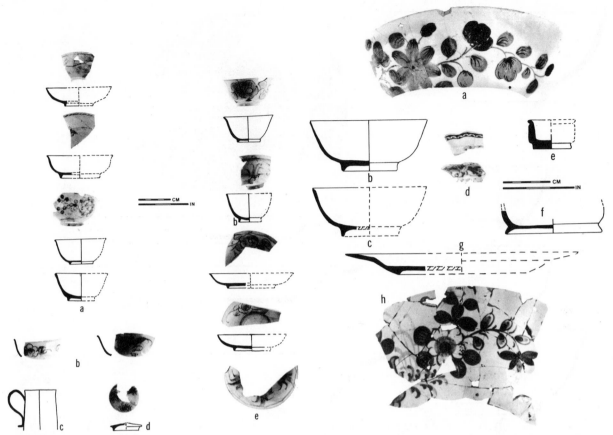

Figure 61. **a,** polychrome painted white salt-glazed saucers and cups from Feature 69, Level I, Feature 34, Level III, the southwest casemate, Level II and Feature 56, Level III; **b,** "Scratch Blue" white salt-glazed cups from the north casemate, Level I, Feature 48, the southwest casemate, Level II and the east scarp, Level III; **c,** "Scratch Blue" white salt-glazed mug from the sally port, Level II; **d,** "Scratch Blue" white salt-glazed sugar bowl lid from Feature 52, Level IV; **e,** "Scratch Blue" white salt-glazed saucers from the west barracks, Level I, the bridge area, Level XI and the east scarp, Level II.

Figure 62. **a,** polychrome painted tin-glazed buffware punch bowl rim in a "Fazackerly" style from the east scarp, Level II; **b,** polychrome painted tin-glazed buffware bowl in a "Fazackerly" style from the north casemate, Level I and the east scarp, Level II; **c,** blue painted tin-glazed buffware bowl from the east scarp, Level II; **d,** French polychrome and blue painted tin-glazed buffware rims from the southeast bastion, Level II and the southwest casemate, Level I; **e,** white tin-glazed buffware drug jar from the north casemate, Level I; **f,** blue painted tin-glazed buffware drug jar from Feature 52, Level III; **g,** blue painted tin-glazed buffware plate from Feature 76; **h,** blue painted tin-glazed buffware punch bowl rim from the southeast casemate, Level II.

six smaller bowls and one drug jar. The plate was represented by a rim sherd decorated in a French style (fig. 62d). All but one of the remaining vessels are decorated in a "Fazackerly" style, named after Thomas Fazackerly of Liverpool, England (Miller and Stone, 1970, p. 36) (fig. 62a, b). These were ascribed to Liverpool, *ca.* 1750-1760 (Miller and Stone, 1970, pp. 34-36). Some of the Fort Stanwix specimens were found in 1776-1781 contexts although they may have

been redeposited. A drug jar, from the east casemate (Level II), with a 4-inch rim and a pink body painted in bright enamel colors appears to be Spanish majolica or French faience. This could not be verified on the basis of comparison. The saucer has a 3-inch foot-ring. One punch bowl has a rim diameter of 9½ inches. A smaller bowl is 4½ inches in diameter and 2 inches high with a 2 inch foot-ring. Others have an 8-inch rim diameter or a 4 inch diameter foot-ring.

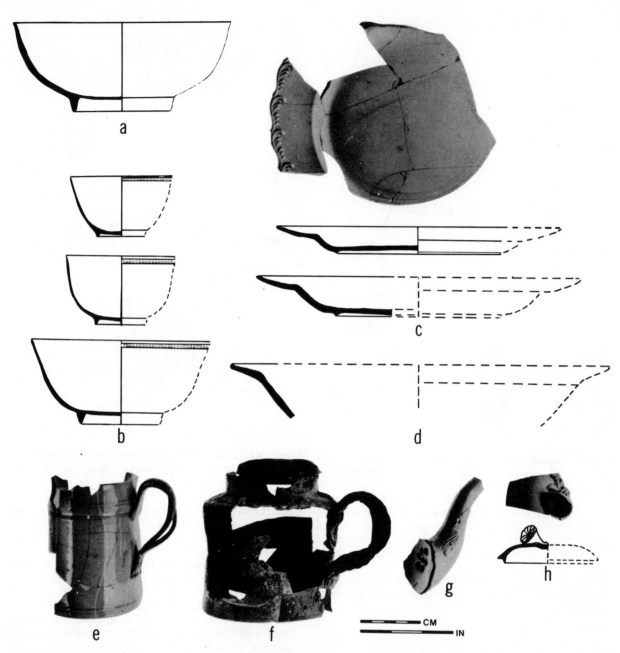

Figure 63. **a,** blue painted tin-glazed buffware bowl from the southwest casemate, Level II; **b,** lead-glazed buffware cups and bowl with beaded band on rim from Feature 56, Level III, the southwest casemate, Level II and Feature 34, Level III; **c,** lead-glazed buffware plates with Featheredge pattern from Feature 34, Level III and Feature 57, Level III; **d,** lead-glazed buffware bowl with beaded rim from the sally port, Level II; **e,** lead-glazed buffware tankard from the sally port, Level II; **f,** lead-glazed buffware teapot (?) with lid which was re-fired when the fort burned from Feature 63, Level III; **g,** lead-glazed buffware teapot spout from Feature 64, Level III; **h,** lead-glazed buffware teapot lid from the east scarp, Level II.

Variety e. Decorated with powdered purple (aubergene) pigment. At least four bowls are decorated on the exterior with a powdered purple pigment. One of these also has a blue painted design on the interior. There may have been unpowdered reserves on the exterior but the sherds are too small to be sure. Two bowls are 7 inches in diameter.

Type 2. Lead-glazed refined buffware. This type is characterized by a cream-colored or buff-colored paste which has all impurities removed. It generally breaks with horizontal cleavage planes. About 1740, this paste was being covered with a light yellow lead-glaze colored with various metallic oxides (South, 1972, p. 85). By 1762, Josiah Wedgwood had perfected a clear lead-glaze and was producing cream-colored earthenware on a commercial basis within a short time (Noël Hume, 1970, pp. 125-126).

Variety a. Clear lead-glaze with no decoration except relief molding. This variety is usually called "creamware" or Queensware." As noted, it was in production by the mid-1760s. At least 81 vessels are represented in the collection: 16 plates, 12 saucers, 16 cups, eight teapots, 17 tankards, one pitcher and 11 bowls (fig. 63b-h). Ten of the plates have a molded feather-edge pattern on the rim dating from *ca.* 1773 (Noël Hume, 1972, pp. 350-355), and one is of the Royal pattern dating from *ca.* 1765 (Noël Hume, 1970 p. 125). Ivor Noël Hume (1970 pp. 126-128) (South, 1972, fig. 1) has observed that creamware is generally darker in color during the period 1762- *ca.* 1780 and that a lighter shade was introduced by *ca.* 1775. This observation, although subjective, seems to be borne out by the presence of both light and dark yellow varieties in pre-1781 contexts, but only light yellow specimens in *ca.* 1802-1825 contexts (Features 71 and 77) (Hanson, 1974, p. 40). However, it should be noted that many pre-1781 specimens are actually lighter than an undecorated pitcher from Feature 77 (see Ramsey 1962, Plate 308d, for vessel of similar shape).

Most of the cups, tankards and bowls are decorated with a beaded band on the exterior rim and some of the saucers have a gadrooned or bead and reel band around the interior bottom. One teapot, tentatively identified because it is missing the spout (fig. 63f), has a gadrooned band around the rim on the lid. One of the plain rimmed plates is 9 inches in diameter, while the feather-edged plates range from 8 to 10 inches in diameter, 1 to 1½ inches high and have 5-inch bases. The saucers are 5 to 6 inches in diameter with 2½-inch foot-rings. Cups are 3 to 4 inches in diameter and 2 inches high with 1½- to 2-inch foot-rings. Creamware cups and saucers tend to be slightly larger than earlier stoneware Type 1a and 1b cups. This may reflect an increase in the practice of tea drinking. Teapots have 2½- to 3-inch rim diameters and 3½-inch bases. One is 4 inches high. A nearly complete tankard is 2½ inches in diameter and 4 inches high with a 2½-inch base. Others are 2½ to 4 inches in diameter or with 2- to 3-inch bases; one pitcher base is 3½-inches across. One bowl is 6 inches in diameter and 2½ inches high with a 2½-inch foot-ring. Others are 5 to 11 inches in diameter or have foot-rings 3 to 4 inches across.

Variety b. With over-glaze red paint. There are at least two saucers, one cup and three bowls decorated with red lines around the interior of the rim. Two saucer fragments include a 5-inch rim and a 2½-inch foot-ring. One bowl has a 5-inch rim diameter.

Variety c. With over-glaze brown paint. There are a minimum of one saucer and one bowl of this variety. The saucer has a brown line on the interior of the rim, while the bowl is decorated with brown panels in a band of raised squares below the lip on the exterior. It appears to have been engine-turned. Both the saucer and bowl are 5 inches in diameter.

Variety d. with over-glaze polychrome paint. These sherds are decorated with floral motifs. Only one saucer is identified by vessel shape and it has painted red and black flowers.

Variety e. With a polychrome glaze (fig. 64a-c). This variety, which has been called "clouded" ware (Noël Hume 1970 p. 123) and under more specific names as "whieldon" ware and "tortoise-shell" ware, was first manufactured about 1740 (South, 1972, p. 85). The clouding was accomplished by sprinkling or sponging oxides of copper, manganese and iron onto the wet glaze and allowing them to "run." This produced a mottled effect or an imitation of tortoise-shell. There are at least 22 vessels of this variety: one plate, one saucer, one cup, 12 teapots, four tankards and three bowls. The plate has a 10-inch diameter castellated rim and a 6-inch base, and is ½ inch high. The teapots have 2- to 3-inch rim diameters and 2½- to 3½-inch bases. The bowls are 5 to

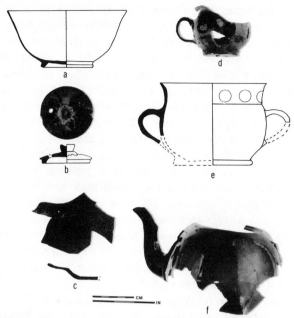

Figure 64. a, polychrome-glazed buffware bowl from the east scarp, Level II, **b,** polychrome-glazed buffware teapot lid from Feature 48; **c,** polychrome-glazed buffware plate from the east scarp, Level II; **d,** lead-glazed white-slipped coarse buffware cup with trailed and dotted red slip from the bridge area, Level XI; **e,** lead-glazed white-slipped coarse buffware bowl with trailed and dotted red slip from Feature 76; **f,** black-glazed refined redware teapot from the bridge area, Level II.

5½ inches in diameter and the latter is 2½ inches high with a 2½-inch foot-ring.

Variety f. With green tinted glaze. There are at least one saucer and one teapot of this variety. This pottery was first produced in 1759 by Josiah Wedgwood (Noël Hume 1970, p. 124). The rich green glaze was produced by adding copper oxides to the basic lead glaze. This saucer has a 4-inch rim diameter and the teapot has a 2-inch foot-ring.

Variety g. With orange glaze. Only one sherd of this ware was found. We are not sure how the glaze was colored, only that it is unique. It was found in the sally port (Level II).

Variety h. With brown glaze. Four sherds from the same vessel, probably a teapot, were found. The glaze is a glossy dark brown with a tendency to flake off.

Variety i. With an over-glaze black transfer print. One sherd with a black transfer print of a sailing ship was found in the ditch (Level XI). It probably came from a pitcher.

Type 3. Clear lead-glazed refined redware.

This type is represented, at most, by three bowls. One of these has a 5-inch rim diameter. The vessel shapes are the same as for Type 2a bowls.

Type 4. Black-glazed refined redware. This type has been called "Jackfield" and was produced after 1740 (South, 1972, p. 85) (fig. 64f). The body is thin and usually has a gray-red or purple color with a glossy black glaze applied over it. A few of our specimens are oil gilded, but no designs could be identified. At least three saucers, 10 teapots, one sugar bowl and one bowl were found. The saucers have rim diameters of 4 inches. One teapot has a 2½-inch rim diameter and a 2-inch base and is approximately 4 inches high. Others have bases 2½ to 4 inches across. The sugar bowl has a 2-inch rim.

Type 5. Lead-glazed slipped coarse buffware. These are vessels with a buff-colored paste containing small grains of sand and grit. Occasionally, a sherd exhibits fine veins of red clay. The surfaces are coated with refined white, red and/or brown slips and are covered with a clear lead glaze. Usually there is no slip or glaze on the pedestal feet of bowls or cups, or the undersides of platters.

Variety a. With red slip and trailed white slips (fig. 65c). There are at least seven large platters of this variety, all with notched lips. A red slip was first applied over the upper surface of the platter; parallel lines of white slip were then laid over the red slip. The upper surface was then lead glazed, changing the colors of the slips to yellow and brown. Because these platters were rarely round, it is not possible to say more than that one was 2 inches high.

Variety b. With combed red slip and trailed white slip. One platter was made the same as Variety a, except that a comb like object was dragged across the surface of the platter at right angles to the slip lines before the glaze was applied.

Variety c. White slipped with trailed and dotted red slip (fig. 64d, e). There are at least 13 vessels of this variety, eight cups and five bowls. The bodies have slips like the platters, except that the white slip nearly obliterates the red, and a row of large red dots was added to the shoulder or rim. The pedestal feet are not slipped or glazed except where the glaze ran. Cups have one thick strap handle and the bowls have two, all on the shoulder of the vessels. The cups have rim diameters of 3 inches with 1½- to 2-inch bases and one is 2 inches high. Bowls are 4½ to 5 inches in diameter with bases 3 to 3½ inches across.

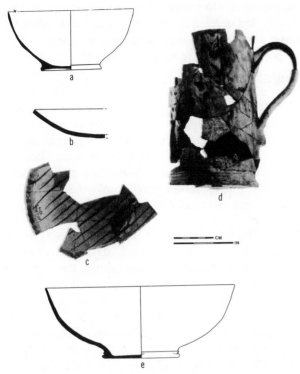

Figure 65. a, lead-glazed coarse redware bowl with a trailed white slip from Feature 72; **b,** lead-glazed coarse redware platter with notched lip from the bridge area, Level I; **c,** lead-glazed coarse buffware platter with red slip, trailed white slip and notched lip from the southwest casemate, Level II; **d,** polychrome-glazed coarse redware tankard with marbled white slip from the east casemate, Level II; **e,** copper-tinted lead-glazed coarse redware bowl with white slip from Feature 72, Level II.

Variety d. With marbled red, white and brown slips. One platter was found which has swirled red, white and brown slips intermingled to produce a marbled effect. It has a notched lip.

Type 6. Lead glazed coarse redwares. This type is largely restricted to utilitarian vessels. It is sometimes difficult to distinguish 18th and 19th century sherds, particularly Variety a. Distinctions were made on the basis of provenience and only those from pre-1781 contexts are described here. All are lead glazed and have inclusions of fine sand and grit in the paste.

Variety a. With no slip (fig. 65b). These vessels are coated with a clear lead glaze. There are at least two bowls, 23 pans and two platters. The pans have thick outrolled rims with straight, flaring walls and are pedestral footed. They are glazed only on the interior. The platters have notches on the lip, but finer than those on the

coarse buffware (Type 5). They are glazed only on the upper surface. One bowl has a 5-inch rim diameter. The bowls are glazed on the interior and exterior. Rim diameters for pans range from 8½ to 15 inches and one fragment of a 7-inch diameter base was found.

Variety b. With white slip. There is a minimum of one bowl and two pans of this variety. The slip, while generally applied, did not coat the entire vessel. The vessel shapes and glazing over the slip are the same as Type 6a. The bowl has a 3-inch-diameter base. The pan fragments are from a 7-inch rim and a 4-inch base.

Variety c. With trailed white slip (fig. 65a). These vessels are decorated with thin lines of white slip. There are at least one bowl, six pans and one platter. The pans are the same shape as Type 6a, and the platter the same as Type 5a. The decoration on the platter is parallel lines, while the lines on the interiors of the pans meander. In some cases the lines might have spelled words, but the sherds are too small for us to be certain. The trailed white slip meanders on the interior of the bowl, while on the exterior it is confined to one small area, suggesting a mark. We could make no sense of it. The bowl is 6 inches in diameter and 3 inches high with a 2½-inch base. Two pan fragments include an 8-inch rim and a 6-inch base.

Variety d. With marbled white slip and metallic oxides in the glaze (fig. 65d). A single tankard of 2-pint capacity, had a swirled white slip covered by a lead-glaze with copper (green) and iron (brown) oxides sprinkled on it. It was 3½ inches in diameter and 6½ inches high with a base 4 inches across.

Variety e. With a copper-lead glaze and no slip. There are at least 16 vessels of this variety: one bowl, 13 pans, one jug and one jar. The pans are the same shape as Type 6a. The jug is a 3½-inch base fragment only, and the jar is a 6-inch open mouthed crock. With the exception of the bowl, which is glazed on both surfaces, all are glazed on the interior only. Copper-lead glazes are common on French buffware vessels in Canada (author's examination). This variety and the following two are probably not of French origin, as the vessel shapes are different and the glaze is not as deep a green. The bowl has a 3-inch basal diameter. One pan has a 10-inch base and two others have 12-inch and 15-inch rim diameters.

Variety f. Copper-lead glazed over a white slip (fig. 65e). Only a single 9-inch bowl, 3½ inches high, with a 3½-inch base could be identified.

Variety g. Copper-lead glazed over a trailed white slip. Two pan fragments 7 inches and 12½ inches in diameter were found.

Type 7. Black glazed coarse. These sherds superficially resemble Type 4, commonly known as "Jackfield," except that the paste is coarser and redder, the vessel walls are thicker, and the glaze is thick and not glossy. There are a minimum of one handled cup, three bowls, one pan, one drug jar and one jug in this type. Identical specimens, in the drug jar form, were found in the Weeden Brigade encampment at Valley Forge (author's examination). The cup has a 3½-inch rim diameter and the bowls are 4 to 10 inches in diameter. The drug jar is 3 inches in diameter and the jug is 3½ inches wide at the base with a 2-inch neck (1-inch opening).

Comparison of the rim and foot-ring dimensions shows that the proportions of plates, saucers, cups and bowls were fairly uniform regardless of the type of pottery or whether made in China or England. The foot-ring diameter is generally one-half to two-thirds as large as the rim diameter. This means that if we have only the foot-ring of one vessel form we should be able to predict the overall size of the vessel with a fair degree of accuracy using a conversion factor. Our sample of measurable vessels was too small to use for calculating conversion factors but the data suggests that plate rims were 1.50 to 2.11 times as large as the diameter of their foot-rings; bowl rims were 1.38 to 2.86 times the diameter of their foot-rings; saucers, 1.30 to 2.25 times as large; and cups, 2.00 to 2.67 times as large. We hope to test this hypothesis with the post-1781 sample of vessels from the site which is large enough to provide adequate samples of each vessel form. The utility of the conversion factor, if its validity can be shown, lies not so much in predicting rim diameters as in demonstrating a relationship, since foot-rings are more durable than vessel rims. It might also be possible to define some temporal changes in the rim to foot-ring proportions. For example, at Fort Stanwix, Type 1 earthenware bowls have rims 2.00 times the size of the foot-ring while Type 2 earthenware is 2.20 to 2.40 times as large, Type 5 earthenware is only 1.33 to 1.43 times as large and Type 6 earthenware is 2.40 to 2.86 times as large. Although the number of vessels involved is small, these observations suggest that there were different standards in the British ceramic industry, and if we can identify those standards we might be able to compare the output of different districts or manufactories.

Bottles

There are five types of bottles, classified according to form. The most common are round free-blown bottles with tooled string rims. Next in popularity are square mold-blown "case" bottles with outrolled lips. Finally, there are round pharmaceutical bottles, octagonal mold-blown bottles and free-blown oval bottles with tooled string rims.

Round Bottles. By far the most common type of bottle is a round, heavy based, dark green bottle with a slight constriction just above the base, a pushed up base, or kick, and a tooled string rim (fig. 66a, b). The count on these specimens was based on the number of necks (table 24). Only one specimen found in Feature 60 (Level II) is complete. Its measurements are: base diameter, 10.7 cm.; kick height, 45 mm.; shoulder diameter, 11.1 cm.; body height, 13.7 cm.; neck height, 10.4 cm.; interior lip diameter, 20 mm. and exterior rim diameter, 36 mm. It has a sand pontil mark 44 mm. in diameter. Composite dimensions for fragmentary specimens are: basal diameter, 9.1 to 11.9 cm., average, 10.6 cm.; kick height, 18 to 52 mm.; average, 34.3 mm.; neck height, 7.7 to 11.0 cm.; average, 9.3 cm.; interior lip diameter, 14 to 20 mm.; average, 16.5 mm.; exterior rim diameter, 32 to 38 mm.; average, 34.1 mm.

Evidence in kicks was found for 37 sand pontil marks ranging in diameter from 36 to 64 mm. with an average of 53.2 mm. (fig. 67a). There are two glass pontil marks 29 mm. and 32 mm. in diameter (fig. 67b). Necks are about evenly divided between those which have slightly flaring fire polished lips with V-shaped string rims below them and those which had the lips pushed down against the V-shaped string rims (fig. 66d). They seemed to be randomly distributed and contemporaneous. Most of the kicks appear to have been formed with a mollette but one was made with a rod 20 mm. square, and another with a quatrefoil rod 30 mm. square (O. Jones, 1971, p. 66). One specimen deserves special mention and this is a bottle from the ravelin (Level II) which has the name "John Sh..o..." scratched into its side (fig. 66b). We have been unable to trace the name to a known occupant of the fort.

Oval Bottles. These are free-blown bottles made in an oval shape rather than round (fig. 66c). The count is based on the number of bases (table 24). The one complete specimen from the north casemate (Level I) has a tooled string rim and is slightly shorter than the round bottles. The greatest width is halfway between the base and neck and there is no shoulder. They are quite similar to modern rosé bottles. They have round sand pontil marks 46 to 53 mm. in diameter. The complete specimen and part of another measure 10.1 by 15.3 cm.; and 10.3 by 15.4 cm. in maximum width. Three kicks are 24 to 37 mm. deep. The base to neck height is 13.1 cm. and the neck of the complete specimen is 9.0 cm. long with an interior lip diameter of 15 mm. and an exterior rim diameter of 33 mm. These bottles are unique so far as we know, but are probably of English manufacture since they differ from the rest only in body shape.

Square Bottles. These have often been referred to as Dutch and as containers for gin (Noël Hume, 1970, p. 62) but the evidence for this is not conclusive. They could just as easily have been English in origin and contained any sort of liquid. The bottles were blown into a square one-piece mold with the neck and shoulder finished off later. The molds were tapered slightly toward the bottom to facilitate the removal of the bottles. Consequently, the measurements taken on the bases fall short of the actual width of the specimens. No complete or reconstructable specimens were found

(table 24). Bases came in two sizes, ranging in width from 73 to 78 mm. with an average of 75.3 mm. and from 86 to 97 mm. with an average of 91.0 mm. The former (four specimens) have kicks of 4 to 8 mm. with sand pontil marks 38 to 47 mm. in diameter (fig. 67d). The remainder have kicks of 13 to 18 mm. with an average of 15.4 mm. and with glass pontil marks 21 to 30 mm. in diameter, averaging 24.4 mm. (fig. 67e). Several of the larger bases have mold marks preserved beneath the glass pontil marks. These include a variety of depressions and crosses. The necks of these bottles are short with everted lips thickened with additional glass (fig. 67c). Interior lip diameters range from 13 to 23 mm., averaging 15.1 mm. and the exterior rim diameters range from 33 to 41 mm. with an average of 37.3 mm.

Octagonal Bottles. These bottles were probably used for pharmaceutical purposes but a few were rather large and may have held liquor (table 24). Grimm (1970, p. 169) suggests that they held shoe blacking or ink. About all they have in common is that four sides are wider than the alternate four sides.

Variety a. Dark green glass. This variety consists of two base fragments, possibly from the same bottle and some side wall sherds. The bases have a sand pontil mark on a slight kick. The bottle resembles the 1770 specimen illustrated by Noël Hume (1970, p. 67).

Variety b. Light green glass. These are four

Table 24.

Distribution of bottles, decanters, wine glasses, tumblers, beaker, glass cup (?), and ink wells.

	Round Bottles	Oval Bottles	Square "Case" Bottles	Octagonal Bottles	Pharmaceutical Bottles	Decanters	Wine Glasses	Tumblers	Beaker	Cup?	Ink Wells
Casements											
North	5	3	2		2	1	1				1
West	1				1						1
Southwest	2	1	1	1	2	1					
Southeast	2					1					
East	2		1			1					
Barracks											
East	2				2						
West	10		2		2				1	1	3
Guardhouse	1						2	1			
Bombproof											
Northeast							1				
Ditch	3		2	1	4	1	3	1			1
Ravelin	1		2			1	1	1			
East Scarp	9			4	3		2				
Sally Port	5		2	1	2	1	4	1			1
Totals	43	4	12	7	18	7	13	5	1	1	7

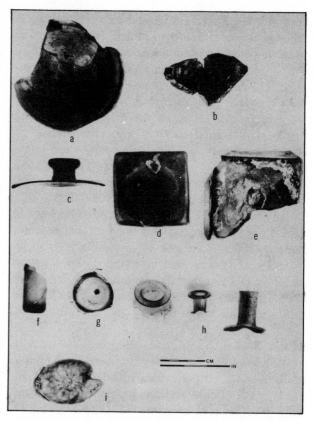

Figure 66. a, round free blown bottles from Feature 60, Levels IV and II; **b,** round free blown bottle with "John Sh..o..." on the side from the ravelin, Level II; **c,** oval free blown bottle from the north casemate, Level I; **d,** free blown bottle necks, probably all from round bottles from the north casemate, Levels II and IV, Feature 56, Level III, Feature 60, Level IV, Feature 57, Level III and Feature 76.

Figure 67. a, round bottle base with sand pontil mark from the southwest casemate, Level II; **b,** round bottle base with glass pontil mark from Feature 76; **c,** neck of square bottle from the north casemate, Level II; **d,** small square bottle base with sand pontil mark from the southwest casemate, Level II; **e,** large square bottle base with glass pontil mark from Feature 56, Level II; **f,** pharmaceutical bottle broken off at the shoulder from the north casemate, Level II; **g,** pharmaceutical bottle base with high kick and sand pontil mark from the sally port, Level II; **h,** pharmaceutical bottles with everted and vertical rims from the north casemate, Level I and the sally port, Levels II and III; **i,** base of a mold blown bottle with a glass pontil mark, possibly a decanter, from the southwest casemate, Level I.

base fragments, none the same shade of green. Only one rectangular specimen can be measured, 66 by 51 mm. This, and one other, have glass pontil marks 20 mm. in diameter. The other two have sand pontil marks 17 mm. and 27 mm. in diameter.

Variety c. Clear glass. This rectangular base fragment is too small for a decanter and is included here. It is 52 mm. long and has a glass pontil mark 15 mm. in diameter.

Pharmaceutical Bottles. The count on these was made on the bases (table 24). There are several shades of glass ranging from clear to dark green, with one blue-green rim fragment which may have come from a French bottle. Five of the bases, three light green and two clear lead-glass, have

kicks 21 to 29 mm. high made with a pointed rod. These are 36 to 53 mm. in diameter with sand pontil marks 20 to 29 mm. in diameter (fig. 67g). Ten bases range in diameter from 24 to 46 mm. and average 30.8 mm. These have sand pontil marks 16 to 20 mm. in diameter with an average of 17.1 mm. (fig. 67f). Four bases, 18 to 44 mm. in diameter and averaging 29.0 mm., have glass pontil marks 10 to 16 mm. in diameter with an average of 13.3 mm. The lips are of two types, sharply everted (nine specimens) or vertical (four specimens) (fig. 67h). The interior lip diameters range from 9 to 28 mm., averaging 14.1 mm., not counting the probable French specimen noted earlier which has a vertical rim with a lip diameter of 41 mm.

Decanters

Parts of seven decanters were found (table 24) five of which are clear lead-glass. One consists of a square base 86 mm. wide on one side with a 6 mm. kick and a glass pontil mark 22 mm. in diameter. Another is a neck fragment and a third is a neck with an interior lip diameter of 31 mm. (fig. 68b). Another two, while not complete, could be reconstructed from fragments. One is cylindrical with cut fluting around the base and neck and a sand pontil mark (fig. 68c). This came from the south ditch (Level II) and is included because it resembles an 1760-1780 style decanter illustrated by Noël Hume (1970, p. 197). The other (fig. 68a) is globular with a glass pontil mark. A stopper fragment (fig. 68d) was found on the parade ground (Level I). The other two are basal fragments of green mold-blown "chestnut"-shaped bottles (fig. 67i) with glass pontil marks. Their identification as decanters is tenuous.

Wine Glasses

These were counted on the basis of stem fragments (table 24). All were made from lead glass and all of the rim fragments appear to have come from trumpet-shaped bowls except one bell-shaped bowl (fig. 68f). One foot was folded at the edge (fig. 68g), and the rest were plain conical in shape (Haynes, 1959, p. 199) (fig. 68h). Five plain stem fragments are from clear drawn stems and four from heavy conical stems in which the trumpet-shaped bowl was a continuation of the stem (fig. 68e). Two air-twist stem fragments with a Z-twist (fig. 68i) had knops (bosses) formed by compressing the glass. There were two enamel-twist stems with a Z-twist, one of which had a central gauze twist as well (fig. 68j).

Tumblers

Fragments of the bases of five lead-glass tumblers were found (table 24), two of which have glass pontil marks 17 mm. across. One has 10 facets around the sides but the others are round. All are less than 40 mm. across at the base.

Beaker

A mold-blown lead-glass beaker 14.2 cm. high and 10.1 cm. in diameter with a glass pontil mark and eight vertical ribs on the exterior (fig. 68k) was found in Feature 56 (Level IV) in the west barracks.

Cup

One mold-blown soda glass cup 32 mm. high and 65 mm. in diameter with a 6 mm. kick and a glass pontil mark was found in the guardhouse area (Level II). It is now opaque white but was once clear glass. It was blown in a mold and there are eight vertical ribs around the exterior (fig. 68l). It may have been a lamp.

Ink Wells

Four glass ink wells were found at Fort Stanwix (table 24). They range in height from 27 to 50 mm. and in diameter from 22 to 42 mm. All are blown glass with inverted lips (fig. 68m). How these ink wells were mounted had never been determined (Noël Hume, 1970, p. 75) but we were fortunate enough to find one intact in Feature 60 (Level III) (fig. 68n). This specimen is encased in a brass jacket with a threaded opening at the top. A brass cylinder was screwed onto the jacket which had a thick paper or cardboard insert in an expansion ring just above the neck to seal the opening when it was screwed on. The function of the remainder of the cylinder remains a mystery. A brass pin and partially hollow wood dowl which may have been a pin case or a stopper was found in it. A similar specimen was found at Fort Montgomery, New York (John Mead, personal communication). Four brass cylinders ranging from 30 to 70 mm. long were found on the site, but three were not associated with ink wells (table 24). Three of the reservoirs were found in the west barracks (Feature 3, Level IV and Feature 60, Level III). The largest was in the northwest corner of the north casemate (Level III) where it had probably been put for safekeeping. This specimen also had brass associated with it which was too poorly preserved to identify as a jacket.

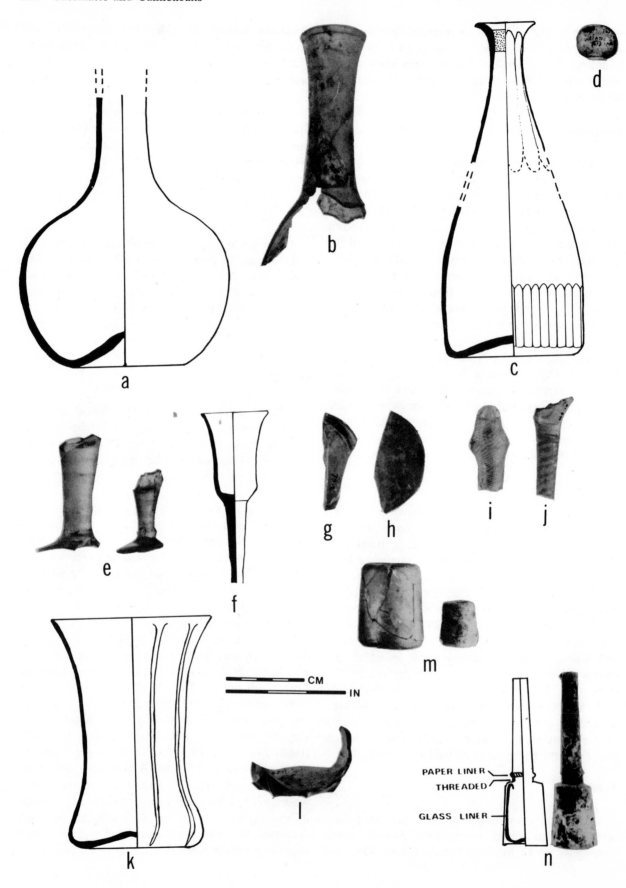

PAPER LINER
THREADED
GLASS LINER

Kettles

Iron kettles were found concentrated in the casemates, barracks and dump areas (table 25). Only two brass kettles were found, one in Feature 51 in the southwest casemate and one in the ditch (Level I). In addition, a brass lid to a pot was found in Feature 57 (Level IV) in the west barracks.

Type 1. Iron with legs. These have the following dimensions: diameter 5 to 12 inches, average 10 $^{11}/_{16}$ inches; height 5¾ to 8¼ inches. The largest pot fragment (fig. 69a) has a raised projection on the lip for a bale attachment and another has an angular handle below the rim. Five of the 14 rim fragments have ridges inside the rim to rest a lid. The largest fragment has a raised "C" on the side but no other markings were found. The smallest kettle has four legs while the rest apparently had three. These were generally welded to the nearly flat base and are D-shaped in cross section. The bases have a casting line or reinforcing ridge under them and reinforcing ridges are common on the sides of kettles.

Table 25.

Distribution of kettle and collander fragments.

	Iron Kettles	Brass Kettles	Collander
Casemates			
North	20		
Southwest	3	1	
Southeast	2		
Barracks			
East	4		
West	10		
Guardhouse	3		
Ditch	9	1	
Ravelin	2		
East Scarp	2		
Sally Port	14		1
Total	69	2	1

Type 2. Brass.

Variety a. Without legs. The example from the southwest casemate (Feature 51) is a shallow basin approximately 9 inches in diameter with an outrolled lip. It has been badly crushed and partially melted. A bale lug or handle is attached to the rim at one point with two copper rivets.

Figure 69. **a,** iron kettle fragments and rim profiles from Feature 56, Level III, the bridge area, Level I, the north casemate, Level II, Feature 19, the southeast casemate, Level II, the bridge area, Level I and the southwest casemate, Level II; **b,** brass pot lid from Feature 57, Level IV; **c,** tin can with folded seams from the northeast bombproof, Level II.

Figure 68. a, decanter from the north casemate, Level II; **b,** decanter neck from the southeast casemate, Level II; **c,** decanter with engraved fluting from the bridge area, Level II; **d,** stopper fragment from Feature 73, Level II; **e,** trumpet-shaped wine glass stems from the east scarp, Level II and the west ditch, Level II; **f,** bell-shaped wine glass from the guardhouse area, Level II; **g,** folded wine glass foot from the north casemate, Level II; **h,** plain wine glass foot from Feature 72, Level II; **i,** air-twist stem fragment from the north casemate, Level I; **j,** enamel-twist stem fragment from the bridge area, Level X; **k,** beaker from Feature 56, Level IV; **l,** cup from the guardhouse area, Level II; **m,** ink well liners from the north casemate, Level III and Feature 3, Level IV; **n,** ink well from Feature 60, Level III.

Variety b. With legs. The specimen from the ditch (Level I) is a shallow basin approximately 8½ inches in diameter with the lip rolled out over an iron wire. There was a handle (broken off) attached to the lip with three copper rivets. Three iron legs were also attached to the lip with two pairs of copper rivets.

Collander

A fragment of a pot about 8 inches in diameter was found in the sally port (Level II) which had its bottom beaten flat and holes punched through it to make a colander. It had been later cut apart and this piece apparently was scrap when discarded.

Category 1. One brass fragment from the ravelin (Feature 76) was found which had been crushed to form a crude cup. There were also two detached brass bale lugs; one from the southwest casemate (Level II) and the other from the guardhouse area (Level II).

Pot Lid

On the floor of Feature 57 in the west barracks lay a brass pot lid 5½ inches in diameter (fig. 69b). The lid consists of a top piece crimped over a circular band to form an insert for the lip of the pot. The handle is cast brass riveted to a square plate on the under side of the top. There is an upside down "IV" stamped on the band under the rim.

Tin Cans

Fragments of tin cans were found throughout the fort but only one complete specimen, from the passageway to the northeast bombproof (Level II) was found (fig. 69c). This is 2⅞ inches in diameter at the base and 2¾ inches high with folded seams which were probably sealed with solder. The top is missing. Some of the other fragments came from rectangular cans and might have been cartridge cannisters but are too corroded and bent to be positively identified.

Buckets

Wood. The charred bases of two buckets were found in the west barracks (Feature 56, Level III). One is made from white oak (*Quercus*) and is 8¾ inches in diameter, while the other is made from eastern white pine (*Pinus strobus*) and is 9¼ inches in diameter and approximately 9 inches high. Comparable buckets were found at Fort Ligonier (Grimm, 1970, p. 55). These were apparently fastened together with wooden strips as no iron bands were found. Staves are 2 to 3 inches wide and ¼ to ½ inch thick on one and 2½ to 3 inches wide and ¼ inch thick on the other. The base of the first fitted into a slot ⅞ inch from the bottom of the staves. The second base has been drilled with 23 holes unevenly spaced around the edge which indicates that it was being used for a purpose other than as a bucket. A few stave fragments from a bucket or barrel made from white ash (*Fraxinus*) were found on the floor of the northwest bombproof (Level III).

Tin. Two tinned bale lugs were found in the west barracks (Feature 60, Level III) and in the ravelin (Level II). The former was held to a bucket with a rolled rim by one rivet. Better preserved specimens were found at Fort Ligonier (Grimm, 1970, pp. 53-55).

Barrel Hoops

Two types were found, iron and copper. The latter were for gunpowder barrels.

Type 1. Iron. Only two iron hoops were identified, one from the southwest casemate (Level II) and the other just north of the southwest casemate (Level II). These are 1½ feet in diameter and 1 3/16 inches wide. The ends are held together with two iron rivets. Other fragments of strap iron were found in most other areas of the fort. These probably came from hoops but we could not be certain. See also: Broilers.

Type 2. Copper. These range in width from ½ to 1 inch, but no hoop diameters could be projected from the fragments found. The narrower straps had holes drilled through them and may not have been barrel hoops. Two of these were found in the north casemate (Level I) with one thin strap in Feature 57 (Level IV) in the west barracks, but most fragments were in Feature 69 (Levels II and III) in the east barracks. Many of these were partly melted and one example was found with two copper rivets. One of the north casemate examples was marked with a broad arrow.

Grimm (1970, p. 98) reported hoops with diameters of 13½ to 17 inches which were used on powder barrels.

Cooking Implements

Griddle Handles

These were wrought iron handles with an eye at one end for suspension and a small hole at the other end for attachment to a broiler (table 26) (fig. 70b). They have the following dimensions: length, 24.4 to 31.1 cm., average, 27.4 cm,; width at center, 12 to 33 mm., average, 19.6 mm.; thickness, 3 to 7 mm., average, 4.3 mm.; diameter at suspension end, 24 to 45 mm., average, 34.9 mm.; eye diameter, 10 to 17 mm.; average, 13.1 mm.; diameter at attachment end, 21 to 36 mm., average, 27.2 mm. Two of these still have rivets through the end and a third has part of a hook through the eye. We believe that these were attached to griddles or broilers and used in cooking.

Pot Hooks

Assorted rods and straps of iron bent into S- or C-shaped hooks and presumably used in fireplaces to hang pots (table 26) (fig. 70c) have the following dimensions: length, 11.5 to 28.9 cm., average, 16.5 cm. Two appear to have been made from old door hinges.

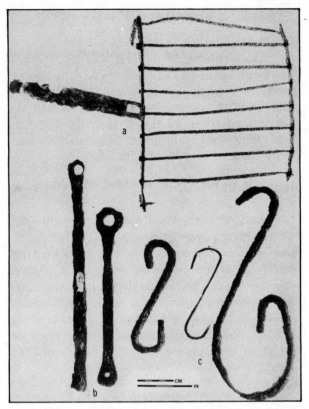

Figure 70. a, broiler from the bridge area, Level I; b, griddle handles from the north casemate, Level I and the sally port, Level II; c, pot hooks from Feature 57, Level III, the sally port, Level II and the northwest bombproof, Level II.

Broilers

Type 1. Made from iron straps. Makeshift broilers to cook meat were made from barrel hoops. Two, from the southwest casemate (Level II) and Feature 68 are bent in a zigzag fashion while another from Feature 57 (Level III) is bent into a spiral.

Type 2. Wrought iron. A specimen from the ditch (Level I) consists of two wrought iron end pieces with legs, one with a handle, which is held together by eight rods approximately 30 mm. apart, welded through holes in the end pieces (fig. 70a). It stands 69 mm. high and is 20 cm. long and 25 cm. wide. The handle is at least 20 cm. long. "Grid irons" and food stuffs were sent in May of 1777 (Gansevoort, May 14, 1777) to Fort Stanwix.

Table 26.

Distribution of griddle handles, pot hooks and broilers.

	Griddle Handles	Pot Hooks	Broilers
Casemates			
North	2		
Southwest	2		1
East		1	
Barracks			
East	3	2	
West	4	1	1
Bombproof			
Northeast	2		
Northwest	1	1	
Ditch	1	1	1
East Scarp			1
Sally Port	2	5	
Totals	17	11	4

Furniture Parts

Key Plates

Two fragments of cast brass ornamental plates from drawers were found (fig. 71a). One came from the west barracks (Level I) and the other from Feature 69 (Level I) in the east barracks. Both were in disturbed areas but their simplicity suggests an 18th-century origin.

Drawer Pulls

Three drawer pulls, two from the sally port (Level II) and one from the ravelin (Level II) were found. They could also have been used for handles on chests or boxes. None are complete, only the handle having survived. Two are made from round rods ¼ inch and ⅜ inch in diameter, and the third from a rectangular strip ⅛ by ¼ inch. All three are approximately 3¾ inches wide and ¼ to 1¾ inches deep.

Tacks

A number of brass tacks were found (table 27).

Type 1. Cast convex head with welded square shank (fig. 71b). These have the following dimensions: length, 11.5 to 19.0 mm.; average, 14.2 mm.; head diameter, 8.0 to 13.0 mm.; average, 11.9 mm. Twenty-four specimens were found in a one-foot square area in Feature 51 in the southwest casemate. These have convex heads and square shanks welded on and look like upholstery tacks. These were also found at Fort Ligonier, 1758-1766 (Grimm, 1970, p. 149).

Type 2. Hammered sheet brass, one-piece construction (fig. 71c). These have the following dimensions: length, 11.5 to 26.0 mm.; head diameter, 6.0 to 13.0 mm. The shanks are rolled sheet brass cones hammered flat at the top to form the heads.

Weights and Measures

Scale

Two fragments of the balance arm of a scale were found in Feature 63 (Level III) in the west barracks (fig. 71d). It is quite similar to the ones illustrated by Peterson (1968, pp. 167-169).

Table 27.

Distribution of brass tacks.

	Type 1	Type 2
Casemates		
North	1	
Southwest	24	
East		1
Barracks		
East	1	
West	2	
Guardhouse		1
Parade Ground	1	
Ditch	3	
East Scarp		1
Sally Port	1	
Totals	33	3

Weight

Part of a conical lead weight was found in Feature 60 (Level III) in the west barracks. It is 23+ mm. long with a diameter of 31 mm.

Rulers

Several ruler fragments were found.

Type 1. Brass rule scaled in .1 inch increments (fig. 71f). Two fragments from the guardhouse area (Level II) and Feature 51 of the southwest casemate probably are from the same ruler. The scale is engraved on one edge of one side. On the opposite edge is another scale numbered in increments of six and tied to the first by diagonal lines. The number 12 is equal to 4.8 inches, 18 to 5 inches and 42 to 7 inches. This ruler is at least 8 inches long and was probably a gunner's instrument, although no comparable example was found in the literature.

Type 2. Copper rule scaled in ⅛-inch increments. This was found in the east casemate (Level II). It is a copper strip with iron pins ¼ inch and 1¾ inches from one end which probably fastened it to a strip of wood. Originally it was at least 22 inches long.

Type 3. Wooden folding rule scaled in ⅛ inch increments. (fig. 71e). These are fragments of folding wooden rules with brass ends and pivots. They were found in the north casemate (Level III) and the ravelin (Level II).

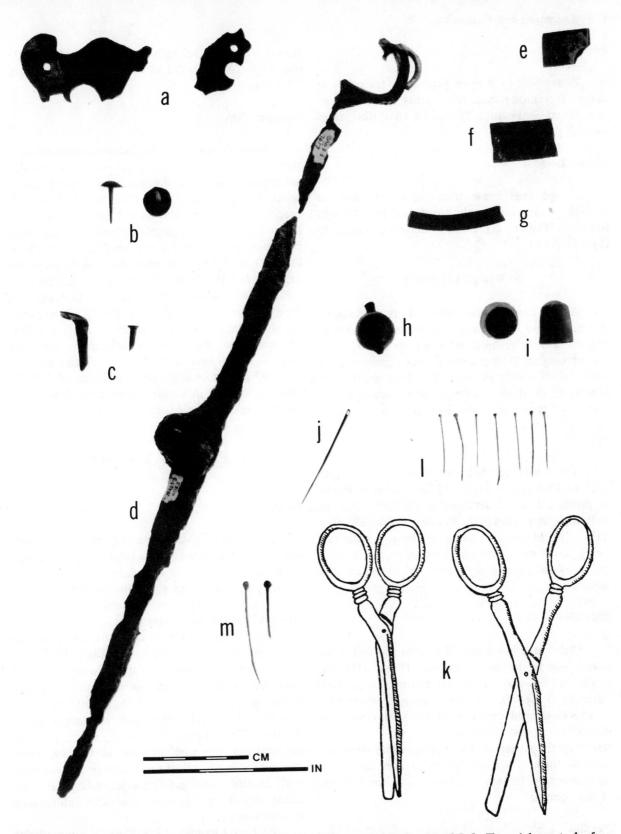

Figure 71. **a,** key plates from Feature 69, Level I and the west barracks, Level I; **b,** Type 1 brass tacks from Feature 51; **c,** Type 2 brass tacks from the east casemate, Level II and the guardhouse area, Level I; **d,** balance arm from scale from Feature 63, Level III; **e,** Type 3 ruler fragment from the north casemate, Level III; **f,** Type 1 ruler fragment from the guardhouse area, Level II; **g,** protractor fragment from Feature 51; **h,** plumb bob from Feature 51; **i,** thimbles from the east casemate, Level II and the north casemate, Level III; **j,** needle from the north casemate, Level II; **k,** scissors from the southwest casemate, Level I and Feature 76; **l,** pins from the southwest casemate, Level II; **m,** hat pins from the sally port, Level II and Feature 48.

Protractor

A segment of a brass protractor scaled in 1-degree increments from 60 degrees to 90 degrees was found in Feature 51 in the southwest casemate (fig. 71g).

Plumb Bob

A spherical brass plumb bob 18 mm. in diameter with a hole at the top for suspension was found in Feature 51 in the southwest casemate (fig. 71h).

Sewing Objects

As the garrison was always short of clothing, it would have been necessary to make constant repairs. The only direct reference to sewing is to the making of a flag out of odds and ends of cloth by the officers in 1777. Presumably the officers mended their own clothes, although this may have been one of the jobs of their "waiters."

Scissors

These have the following dimensions: length, 12.3 to 13.6 cm., average, 12.9 cm.; blade length to pivot, 6.2 to 7.2 cm., average, 6.6 cm. All are iron and have solid loop handles (table 28) (fig. 71k). The blades are isosceles triangles with one being broad and blunt while the other tapers to a point. Two have knops and balusters on the handles.

Thimbles

Only three brass thimbles from the fort were found, one in the north casemate (Level III) one in the east casemate (Level II) and one in the east barracks (Level I). All three have a waffle-like or check-stamped crown with rows of round indentations on the side (fig. 71i). Two have practically no thickening of the opening, while the other is fairly thick. They are 18 to 20 mm. high and approximately 16 mm. in diameter on the interior of the opening.

Needles

Three steel needles were found, one each in the north casemate (Level II), headquarters area (Level II) and the sally port dump (Level II) (fig. 71j). These are 32 to 47 mm. long, averaging 39.0 mm.

Straight Pins

Table 29 presents the distribution of straight pins on the site. All are brass with wire wound spherical heads and the better preserved specimens are tin plated (fig. 71l). We included all specimens from the site except those from documented post-1781 contexts. Round headed pins continued in use on the site until *ca.* 1825 (Features 71 and 77) well after the abandonment of the fort, but this later occupation was confined to the southwest corner of the fort so that there is little chance that the data is skewed. Any skewing would be restricted to the ditch, ravelin, southeast casemate and Campbell collection. The pins range in length from 17 to 35 mm. with an average of 26.97 mm., and a standard deviation of 2.7911. This is somewhat smaller than pins from Fort Michilimackinac (Stone, 1970, p. 611).

Personal Property

Pipes

A total of 7,249 white clay pipe stem fragments were recovered plus a large number of bowl fragments, one ceramic colonial pipe, one ceramic Indian pipe and seven stone Indian pipes.

Series A. English white clay pipes.

The distribution and bore diameters of the pipe stem fragments are shown in Table 30. By far the greatest concentration was a cluster of 3,178 specimens in a 10-square-foot area in the vicinity of the guardhouse north of the southwest casemate (Level II) and spilling into the sleeper trench (Feature 48) along the front wall, which partially accounts for the high number in the southwest casemate as well. All of these appear to have been made by the same manufacturer using the same molds. See Type 9a below for more information on this cluster.

At Fort Ligonier, 1758-1766, (Grimm, 1970, p. 112) the mean pipe stem bore diameter is 4.61/64 inches, while the Fort Stanwix mean is 4.12/64 inches for the period 1758-1781. The sample at Fort Frederica, Georgia, 1737-1750, has a mean bore of 4.91/64 inches (author's examination). Specimens at Crown Point, 1760-1776, have a mean bore diameter of 4.23/64 inches (Gilbert Hagerty, personal communication). These samples merely confirmed what Harrington (1954) observed, that bore diameters decrease through time. Binford (1962) calculated a regression formula for converting the mean bore diameter of a sample to a median date for the sample. We have considerable reservation about the accuracy of this formula because it assumes a constant rate of change which does not seem to occur when plotting documented samples (the four cited above for example.) Nevertheless, Harrington's original premise is valid.

Internally, the Fort Stanwix samples had very consistent means and rather low standard deviations which suggests that the samples are homogeneous. That is: (a) all areas of the site were occupied at the same time, (b) the samples were

Table 28.

Distribution of scissors.

	Scissors
Casemates	
North	1
Southwest	1
Barracks, West	1
Ravelin	1
East Scarp	1
Sally Port	2
Total	7

Table 29.

Distribution of straight pins. (Ratios given are the number of specimens per 10 square feet of excavated area within the structure.)

	Number	Ratio
Casemates		
North	69	2.16
West	10	2.50
Southwest	122	12.20
Southeast	3	2.00
East	62	5.64
Barracks		
East	41	2.91
West	66	5.20
Guardhouse	20	1.67
Headquarters	1	.15
Parade Ground	8	.89
Bombproofs		
Northeast	2	.36
Southwest	6	1.09
Ditch	5	.17
Ravelin	6	1.33
East Scarp	124	18.51
Sally Port	87	4.70
Campbell Coll.	3	.16
Total	635	3.24

Table 30.

Distribution of pipe stems by bore diameter. (Ratios given are the number of specimens per 10 square feet of excavated area within the structure.)

	3/64"	4/64"	5/64"	6/64"	Total	Mean of Sample [1]	Standard Deviation	Ratio
Casemates								
North	4	795	54	1	854	4.06	.263	26.69
West		42	10		52	4.20	.397	13.00
Southwest	1	1,075	141		1,217	4.11	.322	121.70
Southeast		38	6	1	45	4.18	.411	30.00
East		203	28	1	232	4.13	.349	21.09
Barracks								
East	2	69	19		90	4.19	.447	6.38
West		372	32		404	4.08	.270	31.81
Guardhouse	6	2,775	387	4	3,172	4.12	.337	264.33
Headquarters		16	6		22			3.38
Parade Ground	2	483	79		564	4.14	.354	62.66
Bombproofs								
Northeast		57	6		63	4.10	.293	11.45
Northwest		48	11		59	4.19	.392	12.04
Southwest		5	4	2	11			2.00
Bakehouse		3	2		5			
Ditch		61	10	1	72	4.11	.363	2.48
Ravelin		56	8		64	4.13	.333	14.22
East Scarp		152	21	1	174	4.13	.356	25.97
Sally Port		129	20		149	4.13	.342	17.33
Total	15	6,379	844	11	7,249	4.12	.333	37.04

[1] in 64th inches.

thoroughly mixed prior to 1781 or (c) there was little discernible change in bore diameters during the period 1758-1781. We can dismiss (a), above, since we have documentary evidence that the bombproofs were not built before 1776 (W. Willett, 1831, p. 49). Explanation (b) is a strong possibility since the samples from the bombproofs, on the east scarp (Level II) and in the sally port (Level II) can be dated post-1776 on the basis of documents and Revolutionary War buttons. These samples do not differ from other areas of the fort. The evidence, however, favors (c). There was little discernible change in bore diameters between the four sites noted during this period between .3/64 inches per year and .6/64 inches per year. These figures were arrived at by dividing the difference between the means of the samples by the difference between the median dates of the sites, and checked by dividing the standard deviation of each sample by the number of years the sample was accumulating (in these cases, the total time span of the sites). At Fort Stanwix, then, we would expect the mean bore diameter to shift between 4.45/64 inches to 4.81/64 inches for 1758 and 3.43/64 inches to 3.78/64 inches for 1781. In short, any mean within these limits could be considered normal.

The bowls could be typed on the basis of maker's marks and bowl configuration (table 31). These types are not intended to encompass all forms and are based solely on Fort Stanwix specimens. See Hanson (1971a, pp. 92-99) for post-1781 types from the site. The types in this series are defined on the basis of the presence or absence of markings on the bowls. Because most markings are initials (presumed to be the initials of the makers) the procedure in the past has been to judge the age of a pipe by its shape, and then ascribe the pipe to a pipe maker with those initials in that period. This method has its pitfalls and we used it with reservation to identify the source of the pipe, not to date it. No recognizable Dutch or French specimens were found in a pre-1781 Fort Stanwix context, although they occurred later at the site.

Heels are present on only 24 percent of the bowls studied and took two forms, a short truncated heel and a long conical heel which might also be referred to as a spur. The following measurements are used to describe the pipe bowls: bore diameter was taken with the butt ends of drill bits in 64th-inch sizes because standards have been set up on this system (Harrington, 1954). Bowl angle refers to the angle between the back of the bowl and the stem. Where the stem was too broken to get a line, a drill bit, securely fitted into the bore, was substituted. Although the total range was 54 to 77 degrees the bulk fell between 66 degrees and 73 degrees. As a general rule, pipe bowls were at a more acute angle to the stem in 19th-century

Table 31.

Distribution of tobacco pipe bowls (fragmentary bowls not counted).

Series	A																				B	C	D		Totals
Types	1			2						3			4	5		6	7	8	9		1	1	1	2	
Varieties	a	b	c	a	b	c	d	e	f	a	b	c		a	b				a	b					
Casemates																									
North		1		2						1						1					1	1	1		8
Southwest	1	2				1				1				1		1			2	1					10
East	1																						1		2
Barracks																									
East	1																								1
West				2							1	1			1				3				1		9
Guardhouse	1		1																3						5
Parade Ground				2													1	1							4
Bombproofs																									
Northeast					1											1									2
Southwest								1																	1
Ditch	1				1		1						1										1		5
Ravelin							1																		1
East Scarp	3											1												1	5
Sally Port	2								1														2		5
Variety totals	10	3	1	6	2	1	2	1	1	2	1	2		1	1				8	1					
Type totals	14			13						5			1	2		3	1	1	9		1	1	6	1	58

privies on the site than in the pre-1781 components, although there were a few exceptions. Pipe bowls from the 19th-century privies on the site of Fort Stanwix rarely are less than 70 degrees to the stem. Bowl depth was measured from the lip of the back of the bowl to the bottom of the interior of the bowl. These range from 24 to 41.5 mm. in depth with an average of 32.5 mm. A *ca.* 1840-1860 sample (Feature 5) ranges from 26.5 to 45 mm., with an average of 32.0 mm., not significantly different from the Fort Stanwix sample. Length and width of the bowl were measured on the interior of the bowl at the lip. The bowls from the fort tended to be slightly longer than wide, while the Feature 5 bowls tended to be round or slightly wider than long and generally larger. The comparative dimensions are: Fort Stanwix: length, 15.5 to 20 mm., average, 17.1 mm.; width, 11.5 to 15.5 mm., average, 14.2 mm.; Feature 5: length, 15 to 22 mm., average, 17.8 mm., width, 15 to 21.5 mm., average, 17.4 mm. It can readily be seen that the real change in size took place in the width of the bowl rather than the length or depth. This was consistent enough that we suggest it can be used as a means of preliminary identification between 18th and 19th century specimens.

Type 1. Unmarked pipes.

Variety a. Heeless (fig. 72a). These have the following dimensions: bore diameter, 4/64 inches, bowl angle, 61 to 77 degrees, average, 67.7 degrees; bowl depth, 29.5 to 33.5 mm., average, 31.7 mm.; bowl length, 15.5 to 19 mm., average 17.2 mm.; bowl width, 11.5 to 15.5 mm., average, 14.1 mm.

Variety b. Conical heel. These have the following dimensions: bore diameter, 4 to 5/64 inch; bowl angle, 59 to 63 degrees; bowl depth, 33 to 35.5 mm.; bowl length, 20 mm. Evidence from Fort Michilimackinac (L. Stone, 1970, p. 411) suggests this type of heel was in use *ca.* 1750-1780.

Variety c. Truncated heel. This has a bore diameter of 4/64 inch. The bowl is warped. This specimen came from the south ditch (Level II) and might be 19th century. Stone (1970, p. 411) suggests that this type of heel dates *ca.* 1730-1760.

Type 2. "RT" pipes. The initials "RT" have generally been attributed to Robert Tippett of Bristol, England and his family, *ca.* 1660-1720 (I. Walker, 1971a, pp. 19-22), but the initials were used at Fort Stanwix after 1958 and, as in Variety c, even the name "TIPPET" appears on some bowls. I. Walker (1971b, p. 73) notes that

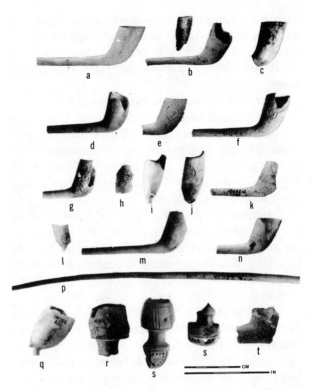

Figure 72. Pipes: **a,** Type A1a from the east scarp, Level III; **b,** Type A2a from the north casemate, Level IV; **c,** Type A2b from the sally port, Level II; **d,** Type A2c from Feature 50; **e,** Type A2d from Feature 56, Level II; **f,** Type A2e from Feature 76; **g,** Type A2f from the southwest bombproof, Level III; **h,** Type A3a from the bridge area, Level XI; **i,** Type A3c from Feature 56, Level III; **j,** Type A4 from Feature 73, Level II; **k,** Type A5a from Feature 63, Level II; **l,** Type A5b from Feature 3, Level III; **m,** Type A9a from Feature 56, Level II; **n,** Type A9a with imbedded gravel from the guardhouse area, Level II; **p,** Series A white clay pipe stem from Feature 56, Level III; **q,** Type B1 from Feature 75; **r,** Type C1 from the north casemate, Level I; **s,** Type D1 from the bridge area, Level XII and the east casemate, Level II; **t,** Type D2 from the north casemate, Level I.

Tippet pipes have been found at Fort Gaspereau, New Brunswick (1750-1756), and in a shipwreck in Baie-des-Chaleurs (*ca.* 1760). It seems likely, therefore, that the Tippet molds were being used into the 1760's, although not necessarily by Tippets. Stone (1970, p. 404) suggests dates of 1740-1780 based on specimens from Fort Michilimackinac.

Variety a. "RT" on the back of the bowl (fig. 72b). These came from the west casemate (Level I), the north casemate (Levels I and IV), the northeast bombproof (Level II), the east scarp (Level II) and the ravelin (Level I). They have the following dimensions: bore diameter, 4/64 inch; heel, none; bowl angle, 64 to 70 degrees; bowl depth, 33 to 37 mm. One also had "TIP,PET" in a circle on the right side of the bowl.

Variety b. "R•T" in heart flanked by hearts on both sides of bowl (fig. 72c). These came from the guardhouse area (Level II) and the sally port (Level II) and have the following dimensions: bore diameter, 4/64 inch; heel, none; bowl angle, 68 degrees; bowl depth, 33.5 mm.; bowl length, 16.5 mm.; bowl width, 14.5 mm.

Variety c. "R, TIP, PET" in sunburst circle on right side of bowl (fig. 72d). This came from the southwest casemate (Feature 50) and has the following dimensions: bore diameter, 4/64 inch; heel, none; bowl angle, 72 degrees; bowl depth, 32.5 mm.

Variety d. "RT" in heart on right side (fig. 72e). These came from Feature 56 (Level II) and Feature 57 (Level IV) and have the following dimensions: bore diameter, 4/64 inch; heel, none; bowl angle, 68 degrees; bowl depth, 32 mm.

Variety e. "RT" with three dots above and below in beaded circle on right side (fig. 72f). This came from Feature 76 and has the following dimensions: bore diameter, 5/64 inch; heel, none; bowl angle, 69 degrees; bowl depth, 34 mm.; bowl length, 17 mm.; bowl width, 15 mm.

Variety f. "RT" in a heart on the right side with flowers around the bowl (fig. 72g). This came from the southwest bombproof (Level II) and has the following dimensions: bore diameter, 4/64 inch; heel, none; bowl angle, 68 degrees; bowl depth, 32.5 mm. Although the size agrees well with other Tippet pipes, the decoration is totally unlike other Tippet products and the letters "RT" are much larger. This is probably a late 18th-century use of the initials by another maker.

Type 3. "TD" pipes. The use of the initials "TD" on pipe bowls dates back to at least 1730 (I. Walker, 1966), and they are still being made. However, changes in the shape of the bowls and the motifs surrounding the initials are clues to the age of the pipes. None of the known English pipe makers with these initials were operating at the time Fort Stanwix was in use, and it would seem that most "TD" pipes were not made by people with those initials (I. Walker, 1966). Indeed, it has not yet been proven that anyone with these initial made "TD" pipes. All we can say, at this point, is that the shape of these bowls suggest

English origin and, therefore, the marks are also probably English. Varieties a and b have been found at Fort Ligonier, 1758-1766 (Grimm, 1970, p. 114).

Variety a. "TD" with curliques above and below in a rope circle on the back of the bowl (fig. 72h). These came from the south ditch (Level XI) and the southwest casemate (Feature 50) and have the following dimensions: bore diameter, 5/64 inch; heel, none; bowl angle, 68 degrees; bowl depth, 41.5 mm.

Variety b. "TD" with curliques above and below in a circle on the back of the bowl. No measurements were possible on this specimen from the north casemate (Level II). Stone (1970, p. 403) suggests a post-1750 date for this type from Fort Michilimackinac.

Variety c. "TD" over a fleur-de-lis in a rouletted heart on the back of the bowl, raised hearts on both sides of the heel (fig. 72i). These were found in Feature 48 and Feature 56 (Level III) and have the following dimensions: bore diameter, 4/64 inch; heel, truncated; bowl angle, 66 to 70 degrees; bowl depth, 29.5 mm.; bowl length, 15.5 mm.; bowl width, 15 mm.

Type 4. "WM" pipe: "WM" with curliques above and below in a rouletted circle on the back of the bowl (fig. 72j). This came from Feature 73 and has a diameter of 5/64 inch and a bowl angle of 66 degrees. This mark has been found on pipes from Williamsburg, ca. 1750-1765, (A. Noël Hume, 1963, p. 22) and Louisbourg, 1747-ca. 1760 (Hanson, 1968, p. 20).

Type 5. "IC" pipes.

Variety a. "I.C., 1" in a rouletted circle on the back of the bowl (fig. 72k). This was found in Feature 63 (Level II) and has the following dimensions: bore diameter, 5/64 inch, heel, none; bowl angle, 65 degrees; bowl depth, 30 mm.

Variety b. "I.C., 14" in a rouletted circle on the back of the bowl (fig. 72l). No measurements were possible on this specimen from Feature 3 (Level III).

Type 6. "WN" pipe: "WN" in a circle on the right side of the bowl. No measurements were possible on these specimens from the southwest casemate (Level II), the northeast bombproof (Level II) and the east scarp (Level II).

Type 7. "WO" pipe: "W" and "O" on sides of heel. This was found in the south ditch (Level II), the north casemate (Level I) and the northeast bombproof (Level II). They have the following dimensions: bore diameter, 5/64 inch; heel, truncated; bowl angle, 66 degrees.

Type 8. "T" pipe: "T" in a sunburst diamond. No measurements were possible on this specimen from the parade ground (Level I).

Type 9. Pipes with symbols instead of lettering.

Variety a. "+" on right side of bowl (fig. 72m, n). These have the following dimensions: bore diameter, 4/64 inch; bowl angle, 66 to 70 degrees, average, 68.5 degrees; bowl depth, 34 mm. Three of these are associated with the large cluster of pipe stems between the southwest casemate and the west barracks (Level II), three came from Feature 56 (Level II) and the remaining two from the southwest casemate (Level II and Feature 48). Both the bowls and the majority of the stems are crude. Inclusion of gravel in the clay, which sometimes fell out after firing left holes through the stem or bowl and there are air bubbles along the upper surface of the stem and back of the bowl. The mean of the bore diameters for this collection is 4.12/64 inch with a standard deviation of .335. All of the bits had been trimmed with a knife before the wire was withdrawn. A count of the bits indicates approximately 441 pipes in the cluster. If these were all made by the same person, he was using wires with diameters of 3/64 to 5/64 inches. Two 6/64-inch specimens in the cluster were probably intrusive, although pre-1781, and all the 3/64-inch specimens could have come from one pipe. Eliminating the 6/64-inch specimens would not change the mean and would lower the standard deviation to only .330. This cluster probably represents pipes broken in shipment and discarded at the site.

Variety b. A cross of five nodes on the right side of the bowl. No measurements were possible on this specimen from Feature 48.

Category 1. Marked fragments which could not be identified (12 specimens). Eight of these have a circle on the right side of the bowl, some of which has illegible lettering; one has a fragment of a circle and a curlique on the back like Type 3b; one has a sunburst circle fragment like Type 2c; and one is marked "?" and "W" on either side of a truncated heel.

Category 2. Fragments which were too broken to tell if they were marked (26 specimens). Seven specimens have conical heels and are probably Type 1b; the rest had no heels.

Series B. Colonial Clay Pipe.

Type 1. Unmarked red clay pipe with a heel (fig. 72q). This has the following dimensions: bore diameter, 5/64 inch; bowl angle, 65 degrees; bowl depth, 34.5 mm.; bowl length, 20.5 mm.; bowl width, 20 mm. This is made from a refined clay fired to a red-orange color. It was found on the east scarp (Level II) and may have come from Virginia.

Series C. Indian Clay Pipe.

Type 1. This was patterned after the stone Micmac pipes described below (fig. 72r). The base and stem hole are broken off but the bowl is 23 mm. in diameter and 25 mm. deep. It came from the north casemate (Level I). It is poorly fired and pinkish-gray in color. It is decorated with four incised circles (probably made with a compass) separated by groups of vertical incised lines, three groups of four lines and one group of five lines, with a row of punctations around the outside of the lip.

Series D. Indian stone pipes.

Type 1. "Micmac" pipes (fig. 72s). Five of these are made of fine grained sandstone and one of dolomite. These came from the north casemate (Level II), Feature 3 (Level III), the east casemate (Level II), the sally port (Level II) and the south ditch (Level XII). The most complete specimen is 60.5 mm. high with a bowl diameter of 19 mm. and a bowl depth of 21.5 mm. The bowl depth of two others is 22.5 mm. The nearly complete specimen has four drilled depressions on the bowl separated by groups of vertically engraved lines, three groups of four lines and one group of five lines opposite the side with the stem hole. There are engraved lines around the lip and bowl base. On both sides of the lower portion containing the stem hole are shield-shaped engraved lines bordered on the inside by drilled holes with a hole drilled transversely below the stem hole, probably for suspension. Two of the other sandstone bowl fragments have engraved lines around the lip and base and one has triangles engraved near the base with drilled depressions at the apex of the triangles. The dolomite specimen is undecorated.

Type 2. "Imitation European" pipe (fig. 72t). This specimen is made from coarse sandstone and is an elbow pipe with a vestigial "heel" at the front of the bowl. It is too broken to obtain measurements, but was obviously made with a European pipe as a model. It came from the north casemate (Level I).

Knives and Razors

Several types of knives were found (table 32). For the most part these are too corroded and fragile to be cleaned and measurements are estimated allowing for the corrosion. All blades are made of steel and are wedge-shaped in cross section.

Type 1. Blade folded into the handle (clasp knife) (fig. 73a, b). These have the following dimensions: small: handle length, 10.9 to 15 cm., average, 12.1 cm.; blade length, 8.8 to 12.2 cm., average, 10.5 cm.; blade width, 15 to 24 mm., average, 20.3 mm. Large: handle length, 17.7 to 18.5 cm.; blade length, 16 to 16.8 cm.; blade width, 21 mm. There is no difference in the large and small clasp knives except size. All have six parts: a blade, two side plates, a divider bar along the upper side between the plates which formed a slot for the blade and served as a spring to lock the blade open or shut and two bone splints for grips which are riveted to the side plates. These bone grips are usually carved with parallel notches and two have initials carved on them. One specimen of an excised brass grip was found in the guardhouse area (Level II) and similar specimens have been found at Fort Michilimackinac and may be French (L. Stone, 1970, p. 502). The blades

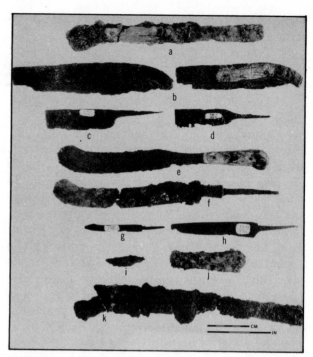

Figure 73. a, Type 1 open clasp knife from Feature 57, Level III; **b,** Type 1 closed clasp knives from the east scarp, Level I and the southwest casemate, Level II; **c,** Type 2a knife blade from the guardhouse area, Level II; **d,** Type 2b knife blade from the north casemate, Level I; **e-f,** Type 3 knives from the north casemate, Level I (2) and the sally port, Level II; **g-i,** Type 4 knives from the north casemate, Level I (2) and the sally port, Level II; **j,** Type 5 razor from the east scarp, Level II; **k,** Type 6 knife from Feature 51.

are notched and squared at the butt to engage the divider bar and the blade tip is convex on both the upper and cutting edges. One blade from the sally port (Level II) has "LUCA" stamped on it near the pivot.

Type 2. Blade has a square tang on it for halfting (sheath knife).

Variety a. Tang an extension of the upper edge of the blade (fig. 73c). These have the following dimensions: blade width, 17 to 30 mm., average, 22.4 mm.; tang length, 39 to 55 mm.; average, 51.0 mm. Other measurements are not possible. At least one is hafted with a wooden handle. The blade tips are straight or slightly concave on the upper edge and convex on the cutting edge.

Variety b. Tang centered on the blade (fig. 73d). These have the following dimensions: blade width, 19 to 25 mm., average, 22.0 mm.; tang length, 36 to 61 mm., average, 50.7 mm. No

Table 32.
Distribution of knives, forks and spoons.

Type	1	2		3	4	5	6	Fork 1		Spoons 1		2
Variety		a	b					a	b	a b c	a b	c
Casemates												
North	6		2	2	2	2		2		1	2	
West	1											
Southwest				2				1	2	2	1	
Southeast	1							1		1		
East	1	1		1		1				3		
Barracks												
East	1		1	2				1				
West	5	1	2					3		1		
Guardhouse	2	2						1			1	
Parade Ground										1		
Bakehouse			1									
Ditch	1		1	1				2	1			
Ravelin	3			2	1					2		
East Scarp	3	1		3	2	2		2				
Sally Port	7	3		2	1	1		2		1 1 1	1	1
Variety totals		8	7					16		3 1 3	1 8 4	1
Type totals	31	15		15	3	7	1	19		5	13	

other measurements can be taken. This variety might be table knives (Type 3) rather than sheath knives but it is impossible to tell without a complete specimen.

Type 3. Blade with upturned blunt tip riveted to handle (table knife) (fig. 73e, f). These have the following dimensions: length, 24 cm. and 25.7 cm.; blade width, 19 to 25 mm., average, 22.0 mm. One example (fig. 73f) has a square tang but is otherwise identical. The handles are of the "pistol grip" type held to the flat tang by two to three rivets. There is usually a short ferrule between the handle and blade. These are somewhat larger than similar specimens from Fort Michilimackinac (L. Stone, 1970, p. 506).

Type 4. Small blade with square tang (surgical knife) (fig. 73g-i). These have the following dimensions: length, 9.5 cm.,? and 14.5 cm.; tang length, 26 mm.,? and 46 mm.; blade width, 8 mm., 13 mm. and 18 mm. These are tentatively identified on the basis of their unusual shape and the high quality of the steel.

Type 5. Narrow blade folding into a handle (razor) (fig. 73j). These have the following dimensions: blade length, 7.9 to 13.2 cm., average, 11.4 cm.; handle length, 8.6 cm. for the shortest specimen; blade width, 15 to 18 mm., average, 16.2 mm. These are constructed similarly to clasp knives; handles have bone grips and the blade tips were squared.

Type 6. Socketed blade (function unknown) (fig. 73k). This has the following dimensions: length: 24.7 cm.; socket length, 11.7 cm., blade width, 28 mm. This was found in Feature 51 in the southwest casemate and is probably a heavy cutting knife.

Forks

Type 1. Steel with bone handles (table 32).

Variety a. Two round tines with a pistol grip handle (fig. 74a). These have the following dimensions: length, 17.5 cm. and 18 cm.; tine length, 32 to 64 mm., average, 46.5 mm.; width at tines, 13 to 19 mm., average, 15.7. All are two-tined iron forks with "pistol grip" bone handles riveted to the tang except one, which has a two-piece antler handle with the tang flattened over the butt. This has two iron rivets while the others have three. Three specimens which have lost their hafts have square tangs for a drilled handle, but the rest have flat tangs with plano-convex bone plates riveted to

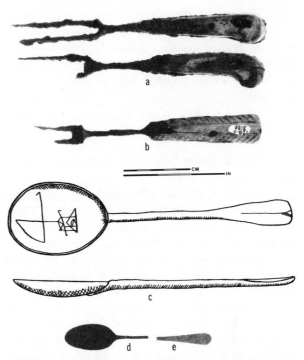

Figure 74. a, Type 1a forks from the southwest casemate, Level II and the sally port, Level II; **b,** Type 1b fork from the west ditch, disturbed area; **c,** Type 2 spoon from the east casemate, Level I; **d,** Type 1b spoon from the sally port, Level II; **e,** Type 1c spoon handle from the sally port, Level III.

them. Handles are generally plain or have small clusters of dots on them.

Variety b. Two flat tines with a ridge across the back of the tines and a straight handle (fig. 74b). These have the following dimensions: length, 15.8 cm., tine length, 26 mm., width at tines, 14 mm. The handle is two flat bone slats held to the flat tang by two rivets. The handles are engraved with chevrons pointing toward the butt except one which has the chevrons stamped into the bone. This variety occurred only in the upper level of the site and might, therefore, be post-1781. A similar example was found in a mid-19th century privy (Feature 5) which contained several early 19th-century artifacts.

Spoons (table 32).

Type 1. Small bowls with thin handles (teaspoons)

Variety a. Pewter. Only a fragment of a spoon bowl is present with a bowl depth of 4 mm.

Variety b. Brass or latten (fig. 74d). These have the following dimensions: bowl length, 34 to 36 mm.; bowl width, 17 to 19 mm.; bowl depth, 3 to 5 mm. These are all spoon bowls with the handles braized to the bottom of the bowl. A silver example of this type at Fort Michilimackinac (L. Stone, 1970, p. 463) had a total length of 10.7 cm.

Variety c. Silver plated brass (fig. 74e). Only a handle fragment was found with an upturned end.

Type 2. Large bowl with thick handle (serving spoons) (fig. 74c).

Variety a. Pewter. One bowl has a depth of 9 mm. No other measurements are possible. Three handle fragments have a central ridge on the top near the end. The bowls are oval. One bowl has engraving in it which appears to be either a small gabled roofed structure, a monogram surmounted by a "4" or a merchant's mark.

Variety b. Brass or latten.

One bowl has a depth of 9 mm. No other measurements are possible. Two bowl fragments and two handle fragments were found. The bowls are more egg-shaped than the pewter variety.

Variety c. Silver plated brass. Only a handle fragment was found.

Combs

These are all made from bone with notching to form teeth. None are complete specimens (fig. 75a). As far as we can tell, they are all toothed on two opposing edges. The number of teeth per inch ranges from 14 to 35. Two specimens have two sizes of teeth, 24 and 35 per inch on one, and 14 and 28 per inch on the other. One was found in the north casemate, (Level I), two in the southwest casemate (Feature 48 and Level II) and two in the west barracks (Feature 57, Level IV and Feature 60, Level II).

Mirrors

Three glass mirror fragments with silver backing were found, two in the southwest casemate (Feature 48 and Level II) and one in the sally port (Level II). All are too fragmentary to obtain meaningful dimensions. Several other mirror fragments were found on the site but they are probably of post-1781 origin.

Hat Pins

Five hat pins (fig. 71m) were found in the north casemate (Level II), west casemate (Level II) and Feature 56 (Level III), Feature 48 and the sally port (Level II). The only complete specimen is 47 mm. long.

Sad Irons

There were women at the fort who washed the laundry of the garrison. They were probably wives of soldiers who had to work in order to stay with their husbands, and to augment the meager wages of the soldiers. With 300 to 400 men stationed at the fort, there was plenty of laundry to keep the women busy, especially in light of the following order:

All the troops, who are able to parade are to be paraded every Sunday morning at 10 o'Clock, with all the Clothing for Examination, when it is expected they will appear neat and in good Order as possible. (M. Willett 3/20/78).

There are no specific references to ironing uniforms, but trousers and shirts made of broadcloth or linen needed to be ironed in order to retain their shape. The sad irons were probably the personal property of the women.

Figure 75. a, bone combs from Feature 48 and Feature 57, Level IV; **b,** sad iron from the surface; **c,** brass jews harp from the north ditch, Level I; **d,** bone whistle from Feature 60, Level III; **e,** 1755 Spanish silver 2 reales coin (reverse) from the north casemate, Level I; **f,** 1741 Spanish silver 1 real coin (obverse) from Feature 3, Level III; **g,** clipped Spanish silver coins (note the broad arrow) from the east barracks, Level I and the west casemate, Level II; **h,** 1723 British George I halfpenny (obverse) from Feature 52, Level III; **i,** 1723 British George I halfpenny (reverse) from Feature 57, Level II; **j,** 1745 British George II halfpenny (obverse) from Feature 42; **k,** 1752 British George II halfpenny (reverse) from Feature 72, Level II; **l,** French or Belgian jetton (?) from Feature 7, Level II; **m,** game counters from the bridge area, Level XV, the north casemate, Level II and Feature 30; **n,** Type 2 bell from Feature 52, Level IV; **p,** Type 1 bell from Feature 72, Level II; **q,** Type 1a lead pencil from the north casemate, Level II; **r,** Type 1b lead pencils from Feature 72, Level III and Feature 76; **s,** Type 1c lead pencil from the north casemate, Level I; **t,** Type 2 lead pencil from the north casemate, Level I; **u,** signet setting from the sally port, Level II; **v,** signet from the north casemate, Level II; **w,** lead bale seal from the south ditch, Level XI.

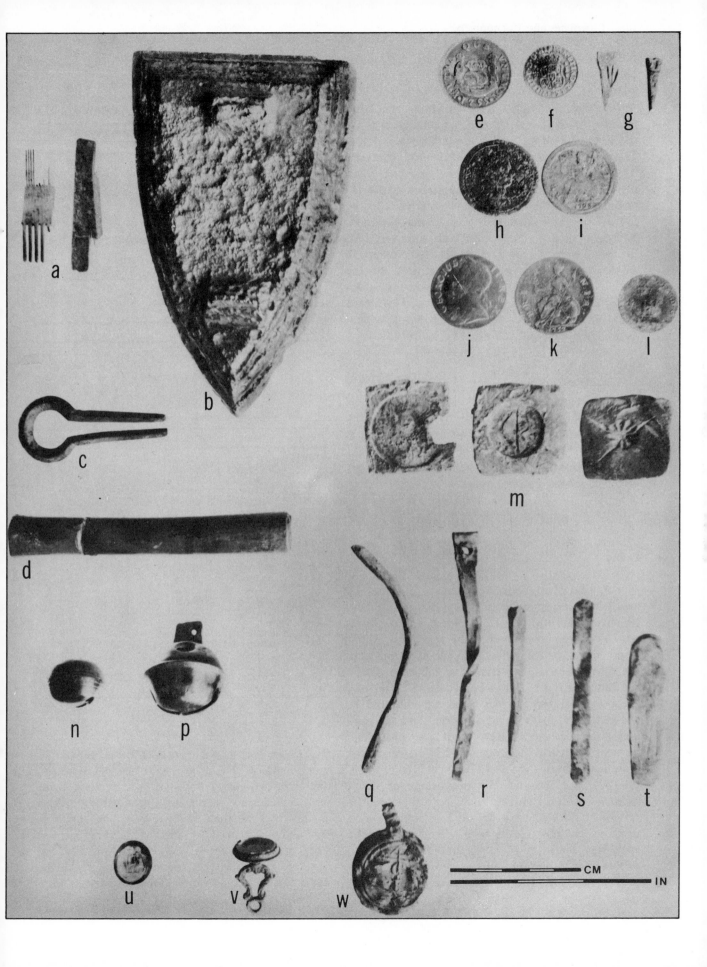

Three sad irons, of a shape generally associated with the early 19th century (Glissman, 1970), were recovered (fig. 75b). The largest is a surface find, the middle sized specimen came from the east scarp (Level II) and the smallest was on the floor of Feature 51 in the southwest casemate. Thus, two are from definite 1758-1781 contexts. The one found on the surface has a raised "7" on the top immediately behind the front handle attachment. Handles of all three were welded to the top of the sad iron near the front and back and had been broken off prior to their discovery. All the irons were probably sand cast. In profile, the smallest and largest irons have four tiers and the middle sized iron has three tiers. They measure 5 1/16 inches long and 3 1/8 inches wide, 5 1/4 inches long and 3 1/4 inches wide, 6 1/8 inches long and 3 7/8 inches wide and all are 1 1/8 inches thick.

Scrub Brush

A scrub brush of white oak (*Quercus*) was found in the sally port (Level III). It is over 11 cm. long and approximately 6.6 cm. wide and 8 mm. thick. The bristles appear to be of pig, held in place by copper wires in holes 6 mm. in diameter and spaced 11 mm. apart.

Coins and Tokens

Coins

A total of 51 coins were found. Of these, 43 are British copper halfpennys and eight are Spanish silver coins (fig. 75e-k). Campbell (1965) listed a 1743 British coin found in the bakehouse which is no longer in the collection. Table 33 presents the distribution of the coins and table 34 shows the range of dates. It will be noted that, with one exception, all the Spanish coins are clustered at the latter end of the time sequence, and the only coin minted during the Revolution is Spanish. This is not surprising since no British copper coins were issued from 1755 to 1770 (Noël Hume, 1970, p. 162). We included the dimensions of dated coins on table 34 and it can be seen that there is no consistent change in British halfpennys (which made up the bulk of the collection) over the time span represented by the collection. Therefore, one cannot date coins by their diameter when the face is worn off. The earliest Spanish coin (1699)

Table 33.

Distribution of coins. (Ratios given are the number of specimens per 10 square feet of excavated area within the structure.)

	British Halfpennies	Spanish Coins	Total	Ratio
Casemates				
North	8	2	10	.31
West	1	1	2	.50
Southwest	6		6	.60
East	2		2	.18
Barracks				
East	8		8	.64
West	4	2	6	.47
Guardhouse	2		2	.17
Bombproof, Northeast		1	1	.18
Ditch	3		3	.10
Ravelin	1		1	.22
East Scarp	4		4	.60
Sally Port	2		2	.23
Campbell Coll.	2	2	4	.22
Totals	43	8	51	.27

Table 34.

Sizes of dated coins in millimeters.

Date	Value	Nationality	Diameter	Thickness
1699	?	Spanish	?	.6
1700	halfpenny	British	28.0	1.9
1722	halfpenny	British	27.8	2.2
1723	halfpenny	British	28.9	2.0
1723	halfpenny	British	27.9	2.1
1730	halfpenny	British	28.1	2.0
1730	halfpenny	British	28.1	2.0
1732	halfpenny	British	28.2	2.0
1732	halfpenny	British	28.3	2.2
1734	halfpenny	British	28.8	2.5
1735	halfpenny	British	28.2	2.3
1737	halfpenny	British	28.9	2.1
1740	halfpenny	British	28.4	1.9
1740	halfpenny	British	28.9	2.0
1741	1 reale	Spanish	20.1	1.2
1745	halfpenny	British	28.1	2.0
1752	halfpenny	British	29.0	2.0
1753	halfpenny	British	28.3	1.9
1755	2 reales	Spanish	26.8	1.2
1766	2 reales	Spanish	25.6	1.2
1768	1 reale	Spanish	21.8	1.3
1779	2 reales	Spanish	27.8	1.1

is a silver disc stamped on both faces, denomination unknown. The other dated Spanish coins are one and two reales and the two undated coins were pie-shaped pieces cut from large Spanish dollars and weighed slightly less than one half real and one real. The larger piece (they are not from the same coin) is stamped with an "M" on one side and a broad arrow on the other. All the dated Spanish coins were minted in Mexico City.

Jetton

One French or Belgian specimen was probably a jetton (Noël Hume, 1970, pp. 171-173) rather than a coin and is made of brass (fig. 75l). On the obverse it has a large block "L" surmounted by a crown with a fleur-de-lis on each side and the bottom. The legend reads: "LUD•XV• D•G•FR•ET•NAV•REX". The reverse has a vine scroll surmounted by a crown and the legend: "(B)ENE-DICTUM•1700•SIT•NOM•DOM". It has a diameter of 21.8 mm. and a thickness of .5 mm.

Game Counters

These are lead pieces, probably used as checkers or counting devices and were locally made (fig. 75m). Six of these came from the north casemate, (Feature 30 and Levels I, II and III), two from the ditch (Levels X and XV), and one each from the southwest casemate (Level I) and the sally port (Level II). Six are square, three round and one oval. Eight are cut on one or both faces with X's or symbols, or impressed with buttons or a Spanish silver coin before the lead hardened. The impressed specimens are too rough for button molds and are not graduated as weights should be, although they might have served that purpose.

Musical Instruments

Jews Harp

A single brass jews harp with a diamond-shaped cross section was found in the north ditch (Level X) (fig. 75c). The iron tongue is broken off. It is 53 mm. long, 24 mm. wide and 6 mm. thick.

Whistle

A carved bone whistle was found in Feature 60 (Level III) in the west barracks (fig. 75d). It is 10 cm. long with a diameter of 15 mm. It was whittled with a knife and smoothed with a file. It has been burned.

Bells

Two brass bells were found in fort contexts. There are three others, larger than these, which probably were post-1781 and were found in the ditch (Levels I and X). The latter have engraved loops and "U"-shaped shanks like the one illustrated by Noël Hume (1970, p. 58). Two post-1781 examples are marked with the initials "WB". Bells found at Fort Ligonier (Grimm, 1970, p. 50) were an entirely different type.

Type 1. Cast with drilled shank (fig. 75p). This has the following dimensions: diameter, 30 mm.; shank height, 10 mm., shank width, 11 mm. The specimen is cast in two halves and braized together at a sharply thickened seam. The shank is a solid piece soldered to the two and drilled with a small hole. There are two holes connected by a slot in the lower half and two holes in the upper half. It has iron clackers. It came from Feature 72 (Level II) in the east barracks.

Type 2. Stamped with a wire shank (fig. 75n). This has a diameter of 21 mm. and a shank height of 7 mm. This specimen is thin brass that was apparently stamped in two halves, each of which was ground by turning and then braized at the seam. A wire loop shank is soldered to the upper half. There are four lines engraved around the sides and a broad arrow is stamped on it. It came from Feature 52 (Level IV) in the east barracks.

Marking Implements

Pencils

Lead pencils were fairly common on the site. There are two types, one made from scrap lead and the other hammered out of musket balls (table 35).

Type 1. Scrap lead pencils.
Variety a. Round cross section (fig. 75q). Dimensions: length, 69.0 to 89.5 mm., average, 76.8 mm.; diameter, 3.0 to 7.5 mm., average, 4.5 mm. Most specimens taper to a flat tip at one end and are blunt at the other end. One is drilled for suspension at one end.
Variety b. Square to rectangular cross section (fig. 75r). Dimensions: length, 33.0 to 115.5 mm., average, 65.6 mm.; width, 2.5 to 12.5 mm., average, 6.2 mm.; thickness, 2.0 to 11.0 mm., average, 5.2 mm. These generally have blunt or pointed tips Two are twisted, probably for greater strength and one is drilled for suspension. They frequently show hammer or trimming marks.
Variety c. Thin rectangular cross section (fig.

Table 35.

Distribution of lead pencils.

Type		1		2	
Variety	a	b	c		Total
Casemates					
North	5	8	3	1	17
West		2	1		3
Southwest	1	5	1		7
East	2		2		4
Barracks					
East	2	4	5		11
West	1	3			4
Guardhouse	1	1		1	3
Parade Ground				1	1
Bombproof, Northeast			1		1
Ditch	1	2	3		6
Ravelin		2			2
East Scarp	2		3	1	6
Sally Port	1	3	2		6
Variety totals	16	30	21		
Type totals			67	4	71

75s). These have the following dimensions: length, 43.5 to 83.5 mm., average, 62.2 mm.; width, 5.0 to 12.0 mm., average 7.3 mm.; thickness, 1.0 to 3.5 mm., average, 2.0 mm.

Type 2. Musket ball pencils (fig. 75t). These have the following dimensions: length, 44.5 to 60.0 mm., average, 53.2 mm.; width, 11.0 to 14.5 mm., average 12.5 mm.; thickness, 5.5 to 10.5 mm., average 8.9 mm. These were musket balls hammered to a blunt point on one end and retaining the musket ball shape at the other.

Signets

Four glass signets were found in the north and east casemates (Level II), the west barracks (Level I) and the sally port (Level II). The specimen from the north casemate is a clear glass oval, 14 by 12 mm. with the impressed bust of a man in Roman garb and a rope border. (fig. 75v). It is mounted with red wax in a brass stamp 29 mm. long. It is not a ring and was probably worn attached by a string through a hole in the mount. The one from the east casemate is 11 mm. in diameter with an impressed large house flanked by trees. The specimen from the west barracks is also 11 mm. in diameter with an impressed rosette pattern of seven flowers. These two might have been insets from sleeve links. The sally port specimen is an oval blue glass setting measuring 16 by 14 mm. It has the design of an impressed four-masted ship (fig. 75u). The back and edges are faceted. These signets were probably used with hot wax to seal letters and documents.

Bale Seal

A single used lead bale seal was found in the ditch (Level XI) south of the southwest bastion. It consists of two discs connected by a strip. One disc has a hole in it and the other a knob on the back which has been pressed through the hole. The obverse is shown in Figure 78w. The reverse has a bisected circle with a "25" molded in the lower half. In the upper half is scratched the number "792" or "292". It is 30 mm. in diameter and may have been British, although what it sealed is unknown. Philip Schuyler (letter dated July 6, 1777) responded to a letter of John Hansen, the fort's commissary, about two bales of cloth for the Indians that were sent from Boston by the firm of Livingston and Trumbull and were numbered 172 and 173. See also: Ink Wells

Miscellaneous

This section is a catchall for those objects we could not identify as to function but which were considered important enough to describe. Many iron objects and lead and brass scraps were encountered which had no apparent function. Most of the iron specimens are probably fragments of tools. Most of the lead specimens appear to have been worked on by persons with nothing better to do and most of the brass specimens appear to be scrap.

Ferrules

Wrought iron ferrules were used to reinforce pieces of wood, especially ends, to prevent them from splitting. Also, they were used to keep wood or bone handles clinched tightly over the tangs of metal implements. They were all made from strips of metal cut to the desired length, bent to the desired shape and the ends welded together. The welds were skillfully done and on some specimens are very difficult to detect. Specimens identical to these types were found at Fort Ligonier (Grimm, 1970, p. 53).

Type 1. Rectangular.

Variety a. Large with rounded corners. Two specimens were found (fig. 76a). They are seven to eight times larger than the other ferrules. One fitted on a piece of wood approximately 2¼ by 3⅜ inches and the other on one 2¼ by 4 inches. The smaller ferrule is ⅝ inch wide and 3/16 inch

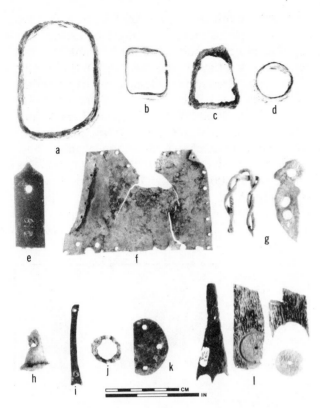

Figure 76. **a,** Type 1a ferrule from the bridge area, Level X; **b,** Type 1c ferrule from the east scarp, Level II; **c,** Type 2 ferrule from Feature 76; **d,** Type 3 ferrule from the ravelin, Level I; **e,** brass gunner's sight (?) from the east scarp, Level I; **f,** brass plate from the sally port, Level II; **g-k,** unidentified lead objects from the west casemate, Level I, the east casemate, Level II, the north casemate, Level II, the east casemate, Level II, Feature 72, Level III and the east casemate, Level II; **l,** iron button bit, bone blanks and finished button from the sally port, Level II.

thick; the larger specimen is 1 inch wide and ⅛ inch thick.

Variety b. Small with no attachment holes. Two specimens were found. One is square and the other rectangular. The rectangular ferrule measures 1¼ inches long and ¾ inch wide. The strap is ½ inch wide and 1/16 inch thick. The other is 1⅜ inches square made from a strap ⅜ inch wide and 1/16 inch thick.

Variety c. Small with one attachment hole. Five specimens were found (fig. 76b). Four are square and one is rectangular. Three of the square ferrules measure 1⅛ inches on a side, the other is 1¼ inches on a side. They are made from ⅜-inch-wide strips, 1/16 inch thick. Three still have nails

up to ½ inch long through a hole bored in the center of one side. The rectangular specimen measures ¾ by 1¼ inches and is made from a strip ½ inch wide and 1/16 inch thick. A nail hole is in the middle of one short side.

Type 2. Bell-shaped. Two were found (fig. 76c). They have a flat bottom, two sides that taper inward and a rounded top. They are identical in size and shape; the bottom measures 1¼ inches long, the sides 1½ inches long, and the top approximately 1 inch in diameter. The metal strips are ½ inch wide and 1/16 inch thick.

Type 3. Round.

Variety a. No attachment holes (fig. 76d). There is a wide range of diameters and widths for these 29 ferrules. The diameters range from ⅞ inch to 2⅞ inches, width of the metal ⅜ to 1 inch and thickness of the metal 1/16 to 3/16 inch.

Variety b. One attachment hole. The three specimens range in diameter from 1¼ to 1⅝ inches, width of strip ⅝ to ⅞ inch and thickness of strip 1/16 to 3/16 inch.

Variety c. Two attachment holes. Two specimens were found. One is 2⅞ inches in diameter and the other is 1½ inches. They are made from strips ¾ inch wide and 1/16 inch thick. The holes are bored approximately 180 degrees from each other.

Type 4. Oval. One specimen is 2 by 1⅛ inches in diameter. The metal strip is ¾ inch wide and ¹⁄₁₆ inch thick.

Rings

Three brass or copper wire loops were found in pre-1781 contexts. We have no idea what they were used for. Dimensions: diameter, 8.5 to 16.0 mm.; thickness, 1 to 1.5 mm. Two were in Feature 60 (Levels II and III) in the west barracks and one in Feature 52 (Level IV) in the east barracks.

Gunners Sight (?)

A brass bar fragment 25 mm. wide was found in Level I on the east scarp (fig. 76e). It is pointed at the unbroken end and has a screw hole drilled through it 21 mm. below the point and the number "219" engraved on the back. Because of its provenience it cannot be definitely related to the fort and it may be a piece of furniture hardware.

Brass Plates

Two similar brass sheets were found on Feature 51 in the southwest casemate and in the sally port (Level II) (fig. 76f). They have the following dimensions: length, 10.5 cm. and 10.4 cm.; width, 8.6 cm. and 8.1 cm.; thickness, .5 mm. Both are pierced with holes around the edge and the one in the southwest casemate still has sheet brass rivets in it.

Unidentifiable Lead Objects

There are a large number of cut scraps of lead which fell into this category, and which are probably the by-products of manufacture. These cannot be described because of their infinite variety. Two are illustrated in figure 76g. The few objects which appear to have been made for a purpose are described below.

Two lead truncated cones with rolled rims were found in the north casemate (Level II) (fig. 76h). One has nail holes in it and they probably were attached to wooden rods. They are 31.5 to 35.5 mm. long (too crushed for other dimensions).

Three lead bars with holes at each end came from the east casemate (Level II), Feature 64 (Level IV) in the west barracks, and the sally port (Level II) (fig. 76i). One is also notched at one end. We suspect these were somehow connected with weaving. Dimensions: length, 64.5 to 66.0 mm., width, 4 to 7 mm., thickness, 4.5 to 5.0 mm.

A lead ring with 10 serrations in one edge came from Feature 72 (Level III) in the east barracks (fig. 76j). It looks like a miniature crown. It is 30 mm. in diameter and 19.5 mm. high.

A D-shaped lead piece with three nail holes was found in the east casemate (Level II) (fig. 76k). Except that it is made of lead and not worn, it looks like a heel plate from a shoe. It is 28 mm. long, 45 mm. wide and 2.5 mm. thick.

A spoked, wheel-shaped object came from Feature 48 in the southwest casemate. It is fragmentary and may have been a pendant or toy.

Prehistoric Indian Artifacts

Scattered over the site, generally in Level I, were prehistoric stone tools and chert flakes. These were identified for us by Dr. Robert E. Funk, New York State Archeologist (personal communication),

and range in time from *ca.* 4000 B.C. to A.D. 1300 with a couple of pieces that might be earlier. The types of projectile points defined by Funk are: one Otter Creek (Laurentian, 4000-3000 B.C.) (fig. 77a), two Brewerton side-notched (Laurentian, 3000-2000 B.C.) (fig. 77b, c), six Brewerton-like (Laurentian, 3000-2000 B.C.), one Lamoka-like (Lamoka *ca.* 2500 B.C.) (fig. 77d), four broad-stemmed (late Archaic), three crude small side-notched (late Archaic ?, *ca.* 2000 B.C.), two Fox Creek (A.D. 400-500) (fig. 77e) and one Levanna (Owasco, A.D. 1100-1300) (fig. 77f). The distribution of these and other tools is shown on table 36.

Figure 77. **a,** Otter Creek projectile point from the north ditch, Level I; **b,** Brewerton projectile point from the guardhouse area, Level II; **c,** Brewerton scraper reworked from a broken projectile point from the guardhouse area, Level II; **d,** Lamoka-like projectile point from Feature 21; **e,** Fox Creek projectile points from Feature 52, Level III and the southeast bastion, Level I; **f,** Levanna projectile point base from the northwest bastion, Level II; **g,** drill fragments from the west casemate, Level II and the east casemate, Level II; **h,** scrapers of Normanskill chert from the sally port, Level II (2).

There are a number of utilized flakes and some drills (fig. 77g) and scrapers which cannot be identified by age. Only the Lamoka point, a bifacial tool fragment, three utilized chert flakes and eight unworked flakes can be associated with an aboriginal feature. This is a hearth (Feature 21) with fire-cracked rocks in the southeast casemate area (Level II). More Indian features were probably destroyed by the construction of the fort and subsequent occupation by the town of Rome. Three scrapers of green Normanskill chert from the Hudson Valley were found (fig. 77h). One came from the west end of the north casemate (Level II), and two from the sally port (Level II). The remainder of the artifacts appear to be local chert.

The Indian artifacts were found in all parts of the fort and many were in the top level suggesting probable disturbance or secondary deposits. Figure 78 shows the two main concentrations in relation to the fort and the original hill contour on which the fort stood. See also: Pendants, Type 4.

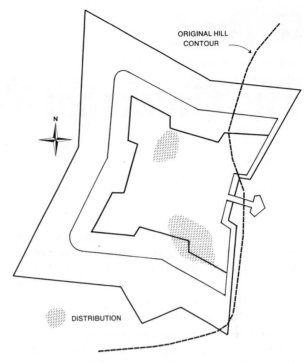

ORIGINAL HILL CONTOUR

N

DISTRIBUTION

Figure 78. Distribution of prehistoric Indian artifacts at Fort Stanwix.

Table 36.
Distribution of Indian stone artifacts.

	Points						Scrapers	Drills	Gravers	Worked Slate	Utilized Flakes	Other Flakes
	Lauren-tian	Lamoka	Late Archaic	Fox Creek	Owasco	Unidentified Fragments						
Casemates												
North	2		1			2	2				13	37
West								1			5	72
Southwest									1		9	80
Southeast		1	1			2			1		23	147
East							1	1			9	25
Barracks												
East				1		1	2		1 [1]		3	31
West											5	15
Guardhouse	2		1			3			1		21	137
Headquarters											4	9
Parade Ground					1	1					8	32
Bombproofs												
Northeast						1					5	11
Northwest	1											1
Southwest	1										1	3
Bakehouse	1		1	1							10	19
Ditch	1		1			5	3		2	1	10	81
Ravelin						1					3	15
East Scarp						1					4	14
Sally Port	1		1			1	2				4	19
Total	9	1	6	2	1	18	10	3	6	1	138	758

[1] Made from a French gunflint and found in a clay-lined cellar.

Chapter 5

The Times that Tried Men's Souls

If Thomas Paine caught the imagination of Americans in 1776, he also captured the spirit of the times. Although America had yet to become the melting pot of the 19th century, the people were nonetheless marked by diversity of thought, background, economic pattern and life style. Certainly, there was more than a geographical separation between Mrs. Eliza Wilkinson in her plantation at Charlestown, South Carolina (E. Wilkinson, 1839) and John Roof in his lob cabin on a piece of cleared land at Fort Stanwix, New York. Yet, both were "patriots," displaced by war, losing most of their possessions. The ties that bound men and women in the common cause of American Independence were as varied as the men and women themselves. Fort Stanwix served as a microcosm in which to study the soldiers through their orderly books, letters and diaries. We must, of necessity, interpret these often cryptic documents so that what we offer here is an interpretation of historic events rather than a chronologue of those events. For example, in May 1778, Lt. Colonel Willett ordered the sentry boxes, "Fix'd so as not to be blown down with every triflng Wind." (M. Willett, 5/15/78). This tells us (a) that they were flimsy structures, (b) they were not securely anchored, and, (c) that at least one probably blew over. Since these were located on the tips of the bastions it could have blown into the ditch which would have been rather hazardous to any sentry that was in it.

Living Conditions

When the first American troops from the 3rd New Jersey Regiment occupied Fort Stanwix on July 13, 1776, they found it in a state of ruin.

While making repairs, they lived in tents and barns or boarded with one of the five settlers in the area. The conditions are best described by one of the junior officers:

Sunday, September 19, 1776 . . . Cold, stormy day, and I obliged to live in a cold wet marquee, which leaks considerable: Whilst the Captain, with the Field officers and other great men, have good rooms in barracks. The way of the world. This is what will try a soldier to live in this manner in this cold country: those who never tried these hardships, know not how to prize good shelters and warm fires to defend themselves from the inclemencies of cold and inhospitable climates. (Elmer, 1848, p. 30).

Tuesday, October 1st, 1776 . . . Being on guard all night we came near perishing, having our bodies exposed to a severe white frost, which froze the ground hard, and some of the men barefoot." (Elmer, 1848, p. 31).

Despite the hardships, or perhaps because of them, they played hard too. They played ball nearly every day and a game called whirl, at which Elmer nearly suffered a broken jaw (Elmer, 1848, p. 31). John Roof's house became a gathering place for drinking and card playing. On October 2nd, after concluding a court martial, several of the officers

Began drinking wine, which they continued successively till about 10 o'clock at night. Many of them got very happy; upon which, appointing Capts. Dickinson and Potter and Major Barber, Sachems, they knocked up an Indian dance, at which they yelled much—all this was done within the Fort . . ." (Elmer, 1848, p. 31). The next morning they seemed . . . very squeamish after last night's merry dance. (Elmer, 1848, p. 32).

In 1778, the men were ordered not to play in the meadows below the fort because they would destroy the forage (M. Willett, 4/23/78). In 1781, the soldiers had to be ordered not to engage in snowball fights in the garrison (Lauber, 1932, p. 557). Evidence for leisure activities was scanty: one Jew's harp, a carved bone whistle and a number of lead pieces identified as game counters.

In October, 1776, the Connecticut regiment of Colonel Samuel Elmore replaced the New Jersey troops. These, in turn, were replaced by the 3rd New York Regiment in April, 1777, although part of the regiment did not arrive until May.

From the beginning, construction of the fort was hampered by a lack of tools, materials, skilled craftsmen and competent engineers. That any progress was made at all was probably due to the fact that they had the British fort to start with and they expected an attack any day. On August 30th, 1776, the men

labored earnestly all the forenoon; but the scout . . . returning with the news that no forces of any kind were at Oswego, or on their march from thence, produced in almost every one a languor and disinclination for labor. (Elmer, 1848, p. 189).

During the Revolution, many Europeans offered their services to the American army. As the pay was low they were largely enticed by high rank, which they could not get in Europe. For every LaFayette, Count Kosciusko and "Baron" von Steuben, there were countless opportunists who talked their way into positions for which they were unqualified. One Captain B. De La Marquise, assigned to rebuild Fort Stanwix, reported for duty on April 20, 1777 (Luzader, 1969, p. 66). By July, his incompetence was evident to everyone and he was replaced by a Major Hubble who was apparently little better as an engineer, but less of a troublemaker. Hubble was replaced in January, 1778, by a Lieutenant Bowen (M. Willett, 1/15/78).

Although De La Marquese made his share of mistakes he had other problems. He arrived

. . . with a Company of 20 carpenters / ./ a few days after / ,/ he was obliged to discharge 10 of them / ,/ being shoemakers, taylors, & Smiths who did not understand . . . / the / business for which they engaged . . . (Luzader, 1969, p. 66).

Civilian carpenters were expensive and the army attempted to get as much work out of them as possible:

Fortifications are at all times expensive; they become more so, when the artificers are suffered to while away their time. Your carpenters must therefore begin to work at day-light, and work until sun-set, allowing an hour for breakfast, and an hour and a half for dinner. No sitting down to smoak and drink at eleven o'clock, or at any other time, except that at meals. In very hot weather, two hours may be allowed at dinner. (Schuyler, 1880, p. 87).

As noted in the section on artifacts, most of the nails used in constructing the fort were probably made on the site or, more likely, were shipped from Albany or the Mohawk Valley. We know that sawed boards were brought in by batteaux (M. Willett, 5/31/77, 6/16/77). There were carpenters and sawyers at the fort (M. Willett, 3/17/78). Axes, spades, hammers, saw fragments, files, rulers and a plumbob were found in the fort and may have been used in its erection. The concentration of these tools in the southwest casemate, coupled with the knowledge that the civilian carpenters were probably living together (M. Willett, 4/8/78, 4/26/78), leads us to conclude tentatively that this casemate was their quarters.

The Gansevoort Plan (fig. 7) depicts a carpenter's shop and a blacksmith's shop outside the fort but it is unlikely that these were living quarters. They would have been in constant danger of British-led Indian attacks. Another anomaly peculiar to the southwest casemate, which supports our conclusion that it was used by carpenters, was the high number of nails found there, particularly since it was a log structure and had an earthen floor. One would expect the frame buildings on the parade ground, particularly the west barracks which was rebuilt twice, to have had the greatest number of nails, but the southwest casemate ranked second and the southeast casemate fourth in the number of nails found per square foot. The presence of a large number of spades in the southwest casemate suggests that the engineer was using this building for storage since these were his responsibility (Clinton, 1900, #1554; M. Willett, 3/10/78). As the artificers were well paid they probably enjoyed a higher standard of living than the soldiers, particularly since they seem to have engaged in a sideline of bootlegging rum to the garrison (M. Willett 4/18/78, 4/26/78). The ratio of porcelain (taken as an indication of wealth) was the highest in the southeast and southwest casemates.

In addition to civilian carpenters, there are occasional references in the orderly books to civilian wagoners and sleighmen, and the fort commissary was a civilian who answered to the Deputy Quartermaster General in Albany. References to bakers and butchers infer that soldiers acted in these capacities (Lauber, 1932, p. 541; M. Willett, 4/19/78). The horseshoes and oxshoes found on the site merely confirm the presence of these animals but tell us nothing about them except that all the oxshoes were found in the ditch and ravelin suggesting that these animals were kept in the ditch and not allowed into the fort proper. We know that cattle and hogs were kept in the ditch during 1777 (Gansevoort to Henry Glen, 12/12/77). The relative number of shoes indicated that horses were far more common than oxen which is supported by the documents which do not mention oxen in connection with the fort.

Records for one company of the First New York which served in 1779-1780 at Fort Stanwix provides some basic information on the men themselves. Of 27 men listed, 15 had been born in Europe, most of them in Ireland. The average age was 27 years with a range of 17-40 years, not counting an 11-year-old fifer and a 12-year-old drummer. The average height was 5 feet, 7 inches. Civilian occupations were farmer (6), carpenter (3), coppersmith, barber, scribe, tanner, weaver, merchant, shoemaker (2) and laborer (7) (Anon., 1916, p. 436).

When the British attacked the fort in August 1777, it was in a defensible state except for a parapet to protect the men from snipers (M. Willett, 1777). This was remedied during the early days of the siege. We have few records of living conditions in the completed fort, but in January 1778, James Wilkinson visited the fort and reported: ". . . the present Barracks must Necessarily be pulled down, being so constructed, as barely to cover 200 Men: the rest of the Garrison I found in Sod Hovils in the Ditch . . ." (J. Wilkinson 1778). He also noted that Major Hubbell "is a stupid fellow unfit for any other appointment than a Sergeant of Posts . . ." As we have seen, he was soon replaced. No evidence was found for sod hovels in the ditch but the fireplace on the east scarp (Feature 68) and the hearth in the south ditch Feature 2) may have dated from this period.

One of the unsolved mysteries of Fort Stanwix involves the question of where all the troops were housed during the siege of 1777. There were from 700 to 750 men in a fort that was built to quarter 400 under optimum conditions. Yet from the records there was no hint of overcrowding. The Third New York had about 40 officers while it was at Fort Stanwix (Fernow, 1887), The three senior officers could have been housed in the headquarters building. If the north casemate was also officers' quarters, as the size of the rooms and fireplace locations indicate, then it probably held 12 more. The Barr diary (Lauber, 1932, p. 843) indicates two officers to a room in this structure. This leaves about 25 officers, or 13 more rooms to be located in the fort. The arrangement of chimneys and doors on powderhorn drawings of Fort Stanwix suggest that each barracks on the parade ground may have contained officers' quarters, perhaps enough to meet the remaining needs of the garrison.

Casualties and Desertions

There is some difficulty in resolving various accounts of events, although most accounts agree on the major points. For instance, on July 3, 1777, Ensign Spoor led a fatigue party which was attacked by Indians. Colonel Gansevoort reported in a letter dated July 4, that a party of 17 were attacked. In another letter of his dated July 5, the party was 26 strong, two men were killed, one wounded and seven captured. The Colbraith Diary (Reid, 1905) lists one killed, one wounded and five captured while the muster rolls (Fernow, 1887) list two killed, one wounded and five taken prisoner. Finally, the Indians showed up at Oswegatche with five prisoners and four scalps (O'Callahan, 1854, Vol. 8, p. 719). By comparing various documents we feel we have arrived at a close approximation of the American casualties at Fort Stanwix during the Revolution (Table 37).

Table 37.

American casualties and desertions at Fort Stanwix, including civilians.

	Killed	Wounded	Captured	Died	Deserted
1776	3		2	8	19
1777 [1]	14	23	6	6	52
1778	2		2	7	47
1779	3	3	41	1	9
1780	14 [2]		1	4	52
1781	1	1	14	1	2
Total	37	27	66	27	181

[1] During the siege, August 2-22, there were eight killed, 21 wounded and one captured.

[2] Thirteen of these were killed on May 23 while trying to desert.

Any assessment of these figures must take into account the fact that most of these casualties took place outside the walls of the fort where work parties were subject to ambush. The only casualties inside the fort occurred during the siege. Although 1779 was known as the year of the Sullivan Expedition, there were Indian raids around Fort Stanwix as well. On June 4, eight men were captured and one of these was killed by the Indians (Fernow, 1887). Then on July 23, 28 more were captured while two were killed and one was wounded (Fernow, 1887). One of the captives later escaped but the rest were held almost to the end of the war.

In addition to casualties, the commanders worried about desertions. Because Fort Stanwix was an isolated post, it was relatively easy to desert. Various methods of stemming the tide were tried, from forbidding the soldiers to go outside the fort without orders from their company commanders to stationing a quarter guard on the covered way with orders to shoot anyone climbing over the walls. A small fire hearth found on the covered way (Feature 47) may have been a post of the quarter guard. The 3rd New York was relieved by the 1st New York in December 1778. On May 22, 1780, 31 men of this regiment left in a body for Canada (Washington, 1932, Vol. 19, 6/20/80). The commanding officer did not want to weaken the garrison further by sending a detachment after them (he may have been concerned that they would join the deserters), so he sent an officer with a large party of Oneida Indians in pursuit. They caught up with the deserters the next evening while they were crossing a river. Thirteen of the deserters were reported killed and three taken prisoner. The remainder made their escape during the night leaving most of their food behind. Some of these managed to get to Fort Haldeman (Pat Wilder, personal communication) although one returned to Fort Stanwix in October. Washington was so alarmed by this "mutiny" that he ordered militia to man the fort in October 1780. The 1st New York went on to distinguish itself at Yorktown so the problem probably stemmed from conditions at Fort Stanwix. In November, 1780, the 4th New York arrived at Fort Stanwix (Lauber, 1932).

It can be seen in table 37 that there was an inverse ratio between casualties and desertions. It appears clear that when there was a danger of being captured by hostile Indians, the men stuck close to the fort and when this danger was removed, the conditions in the fort were bad enough to cause the men to desert. Weather was probably a factor too as the four most favored months for desertion were May, June, August and October with very few leaving in July, or December through February.

Crime and Punishment

Desertion was the most common offense committed at Fort Stanwix. At least three were later executed (Fernow, 1887) and several others were whipped, one receiving 400 lashes (M. Willett 1/31/78). Other serious crimes included drunkeness, theft, insulting officers and the sale of issued clothing. The whipping post, located on the parade ground, was capable of holding four men at once for punishment (Elmer, 1848, p. 135; M. Willett, 1/31/78) which usually consisted of 50 to 150 lashes administered by the drummers, Although the drummers may have had strong arms, they were mostly boys. Even if they took turns on the more severe punishment, they may not have inflicted excessive injury to the offenders. There were no reported instances of death from whipping. Other forms of punishment were confinement in the guardhouse or a bombproof, running a gauntlet through the regiment preceded by a sergeant with a fixed bayonet to impede progress, and having a two-foot-long log chained to one leg while cleaning garbage from the fort (Lauber, 1932, pp. 547, 577).

Another offense, which seldom was punished because of the difficulty of catching the culprit, was the firing of weapons. Besides wasting ammunition, such an alarm could easily lead the men to the conclusion that Indians were attacking the fort. Commanders tried everything from counting cartridges and charging a shilling for each shot (Elmer, 1848, p. 135) to forbidding the men to take weapons from the fort except on duty (M. Willett, 4/1/78).

Indian Relations

At the outset of the Revolution, the Americans made an effort to placate the Indians. They realized that most of the Indians favored the Crown and, therefore, made special efforts to persuade them to remain neutral. In writing to Congress January 25, 1777, Philip Schuyler complained:

I have Indians, more or less, every day with me, complaining of the want of clothing, blankets especially, of which we have not one. I clearly perceive that our cause will be most essentially prejudiced, unless a large stock of Indian goods be immediately sent here. To transact business with Indians, at any time is a most disagreeable task, to do it with empty hands greatly encreases the difficulty. (Schuyler 1880, p. 68).

Only two tribes in the New York area remained friendly to the American cause, the Oneida and the Tuscarora. Fortunately, the Oneida were the nearest neighbors of Fort Stanwix. Their principal role was to serve as scouts for the fort but they took little active part in the war except for an expedition against the Onondaga in 1779. This expedition was equipped at the fort and provided with two officers from the garrison. They were also ordered to track down the large party of deserters in 1780 (Washington, 1932, Vol. 19, 6/20/80).

The Indians were kept out of the fort at night, although no explanation was given for this policy (M. Willett, 12/25/77). Probably the garrison couldn't be certain who was friendly and who was not. Apparently there was little difficulty in communicating with the Indians. In 1776, missionary Samuel Kirkland acted as an interpreter and later James Dean served in this same capacity. Only in the fall of 1777 did there appear to have been a communications problem, because both the Oneida and the garrison asked that an interpreter be sent up (Gates Papers, 10/27/77, 11/18/77).

Although the Indians may have provided some food for the garrison, the only reference was to fish brought to the fort in 1777 (W. Smith, 1956, p. 339). Several letters from the commanders of the fort complained of the heavy drain on the fort's provisions by the Indians coming in for food. In the years 1776-1778, several references were made to shipments of Indian goods to the fort for distribution to the Indians (Schuyler, 1880; M. Willett, 4/23/78; Gates Papers, 10/11/77), but in later years there were no references to such practices. In late 1780, the Oneida moved down the Mohawk where they felt more secure from attack by other Indians. During the winter, parties from the fort looted Oneida Castle of two swivel guns, approximately 1,000 bushels of corn and some potatoes (Lauber, 1932, p. 844). Only a few artifacts such as Micmac pipes, brass tinkling cones and beads suggest an Indian presence at Fort Stanwix. This tends to confirm the documents and conclusions of

historians that the Indians were kept out of the fort as much as possible. Of course, we are dealing with Iroquois who had been greatly acculturated by the second half of the 18th century, and who shared much of the material culture of the garrison. Thus, a clasp knife intended for trade or lost by an Indian would be indistinguishable from one lost by a member of the garrison.

Sickness and Disease

Sickness and disease were major concerns of the American army, especially after the 1775 Canadian expeditions. The men were ordered to clean their quarters daily and air their bedding periodically. They were to get fresh straw for their beds every three months although we suspect straw was not always available. One or more necessaries, or latrines, were maintained for the troops. Apparently it was a long cold walk and orders were issued for the men not to ease themselves elsewhere. The spring brought campaigns to clean up the "filth" in the garrison (M. Willett, 3/24/78). In May, 1778, tubs were ordered put in each room for the men to use at night (M. Willett, 5/21/78). The Quartermaster's job included supervising men who picked up the dirt and filth in the garrison (M. Willett 5/30/77).

Animals that were kept in the fort contributed to the problem. At various times there were references to horses, cows and pigs being quartered. Some animals apparently were community property but most were privately owned by the soldiers and civilians residing in the fort. The owners of cows were allowed to charge for milk even though the cows were fed from the public stores. In September, 1777, a quart of milk sold for 6 shillings (M. Willett, 9/23/77). One individual who charged more had his cows confiscated for a time and the milk given to the hospital. (M. Willett, 5/1/78).

Some form of hospital existed throughout the occupation of the fort, staffed with a surgeon and a surgeon's mate. Undoubtably it was a small structure where only the most seriously ill were kept, for the available returns show four to 11 men in the hospital with four times as many sick staying in their own quarters. In 1776, Ebenezer Elmer

Visited the sick in their old lousy hospital, which represents such a scene of wretchedness that one could hardly bear to behold the abject souls therein confined. But the Colonel moving into the barracks, they were permitted to remove into his house. (Elmer, 1848, p. 32).

During the siege of 1777, the southwest bomb-proof apparently served as a hospital, for a woman who had been wounded gave birth to a baby there (Reid, 1905, p. 103). Just before the siege, the sick were sent downstream because of a lack of facilities (Reid, 1905, p. 94)

In 1777, Elmer (1848, p. 32) who had studied medicine, listed catarrh, diarrhea, cutaneous eruption (epidemic) and ague, as the major maladies. The primary causes of these were probably exposure and a poor diet. The smallpox epidemic in the Albany area in December, 1777, apparently did not reach Fort Stanwix. Nevertheless, the commander would not let men who had not had the disease leave the fort (M. Willett, 12/24/77). In March of 1778, 10 men were in the hospital with the following ailments: rheumatism, venereal disease, inflammatory fever, lameness (2), debility, convulsive asthma, weakness and remitting fever. Another 22 were in their quarters with: hamoptoe (hammer toe?), lameness (8), debility (2), itch (4), ulcerous leg, asthma, venereal disease, inflammatory fever, remitting fever and pleurisy. Two were listed merely as sick (Anon., 1916, p. 390). There were no concentrations of pharmaceutical bottles or medical instruments to indicate the location of the hospital or surgeon's quarters.

Duty

The three most common tasks performed in the fort were guard duty, fatigue, and drill. There was a set routine for the day (orderly books) beginning at sunrise with the waking of the troops and roll call. The guard for the fort was paraded at 8 a.m. and the old guard relieved. At the same time the fatigue parties for the day were paraded and as soon as the gates opened, they marched to their jobs. At 10 a.m. the remaining troops were formed on the parade ground for drill. In 1778, these were divided into three groups, a "grand squad," an "awkward squad," and a special drill unit for the extremely awkward (M. Willett, 5/3/78). The first was to drill for an hour, the second for 1½ hours and the last until noon. In the winter these times were reduced but drill continued as weather permitted. Everyone, except the carpenters whose hours were described above, took an hour for lunch. By 1 p.m. the fatigue parties

were back at work until Retreat at about 7 p.m. At 4 p.m. the grand squad was drilled another 1½ hours, the awkward squad 2 hours and the remainder until Retreat. Tattoo was about 8 or 9 p.m. when the lights and all fires were to be extinguished.

Sundays were days of rest; Kirkland sometimes preaching when he was at the fort (Elmer, 1848). Occasionally, the garrison would have a field day on Sunday, demonstrating manuevers and manual of arms. Clothing and equipment were inspected for cleanliness and deficiencies at this time.

Fatigue parties were usually formed to cut and haul firewood but also cleared the woods around the fort, obstructed Wood Creek, cut sod for the fort walls, gathered hay and made repairs on the fort (orderly books). They were allowed an extra ration of a gill of rum (2 drams) a day, half in the morning and half in the evening. Most of the tools found in the fort were probably related to fatigue activity. Their concentration in the southwest casemate has already been noted as evidence that the engineer kept his stores there.

Patrols were constantly out to the west toward Oneida Lake to look for evidences of British advances. These men had to wade swollen creeks, brave sudden storms and evade British parties. Sometimes they did not return.

Communications

The isolation of Fort Stanwix was a major problem for the garrison There was only one way —up the Mohawk River—for supplies and news to reach the fort. Under ordinary conditions, it took three to four days for messages arriving from Albany by express courier, and two to three days for a return trip (based on letters and replys which can be tied to each other by reference). A body of troops took considerably longer to make the journey. Willett's detachment in May, 1777, required 7 days to get from Albany (M. Willett, 5/25/77) while the detachment of the 9th Massachusetts which escorted supplies to the fort on August 2, 1777, took 14 days to make the same trip, although they stopped at Fort Dayton for several days (Rix, 1938).

A resolution of Congress, passed on October 4, 1777, congratulating the garrison for its defense of the fort, was not read to the troops at Fort Stanwix until December 2 (M. Willett, 1/2/77). However, there is reason to believe that Colonel

Gansevoort carried the resolution in his pocket for several weeks in Albany so he could be present when it was read to the men. News of the American victory at Cowpens, South Carolina, on January 17, 1781, did not reach the fort until February 27, 41 days later. (Lauber, 1832, p. 566).

Travel was generally made by bateau because of bad roads, but the 2nd New York arrived in November 1781, with 98 wagons of baggage; the troops required 6 days to make the 50-mile trip from Fort Plain to Fort Stanwix (Lauber, 1932, p. 842). In the wintertime, sleighs were used to supply the fort. The finding of horseshoes and ox-shoes indicates that these animals were used for transportation and hauling supplies. We also recovered a few objects which were interpreted as wagon parts.

Food

If one single problem worried the commanders of the fort more than an Indian attack, it was where their next meal was coming from. On November 24, 1780, the following daily rations were to be issued: 1¼ pounds of bread or one pound of flour, 1 pound of fresh or salted meat, 1 quart of salt per 100 pounds of meat, one pound of candle tallow per week for every 12 men, including women, and 8 pounds of soap for every 100 men per week. The head and heart of a beef might be substituted for five pounds of meat and three "points" (pints?) of peas per week might be issued on special order (Lauber, 1932, p. 542). The same day some cow tongues and flour were condemned and ordered destroyed. On December 5, the bread ration for troops was reduced to 1 pound but the artificers, waggoners, colliers, boatmen and woodcutters were allowed 2 pounds of bread or flour, 2 pounds of beef or 18 ounces of pork or fish per day and one gill of rum, if available. Officers were issued a pound of tallow for candles per week. The guard received 4 pounds per week. When vegetables were available, the flour ration was to be reduced ¼ pound per man and 2½ bushels of peas, 2½ bushels of beans, 8 bushels of potatoes or 12 bushels of turnips were to be issued for every 100 pounds of flour so reduced (Lauber, 1932, pp. 549-550). The commissary's job consisted largely of keeping the books straight and convincing everyone they weren't being shortchanged.

By February 8, 1781, the salt beef was running low and the ration was cut back to ½ pound per day augmented with 1½ pounds of bread. On February 28, the accumulative deficiency was made up when the fort was re-supplied; except for three barrels which were stolen after delivery (Lauber, 1932, pp. 562, 567).

At various times references were made to pigeons and fish supplementing the diet, and in the winter of 1781 the garrison took about 1,000 bushels of corn from an abandoned Oneida village (Lauber, 1932, p. 844). Cow, pig, deer, chicken and pigeon bones were found in the excavation (Appendix B). The number of feral species indicates the need of the garrison to supplement their diet. Cattle were driven to the fort periodically and slaughtered as needed. The cattle were targets of Indian raids, and in September 1778, about 100 head being driven to the fort were lost (Clinton, 1900, #1774). These animals apparently were kept in the fenced meadow near the fort and hay was fed to them in the winter.

More reliable, but no more plentiful, were hogsheads or barrels of salted beef, pork and fish. Between May, 1780, and May, 1781, George Washington ordered at least 334 barrels of salted meat sent to Fort Stanwix, along with 250 barrels of flour (Washington, 1932). The beef averaged 24 pounds to the barrel and 900 to 1,000 pounds per hogshead (Gates Papers, Reel 3; 5/15/77) and the flour averaged 200 pounds to the barrel. The barrels presented a storage problem. In 1777, the barracks were used to store provisions but during the siege the provisions had to be moved onto the parade ground (Reid, 1905, p. 100). The following spring, probably as a result of thawing conditions, the provisions again were put on the parade ground for lack of adequate storage space (M. Willett, 3/15/78). A month later, the northwest and southwest bombproofs were modified to store provisions (M. Willett, 4/16/78). A small building on the parade ground was identified on the Gansevoort plan, ca. 1777, (fig. 7) as a commissary store. This probably was the quarters of the commissary and the place where unissued clothing was kept. The structure was in an area we chose not to excavate because city maps indicated that it would be highly disturbed by post-fort construction and a paved parking lot.

The types of stores known to have been kept at Fort Stanwix are, of course, indicative of storage needs. In November 1780, the garrison had in stores:

12,707 pounds of flour in 64 barrels

17 pounds of meal

176 pounds of rice

14 barrels and/or 42 bushels of peas

500 pounds of cattle on the hoof

960 pounds of salted beef in 40 barrels

6 hogsheads, 1 barrel, 86 bushels and 16 quarts of salt

2,335 pounds of soap in 19 boxes

209 pounds of candles in 3 boxes

1,512 pounds of tallow in 7 barrels

113 hides weighing 6,215 pounds (Lenard, 1780)

With a garrison of approximately 160 men, provisions were on hand for a 9-day supply of beef and a 63-day supply of flour.

At one point, officers were allowed 1½ gallons of rum, ¼ pound of tea and 5 pounds of sugar per month (Lauber, 1932, p. 843). The higher ranking officers were also entitled to extra rations. When St. Leger's emmissaries came into the fort in August, 1777, they were served wine, crackers and cheese (W. Willett, 1851, pp. 56, 60). There was, then, some variety available if the men had the money to indulge. Farmers and members of the garrison brought food to the fort to sell to the soldiers. Apparently, they were charging high prices for these commodities because the men were ordered not to buy anything from them in October, 1777 (M. Willett, 1/30/77). A price freeze was put into effect in February, 1778. The items listed were:

Turnips—3 shillings per skipple

Potatoes—5 shillings, 4 pence per skipple

Cabbages—2 pence per head

Apples—6 shillings per skipple

Sugar—5 shillings, 4 pence per pound

Fowl—2 shillings apiece

Geese—6 shillings apiece

Turkeys—8 shillings apiece

Butter—5 shillings, 4 pence per pound

Cheese—4 shillings per pound

Onions—16 shillings per skipple

Tobacco—4 shillings per pound untreated or 5 shillings, 4 pence per pound manufactured into cut pig or hogtail.

Cider—1 shilling, 4 pence per quart or 1 shilling, 6 pence if boiled (M. Willett, 2/7/78).

The preparation of this food required kettles and broilers, or griddles which were found scattered about the fort, nearly always broken. In a few instances these were found associated with fireplaces but most were in the brick rubble in the cellar holes and in the dumps. Pottery vessels were used to serve the food but the number found, 697, was well below the needs of the garrison at any one time. We may conclude that most of the soldiers ate from kettles or had wooden trenchers, bowls and cups. The absence of forks and spoons indicate that wooden spoons, knives and fingers were used to convey food to their mouths.

Clothing

In November, 1780, the 2nd New York Regiment was ordered supplied with two shirts, two pairs of stockings, two pairs of shoes and a suit of clothes for each man. The suit presumably consisting of a blouse, waistcoat and trousers (Washington, 1932). Apparently the men were poorly clothed at most times since the commanders were constantly ordering clothing from Albany. In February, 1778, fires were allowed at night because there was a shortage of bedding (M. Willett, 1/24/78). There were scattered references to men going barefoot and in January, 1781, the men were ordered not to cut up their blankets to make clothing (Lauber, 1932, p. 559). Despite the order, one of the more common offenses was for a man to sell or trade his issued clothing or blanket for rum. Items of clothing were among the more common artifacts found, particularly buttons and broken buckles. The great variety may be a reflection in part of the number of units stationed in the fort at various times, but is more likely the result of shortages which forced the American army to use anything that was available.

Holidays and Celebrations

The soldiers did not enjoy many holidays, although occasionally the officers apparently held evening social get-togethers. December 18, 1777, was proclaimed a day of thanksgiving and prayer by Congress (M. Willett, 12/18/77) and Governor Clinton of New York declared a day of fasting and prayer for April 22, 1778 (M. Willett, 4/21/78). Samuel Kirkland arrived that day and preached to the troops. On May 20, 1778, the men were assembled to fire a Feiux-de-joy in honor of the treaty with France (M. Willett, 5/20/78). This consisted of the troops lining up and firing their muskets in rapid succession. They probably mounted the ramparts inasmuch as that many guns discharging on the parade ground at once would have produced a thick cloud of smoke.

New Year's day was the only regularly scheduled holiday for the troops. Toasts were drunk to Congress, Washington and others. Only one reference was made to Christmas being celebrated with an evening social (Lauber, 1932, p. 844). July 4 was never celebrated so far as we know.

Whatever the flag may have looked like, it was ordinarily flown from the southwest bastion and only on Sundays except during the siege (Lauber, 1932, p. 541). A morning and evening gun was fired when the flag was raised or lowered until the garrison ran short of powder and this ceremony was discontinued (Lauber, 1932, 556).

Civilians

Women were in the fort from the beginning. In 1758, a group of camp followers had established a small town on the Mohawk River below the fort (Dorr, 1970, p. E-5). The commander ordered the huts burned. These women left with the British and by 1775 the only women remaining were servants or members of the five families in the area. Other women came to the fort with the American army but, as their presence was condoned, they were probably wives of soldiers. De La Marquise was advised to obtain women to cook for the carpenters (Schuyler, 1880, p. 87) but we do not know if he succeeded. The women supported themselves by doing the soldiers' laundry (M. Willett, 5/21/78). On at least one occasion the army furnished the soap (Lauber, 1932, p. 581).

Civilians sought refuge in the fort in 1777, but three girls picking blackberries near the fort on July 27 were surprised by Indians and two were killed (Reid, 1905, p. 94). Shortly thereafter, all women with children, the sick and the wounded were shipped down the Mohawk River. At least two women stayed in the fort for both were wounded by shrapnel and one gave birth to a daughter during the siege (Reid, 1905, p. 102).

We do not know what accommodations were furnished the women. In 1781, Captain Moody, commander of the artillery detachment at the fort, was allowed a room which he shared with his wife and daughter (Lauber, 1932, p. 570).

Summary

The general picture one gets of living conditions in Fort Stanwix is rather bleak. Isolation, boredom, fatigue, hunger, danger and cold were the elements of everyday life, and the fact that only about one man in 20 deserted seems rather remarkable under the circumstances. These were not summer soldiers or sunshine patriots and they did not conquer so much as they survived. They persevered because they believed their cause was just. Although there were a few radicals and a few traitors, a letter from James Rix of the 9th Massachusetts to his wife, dated September 3, 1777, expressed the quiet determination of most of the soldiers:

Dear Wife having an opportunity to write a few lines to you I embrace it with grate Pleasure.

I would informe you that I am well considering the hard Fatigue that we have had for about Six weeks Past. We have been on the march the Chiefs of the time Since we left Albany which was July 20. We marcht to Fort Dayton in the Germanflats Stayed there a few Days and then marcht to Fort Stanwix which is 112 miles from Albany. We got there just as the Enemy Did . . .

Their was none belonging to Haverhill was hurt. they are all well even to a man. I have sent three Letters to you Before this and have Never Receved any from you. We have drawn the half of our clothing. Our wages we Expect to draw in about 10 Days and then some of Haverhill men Either officer or soldier will Come Home I shall send by him if I Do not come myselfe. I want to hear from you very much. I arrived hear yesterday from Fort Stanwix our Regiment expects now to join this Main army which will be Much better for us than to be the Flying Camp . . .

I am allmost beat out with hardship for I never had so Hard a Capaign Before and I hope I Shall Do the Most Good that ever I Did in one before. I Desir to thank God for all his Mercys and Favours toward us. ever Trusting in him more than all the world of men and Riches and Friends tho I Desir to be Remembered to all enquiring Friends and pray God to Proteck you under his wing. (Rix, 1938, p. 70).

Appendices

Appendix A: Cemetery

It is known that a large number of troops died in 1758 during the construction of Fort Stanwix and that there were other deaths after. that time. While some bodies may have been shipped home it is certain that some were buried in the vicinity of the fort (Dorr, 1970).

In reference to some buildings erected *ca.* 1844 on the northeast corner of James and Dominick Streets, it has been noted that: "In excavating for the foundation of the Merrill Block, or while digging near there, the skeletons of three or four Indians were found." (Wager, 1896, p. 54). The *Rome Daily Sentinel* (Anon. 1872) reported a number of human skulls and bones dug up in front of its office on North James Street, about 200 feet north of the Merrill Block. In 1972, backhoe excavations for sewer and telephone lines in James Street uncovered eight more skeletons (fig. 79). We were able to determine burial position and salvage a few bones from each. In all cases they were adult males laid in an extended position. One was definitely Caucasian and the others probably were since one was buried in a coffin, two had brass sleeve links associated and one had a garment with at least nine plain pewter buttons. We suspect that the "Indians" dug up in 1844 also were Caucasian.

The burials did not appear to be oriented in any particular direction, although the heads were generally north-northeast to northwest. They were not placed in neat rows but it should be noted that the amount of disturbance in the area probably removed or dislocated a number of burials. Some of the burials we recovered had been cut through by utility lines prior to 1972.

Stature estimates could be obtained from only three of the interments. These were approximately

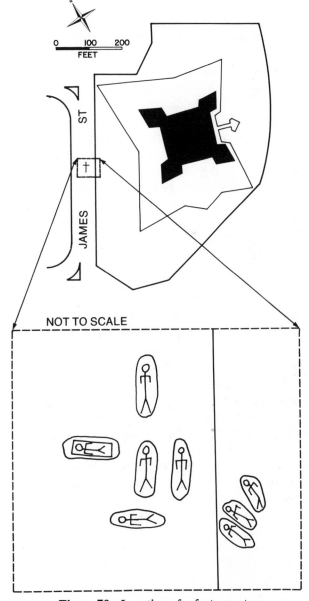

Figure 79. Location of a fort cemetery.

163

5' 8", 5' 10½" and 5'11", estimated from the long bones and using the Trotter and Gleser tables (Bass, 1971, p. 24).

Reportedly, other human bones were dug up north of the site at the rectory of a large church but these accounts could not be verified.*

In 1758, an Oneida Indian was buried in the southeast bastion of the fort (Dorr, 1970), but his remains were not uncovered. If he was in the center of the bastion his remains were probably destroyed with the building of the bakehouse, and if he was anywhere else in the bastion his remains were probably destroyed through erosion or landscaping in the early 19th century.

Appendix B: Food Remains

Foods available to the garrison at Fort Stanwix have already been described in the last chapter. Here, we propose to discuss the actual archeological remains of food stuffs. Dr. Benjamin Clark, New York Department of Agriculture and Markets, Dr. W. O. Sack, New York State Veterinary College, Cornell University and Dr. E. M. Reilly, Jr., New York State Museum, assisted us in identifying the remains.

A small sample of phlox seeds (*Polemonium sp.*) were found on the counterscarp of the north ditch but the purpose to which this herb was put is uncertain. There is the possibility that the sample was 19th-century in origin but stratigraphically it should have been 18th century.

In Feature 56 (Level III) in the west barracks, four small sacks of grain were discovered. Two of these were identified as wheat (*Triticum sp.*) and the other two were a mixture of wheat and oats (*Avena sativa*). Other seeds in the same area which could not be identified as coming from a discrete unit were *Compositae sp.* These were too badly charred to identify more precisely.

A large quantity of animal bone was recovered from cellar holes, the sally port area, and an area

---

* During fort construction the presence of this second cemetery was confirmed by the recovery of two more skeletons.

beneath the north end of the bridge. Time did not permit us to make a thorough study of these remains and as this was certainly not representative of a total population it was felt that there was no need. The largest sample, from the sally port area (Level II) was selected for study. This material came from a deposit about 30 feet long, 10 feet wide and 2 feet deep over the communication and into the redout. Undoubtedly it was placed there deliberately and late in the fort's history since it made the communication unusable. The deposit contained Revolutionary War buttons suggesting a post-1776 date, and ash lenses and articulated joints indicate that it was a primary deposit and not washed in from another area.

The method of analysis used to identify the bones by species and body parts (tibia, ulna, etc.) was based on past experience, using Olsen (1964) and Ryder (1968) as guides. Selected samples of each "bone type" were then sent out for corroboration of identification and minimum animal counts were prepared (table 38) based on the highest count for a single bone of each species.

The only surprise in table 38 is the absence of rabbits. his cannot be accounted for and given the known environment, they should have been plentiful. The table serves to confirm the documentary evidence, that the garrison's diet was dominated by domesticated species, but was supplemented by wild animals and birds. Duck, grouse and passenger pigeons (the latter now extinct) were hunted for sport. At Fort Ligonier, there were more remains of sheep than pig (Grimm, 1970, p. 184) which was just the opposite at Fort Stanwix. Only cattle are mentioned in written accounts as having been sent to Fort Stanwix to supplement salted meats. Apparently pigs were private property, owned by both soldiers and settlers (M. Willett, 4/5/78). If the faunal remains from the sally port garbage dump (Level II) is representative of the entire site, beef made up 55 percent of the fresh meat available to the garrison. Pork and venison made up most of the remainder. At Fort Ligonier venison accounted for about 25 percent of the fresh meat (Grimm, 1970, p. 184), while it was about 22 percent at Fort Stanwix. The principal difference was the absence of sheep and the higher number of pigs.

Fish might have provided a brief change in diet in the spring. Even in today's polluted, dammed and diverted streams and rivers near Rome, there are large runs of pike each spring. There are many references to pike and salmon runs up the Mohawk in the 19th century. Some fish bones were recovered during excavations, but they are not identified as to species or the possible number of fish involved.

All of the larger bones had been split to get at the marrow and the condition of the skull fragments indicates that the brain cases were broken to remove their contents. Not a single saw mark was found on the 18th-century bones, while the 19th-century bones were almost exclusively sawed. A few articulated leg joint were found with splintered ends, but we cannot infer much concerning butchering techniques except that it was designed to get as much nourishment from the animals as possible.

Table 38.

Minimum number of animals in the garbage dump in the Sally Port.

Species	Minimum Number	Count Based On:
Cow	24	Right radii, left femora, right calcanei and horn cores
Pig	13	Lower left second molars, left radii
Goat	1	Horn core
Deer	13	Right calcanei
Bear	1	Premolar
Fox	2	Left calcanei
Muskrat	1	Lower jaw
Dog	2	Right humeri
Turtle	2	Scapulae
Snake	1	Lower jaw
Chicken	9	Right femora
Pigeon	5	Right ulnae
Duck	1	Left coracoid and carpometacarpus
Goose	1	Right tarsometatarsus
Grouse	1	Right tibiotarsus
Rail	1	Right tarsometatarsus
Fish	?	Vertebrae and ribs

Appendix C: Archeological Features

Number	Function	Location	Level	Dates
1.	Privy	Southwest bastion	I	*ca.* 1828-1890
2.	Fire hearth & ash lens	Ditch west of bridge	XI	post-1764
3.	Clay-lined cellar	West barracks	II	*ca.* 1764-1781
4.	Ash & trash deposit	Northwest bastion	I	post-1891
5.	Privy	Northwest bastion	I	*ca.* 1841-1870
6.	Well	North ditch	I	*ca.* 1840-1900
7.	Flagstone pavement around Fea. 6	North ditch	I	*ca.* 1840
8.	Privy	Northwest bastion	I	*ca.* 1839-1860
9.	Privy	North ditch	I	*ca.* 1839-1900
10.	Fireplace	North casemate	II	*ca.* 1764-1781
11.	Cistern	Southeast bastion	I	*ca.* 1875-1927
12.	Fireplace	North casemate	II	*ca.* 1764-1781
13.	Fireplace	North casemate	I	*ca.* 1764-1781
14.	Trash pit	Southwest bastion	I	post-1927
15.	Stone building foundation	North casemate		*ca.* 1850-1870
16.	Pit or animal burrow	Hearth of bakeoven	II	post-1781
17.	Fireplace	North casemate	II	*ca.* 1764-1781
18.	Powder magazine	Southeast bastion	II	*ca.* 1758-1774
19.	Stone building foundation	North casemate	I	*ca.* 1870-1909
20.	Building foundation	Southeast bastion	I	20th century
21.	Rock fire hearth	Southeast bastion	I	*ca.* 2500 BC.
22.	Exterior stone stairwell	Southeast bastion	I	19th century
23.	Privy	Northwest bastion	I	*ca.* 1860-1874
24.	Trash pit	Southeast bastion	I	post-1927
25.	Trash pit	Southeast bastion	I	post-1927
26.	Privy	Northwest bastion	I	*ca.* 1890-1930

Number	Function	Location	Level	Dates
27.	Cobblestone paving	Southeast bastion	I	post-1825
28.	Water sump	West side glacis	I	post-1804
29.	Water sump	North casemate	I	post-1781
30.	Fireplace	North casemate	II	*ca.* 1764-1781
31.	Burned wood	Northwest bastion	I	post-1781
32.	Natural gas well	Northwest bastion	I	post-1890
33.	Passageway of northwest bombproof	Northwest bastion	II	1777-1781
34.	Trench	North casemate	III	1758-1781
35.	(number not assigned)			
36.	Cobblestone foundation	Northwest bastion	I	19-20th century
37.	Privy	Northwest bastion	I	*ca.* 1850-1870
38.	Northwest bombproof	Northwest bastion	II	*ca.* 1777-1781
39.	Privy	Northwest bastion	I	*ca.* 1830-1850
40.	Water sump	Southwest bastion	I	post-1840
41.	Trash pit	Southwest bastion	I	post-1840
42.	Fireplace	North casemate	I	*ca.* 1764-1781
43.	Cobblestone foundation for porch	Main gate area	I	post-1850
44.	Trash pit	Guardhouse area	I	*ca.* 1910
45.	Privy	Northwest bastion	I	*ca.* 1870-1890
46.	Palisade trench	West covered way	II	1777-1781
47.	**Hearth**	West covered way	II	*ca.* 1777-1781
48.	Wall trench	Southwest casemate	II	1758-1781
49.	Cellar	Parade Ground	I	post-1781
50.	Fireplace	Southwest casemate	II	1758-1781
51.	Wood box	Southwest casemate	II	1758-1781
52.	Wood-lined cellar	East barracks	II	*ca.* 1764-1781
53.	**Pit**	East barracks	I	post-1950
54.	Trench	East casemate	I	post-1781
55.	Stone-lined cellar	East casemate	I	*ca.* 1840-1920
56.	Wood-lined cellar	West barracks	II	*ca.* 1764-1781
57.	Clay-lined cellar	West barracks	II	*ca.* 1764-1781
58.	Pit, possible privy	Parade ground	II	*ca.* 1758-1781
59.	Privy	Main gate area	I	*ca.* 1870-1910
60.	Wood-lined cellar	West barracks	II	ca. 1764-1781
61.	Sally port	East casemate & scarp	II	*ca.* 1758-1781
62.	Buried barrel base	West barracks	I	*ca.* 1910
63.	Wood-lined cellar	West barracks	II	*ca.* 1764-1781
64.	Clay-lined cellar	West barracks	II	*ca.* 1764-1781
65.	Privy	South ditch	I	*ca.* 1850-1870
66.	Privy	South ditch	I	*ca.* 1825-1851
67.	Ash pit	East barracks	I	post-1900
68.	Fireplace	East scarp	II	*ca.* 1776-1781
69.	Clay-lined cellar	East barracks	II	*ca.* 1764-1781
70.	Pit, possible privy	Parade ground	II	*ca.* 1758-1781
71.	Privy	South ditch	I	*ca.* 1800-1825
72.	Clay-lined cellar	East barracks	I	*ca.* 1764-1781
73.	Pit, possible privy	Parade ground	II	*ca.* 1776-1781
74.	Brick foundation	Parade ground	I	20th century

Number	Function	Location	Level	Dates
75.	Ash deposit	East scarp	II	*ca.* 1758-1781
76.	Trench	Outside ravelin	II	*ca.* 1758-1781
77.	Privy	South ditch	I	*ca.* 1800-1825
78.*	Privy	Northwest bastion	I	19th century
79.*	Privy	North curtain wall	I	19th century
80.*	Clay-lined cellar	Headquarters	II	*ca.* 1764-1781
81.*	Trash deposit	Parade ground	I	19th century
82.*	Wood-lined cellar	Headquarters	II	*ca.* 1764-1781
83.*	Privy	East casemate	I	19th century
84.*	Pit	Storehouse	II	*ca.* 1758-1781
85.*	Pit	Storehouse	II	*ca.* 1758-1781
86.*	Clay-lined cellar	East barracks	II	*ca.* 1764-1781
87.*	Privy	North curtain wall	I	19th century
88.*	Privy	Northwest bastion	I	19th century
89.*	Privy	Northwest bastion	I	19th century
90.*	Burned area	Southeast casemate	III	*ca.* 1758-1781
91.*	Burned area	West casemate	III	*ca.* 1758-1781
92.*	Privy	Northwest bastion	I	19th century
93.*	Trash deposit	Northeast bastion	I	19th century
94.*	Privy	West side glacis	I	19th century
95.*	Privy	West side glacis	I	19th century

* Located during reconstruction of the fort in 1974 and not included in this report.

References

Abercromby, James
n.d. James Abercromby Papers. Ms. in Huntington Library.

Anonymous
1872 Rome Daily Sentinel. August 13, 1872. Rome, New York.
1879 Roman Citizen. August 15, 1879. Rome, New York.
1916 Collections of the New York Historical Society, vol. 1 (for the year 1914). New York.

Bass, William M.
1971 Human Osteology: A Laboratory and Field Manual of the Human Skeleton. Missouri Archaeological Society. Columbia, Mo.

Binford, Lewis R.
1962 A New Method for Calculating Dates from Kaolin Pipe Stem Samples. Papers presented at the 1st and 2nd Conference on Historical Archaeology. Southeastern Archaeological Conference, Cambridge, Mass.

Bird, Harrison
1963 March to Saratoga, 1777. Oxford University Press. New York.

Bridenbaugh, Carl
1950 The Colonial Craftsman. New York University Press. New York.

Buffington, Arthur H.
1933 The Colonial Wars and their Results. In: History of the State of New York, vol. 2. Alexander C. Flick, ed. New York State Historical Society. Albany.

Calver, William L. and Reginald P. Bolton
1950 History Written with Pick and Shovel. New York Historical Society. New York.

Campbell, J. Duncan
1965 Archeological Survey, Site of Fort Stanwix, Rome, N.Y. 24 May-13 August, 1965. Ms. on file at Fort Stanwix National Monument, Rome, N.Y.

Carroll, Orville
1973 Fort Stanwix Historic Structure Report, Architectural Data Section. Denver Service Center, National Park Service.

City Directory
1857-1970 Rome City Directories on file at the Jervis Library, Rome, N.Y.

Clark, Victor S.
1929 History of Manufactures in the United States. 3 vols. Carnegie Institute, Washington, D.C. (reprinted by Peter Smith, New York, 1949.)

Cleland, Charles E.
1972 From Sacred to Profane: Style Drift in the Decoration of Jesuit Finger Rings. In: American Antiquity, vol. 37, no. 2. Washington, D.C.

Clinton, George
1900 The Public Papers of George Clinton. 10 vols. Albany, N.Y.

Cookinham, Henry J.
1912   History of Oneida County, New York. 2 vols. S. J. Clarke Publishing Company, Chicago. (Contains map of Rome in 1802, first published in 1857.)

Crown Collection
n.d.   British Museum, Crown Map Collection, Copies and Map Divisions, Library of Congress. Washington, D.C.

Darling, Anthony D.
1970   Red Coat & Brown Bess. Museum Restoration Service, Historical Arms Series, no. 12, Ottawa.

Dorr, Moses
1970   Journal of an Expedition against Canaday. In: The Rome Daily Sentinel, August 1, 1970. Rome, N.Y.

Duncan, Richard
1969   Letter to William Livingston dated April 23, 1775. In: The Rome Daily Sentinel, March 3, 1969, Rome, N.Y.

Dupuy, R. E. and T. N. Dupuy
1963   The Compact History of the Revolutionary War. Hawthorne Books, Inc. New York.

Durant, Samuel W.
1878   History of Oneida County, New York. Everts & Fariss. Philadelphia.

Elmer, Ebenezer
1848   Journal Kept During an Expedition to Canada in 1776. In: Proceedings of the New Jersey Historical Society, 1847-1848. vols. II, III.

Fernow, Berthold, ed.
1887   Documents Relating to the Colonial History of the State of New York, vol. XV. Weed, Parsons & Co., Albany, N.Y.

Gage, Thomas
1931   The Correspondence of General Thomas Gage with the Secretaries of State. 2 vols. Clarence Edwin Carter, ed. Yale University Press. New Haven.

Gansevoort-Lansing Papers
n.d.   New York Public Library. New York.

Gates Papers
n.d.   New York Historical Society. New York.

Glissman, A. H.
1970   The Evolution of the Sad Iron. M. B. Printing Co., Oceanside, Calif.

Godden, Geoffrey A.
1966   An Illustrated Encyclopedia of British Pottery and Porcelain. Crown Publishers. New York.

Graymont, Barbara
1972   The Iroquois in the American Revolution. Syracuse University Press. Syracuse, N.Y.

Green, Nelson
1915   The Story of Old Fort Plain & The Middle Mohawk Valley. Fort Plain, N.Y.

Grimm, Jacob L.
1970   Archeological Investigation of Fort Ligonier, 1960-1965. Annals of the Carnegie Museum, vol. 42. Pittsburg.

Hagerty, Gilbert
1971   Massacre at Fort Bull. Mobray Press. New York.

Hanson, Lee
1968   The Excavation of the New Ordnance Storehouse at the Fortress of Louisbourg. Manuscript Report Number 54, National Historic Sites Service, National and Historic Parks Branch, Department of Indian Affairs and Northern Development.

1970   Gunflints from the Macon Plateau. In: Historical Archaeology, vol. IV. The Society for Historical Archaeology. Lansing, Michigan.

1971a Pipes from Rome, New York. In: Historical Archaeology, vol. V. The Society for Historical Archaeology. Lansing, Mich.

1971b A Reply to Gunflints and Chronology at Ocmulgee National Monument. In: Historical Archaeology, vol. V. The Society for Historical Archaeology. Lansing, Michigan.

1974   Outhouses in Rome, New York. In: Northeast Historical Archaeology, vol. 3, no. 1. Journal of the Council for Northeast Historical Archaeology. Dover, Del.

Harrington, J. C.
1954   Dating Stem Fragments of Seventeenth and Eighteenth Century Clay Tobacco Pipes. In: The Quarterly Bulletin of the Archaeological Society in Virginia, vol. 9, no. 1. Richmond.

Haynes, E. Barrington
1959   Glass Through the Ages. (rev. ed.) Penguin Books, Ltd. Baltimore.

Hodgkinson, Ralph
1965   Tools of the Woodworker, Axes, Adzes and Hatchets. In: Technical Leaflet 28, History News, vol. 20, no. 5. American Association for State and Local History. Nashville, Tenn.

Hsu, Dick Ping
1969   The Arthur Patterson Site, A Mid-Nineteenth Century Site, San Jacinto County, Texas. In: Archeological Survey Report, no. 5, July-August. Texas State Building Commission and Texas Water Development Board. Austin, Texas.

Jones, Olive
1971   Glass Bottle Push-ups and Pontil Marks. In: Historical Archaeology, vol. V. The Society for Historical Archaeology. Lansing, Mich.

Lauber, Almon W.
1932   Orderly Books of the Fourth New York Regiment, 1778-1780, The Second New York Regiment, 1780-1783, with Diaries of Samuel Tallmadge and Others. University of the State of New York. Albany.

Lefferts, Charles M.
1926   Uniforms of the American, British, French, and German Armies in the War of the American Revolution. Reprinted by WE, Inc., n.d. Old Greenwich, Conn.

Lenard, Enoch
1780   Return of Stores for the Northern Department, November 1780. Document 22180 in the National Archives. Miscellaneous numbered records (manuscript file), War Department Collection of Revolutionary War Records, 1775-1790's, RG 93. Washington, D.C.

Luzader, John
1969   The Construction and Military History of Fort Stanwix. National Park Service, U.S. Department of the Interior. Washington, D.C.

Mercer, Henry C.
1960   Ancient Carpenters' Tools. Bucks County Historical Society. Doylestown, Pa.

Miller, J. Jefferson III and **Lyle M. Stone**
1970   Eighteenth-Century Ceramics from Fort Michilimackinac. Smithsonian Studies in History and Technology, no. 4, Washington, D.C.

Mountford, Arnold R.
1971   The Illustrated Guide to Staffordshire Salt-glazed Stoneware. Praeger Publishers. New York.

Muller, John
1746   Treatise of Fortifications. Reprinted by Museum Restoration Service, 1968. Ottawa.

Nelson, Lee H.
1968   Nail Chronology as an Aid to Dating

Old Buildings. In: Historical News, vol. 24, no. 11, Technical Leaflet 28. American Association for State and Local History. Nashville, Tenn.

Neumann, George C.
1967 The History of Weapons of the American Revolution. Harper & Row. New York.

Noël Hume, Audrey
1963 Clay Tobacco Pipe dating in the Light of Recent Excavations. Quarterly Bulletin of the Archaeological Society of Virginia, vol. 18, no. 2. Richmond.

Noël Hume, Ivor
1970 A Guide to Artifacts of Colonial America. Alfred A. Knopf. New York.
1972 The What, Who, and When of English Creamware Design. In: The Magazine Antiques, vol. CI, no. 2. New York.

O'Callaghan, Edmund B.
1854 Documents Relating to the Colonial History of the State of New York. 10 vols. E. B. O'Callaghan and Berthold Fernow, eds. Weed, Parsons and Co., Albany.

Olsen, Stanley J.
1964 Mammal Remains from Archaeological Sites, Part 1, Southeastern and Southwestern United States. Papers of the Peabody Museum of Archaeology and Ethnology, vol. LVI, no. 1. Harvard University. Cambridge.

Pascale, Gus V.
n.d. Resource Book on Ceramic Materials. State of New Jersey, Department of Education, Vocational Division. Union City, N.J.

Peckham, Howard H.
1961 Pontiac and the Indian Uprising. 2nd ed. The University of Chicago Press.

Peterson, Harold L.
1968 The Book of the Continental Soldier. Stackpole Company. Harrisburg, Pa.

Ramsey, L. G. G. ed.
1962 The Complete Encyclopedia of Antiques. Hawthorn Books. New York.

Ransom, James M.
1966 Vanishing Ironworks of the Ramapos. Rutgers University Press. New Brunswick, N.J.

Reid, Max W.
1905 A Diary of the Siege of Fort Schuyler. In: The Magazine of History, vol. 3. William Abbatt. New York.

Rix, James
1938 Letter Written by James Rix. A Revolutionary Soldier, to His Wife. In: The National Historical Magazine of the Daughters of the American Revolution.

Ryder, Michael L.
1968 Animal Bones in Archaeology. Blackwell Scientific Publications. Oxford and Edinburgh.

Schuyler, Philip
1777 Letter to John Hansen dated July 6, 1777. Ms. letter #1797. American Antiquarian Society. Worcester, Mass.

1880 Proceedings of a General Court Martial for the Trial of Major General Schuyler, October 1, 1778, Near Quaker Hill, New York. Collections of the New York Historical Society for the Year 1879. New York.

Scott, Albert
1927 Fort Stanwix and Oriskany. Rome Sentinel Publishing Company. Rome, N.Y.

Simms, Jeptha R.
1882 Frontiersmen of New York. 2 vols. Riggs Publishing Co. Albany, N.Y.

Smith, Carlyle, S.
1960 Report on the Art of Making Gunflints (fire flint) by Citizen Dolomieu, 1796-1797. C. S. Smith, translator. In: Missouri Archaeologist, vol. 22. Columbia, Mo.

Smith, George
1779 An Universal Military Dictionary. Reprinted by Museum Restoration Service, 1969. Ottawa.

Smith, William
1956 Historical Memoirs from 16 March 1763 to 25 July 1778 of William Smith. William H. W. Sabone, ed. Reprinted by Arno Press, 1969. New York.

South, Stanley
1964 Analysis of the Buttons from Brunswick Town and Fort Fisher. In: The Florida Anthropologist, vol. 17, no. 2. Gainesville.

1972 Evolution and Horizon as Revealed in Ceramic Analysis in Historical Archaeology. In: The Conference on Historic Site Archaeology Papers, 1971, vol. 7, pt. 2. Columbia, S.C.

Stone, Lyle
1970 Archaeological Research at Fort Michilimackinac, an Eighteenth Century Historic Site in Emmet County, Michigan: 1959-1966 Excavations. PhD. dissertation. Michigan State University. East Lansing, Mich.

1971 Gunflints from Eighteenth Century Fort Michilimackinac, Michigan: A Formal Analysis and Description. In: The Conference on Historic Sites Archaeology Papers, vol. 6. Columbia, S.C.

1972 Gunflints from Fort Michilimackinac. In: Northeast Historical Archaeology, vol. 2, no. 1. The Council for Northeast Historical Archaeology. Providence, R.I.

Stone, William L.
1838 Life of Joseph Brant, Thayendanega. 2 vols. Reprinted by Krause Reprint Company, New York, 1969.

Thatcher, James
1862 Military Journal of the American Revolution. Reprinted by Arno Press, 1969, New York.

Van Dyck, Cornelius
1780 Letter to Colonel Van Schaick, April 17, 1780. Transcribed copy on file at Fort Stanwix National Monument, Rome, N.Y.

Wager, Daniel
1871 Growth of Rome—Changes and Improvements. The Rome Sentinel, November 21. Rome, N.Y.

1896 Our City and Its People. The Boston History Company, Boston.

Waite, Diana S.
1972 History of a 19th Century Urban Complex on the Site of Fort Stanwix. New York State Historic Trust. Albany, N.Y.

Walker, Iain C.
1966 T D Pipes—A Preliminary Study. In: The Quarterly Bulletin of the Archaeological Society of Virginia, vol. 20, no. 4.

1971a The Bristol Clay Tobacco–Pipe Industry. City Museum. Bristol.

1971b An Archaeological Study of Clay Pipes from the King's Bastion, Fortress of Louisbourg. Occasional Papers in Archaeology and History, no. 2. National Historic Sites Service, National and Historic Parks Branch, Department of Indian Affairs and Northern Development. Ottawa.

Walker, John
1971 Excavation of the Arkansas Post Branch of the Bank of the State of Arkansas. National Park Service, Department of the Interior. Washington, D.C.

Washington, George
1932 The Writings of George Washington from the Original Manuscript Sources, 1745-1799. U.S. Govt. Printing Office. Washington, D.C.

Watson, Aldren A.

    1968   The Village Blacksmith. Thomas Crowell. New York.

Wilkinson, Eliza

    1839   Letters of Eliza Wilkinson. Reprinted by Arno Press, 1969.

Wilkinson, James

    1778   Letter to General Horatio Gates, dated February 3, 1778. In: Gates Papers. New York Historical Society.

Willett, Marinus

    1777   Letter Forwarded by Jonathan Trumbull Jr. and published August 18, 1777. In: New York Journal and G. A. Transcribed copy in Rome Historical Society. Rome, N.Y.

  1777-78   Collonel (sic) Willett's Orderly Book, February 18, 1777 to May 21, 1778. Ms. at New York Historical Society. Transcription by W. E. Scripture on file at Fort Stanwix National Monument. Rome, N.Y.

Willett, William

    1831   A Narrative of the Military Actions of Colonel Marinus Willett. Reprinted by Arno Press, 1969. New York.

Witthoft, John

    1967   A History of Gunflints. In: The Pennsylvania Archaeologist, vol. 36, nos. 1, 2. Gettysburg.

Woodward, Arthur

    1960   Some Notes on Gunflints. In: The Missouri Archaeologist, vol. 22. Columbia, Mo.

Index

174

Publications in Archeology

1. Archeology of the Bynum Mounds, Natchez Trace Parkway, Mississippi, by John L. Cotter and John M. Corbett. 1951. (PB 177 061)*
2. Archeological Excavations in Mesa Verde National Park, Colorado, 1950, by James A. Lancaster *et al.* 1954. (PB 177 062)*
3. Archeology of the Funeral Mound, Ocmulgee National Monument, Georgia, by Charles H. Fairbanks. 1956. (PB 177 063)*
4. Archeological Excavations at Jamestown, Virginia, by John L. Cotter, 1958. (PB 177 064)*
5. The Hubbard Site and Other Tri-wall Structures in New Mexico and Colorado, by R. Gordon Vivian. 1959. (PB 230 988/AS)*
6. Search for the Cittie of Ralegh, Archeological Excavations at Fort Raleigh National Historic Site, North Carolina, by Jean Carl Harrington. 1962.
7A. The Archeological Survey of Wetherill Mesa, Mesa Verde National Park, Colorado, by Alden C. Hayes. 1964. (PB 234 542/AS)*
7B. Environment of Mesa Verde, Colorado, by James A Erdman *et al.* 1969. (PB 234 541/AS)*
7C. Big Juniper House, Mesa Verde National Park, Colorado, by Jervis D. Swannack, Jr. 1969. (PB 234 537/AS)*
7D. Mug House, Mesa Verde National Park, Colorado, by Arthur H. Rohn. 1971. (PB 234 539/AS)*
7E. Badger House Community, Mesa Verde National Park, Colorado, by Alden C Hayes and James A. Lancaster. 1975.
7F. Skeletal Remains from Mesa Verde National Park, Colorado, by Kenneth A. Bennett. 1975.
7G. Orthopedic Problems of the Wetherill Mesa Populations by James S. Miles, M.D. 1975.
8. Excavations in a 17th-Century Jumano Pueblo, Gran Guivera, New Mexico, by Gordon Vivian 1964.
9. Excavations at Tse-Ta'a, Canyon de Chelly National Monument, Arizona, by Charlie R. Steen. 1966. (PB 234 540/AS)*
10. Ruins Stabilization in the Southwestern United States, by Roland Von S. Richert and R. Gordon Vivian. 1974.
11. The Steamboat Bertrand: History, Excavation, and Architecture, by Jerome E. Petsche. 1974.
12. The Bertrand Bottles: A Study of 19th Century Glass and Ceramic Containers, by Ronald R. Switzer. 1974.
13. Investigations in Russell Cave, Russell Cave National Monument, Alabama, by John W. Griffin *et al.* 1974.
14. Casemates and Cannonballs: Archeological Investigations at Fort Stanwix National Monument, Rome, New York, by Lee Hanson and Dick Ping Hsu. 1975.

* These publications are no longer available from the Superintendent of Documents. They are available in microfiche or paper form from the National Technical Information Service. Cite the title and parenthetical code number, and apply for prices to NTIS, U.S. Department of Commerce, 5285 Port Royal Road, Springfield, Virginia 22161.

NPS 129